A WOMAN UNDER SURVEILLANCE

A WOMAN UNDER SURVEILLANCE

MY FIGHT WITH THE KGB TO FREE MY HUSBAND FROM THE SIBERIAN GULAG

TATIANA ZUNSHINE

PUMPKIN HOUSE PUBLISHING

Published by:

Pumpkin House Publishing
San Diego, California
pumpkinhousepublishing@gmail.com

ISBN: 979-8-218-43103-7 (Print)
ISBN: 979-8-9916184-0-3 (E-book)
Library of Congress Control Number: 2024942687

Cover and Book Design by Peri Gabriel Design, perigabriel1@gmail.com

TO MY SON AND MY HUSBAND.

CONTENTS

PART 2: 1985

PART 3: 1986

PART 4: 1987

PROLOGUE

My name is Tatiana. I am twenty-eight years old and the wife of a political prisoner. In the Orwellian year of 1984, I live in Riga, the capital of Latvia, in the Soviet Union.

I am under constant surveillance. Who are my trackers? Mostly men, but sometimes a woman or two. I have developed a sixth sense, instinctively knowing if and when I am being followed. I leave my apartment with no agents in sight, but within seconds, I know. A prickly feeling of awareness creeps up my spine. It never fails. Minutes later, I spot them. Plainclothes creatures in their thirties and forties, they are utterly nondescript. Neither tall nor short. Neither skinny nor fat. These are cellophane men. They are meant to blend in, and blend they do. But . . . if you pay attention, their tactics give them away. They come in clusters. Some walk directly behind you, following your every move. Others appear on either side of you, crisscrossing, changing positions, but always keeping you in sight. If you happen to look at one directly, they turn their head away, further betraying their status as strangers who do not wish to be recognized.

I've learned the fundamental rule of surveillance: stalkers never speak to their subjects. I play a trick on them once in a while—stop abruptly, turn around, and ask for directions. Being seen and questioned throws them off. Now they flee for a change. I laugh, keep walking. They resume the surveillance.

The days I am left alone feel different. It's hard to describe the joy I experience when I realize I don't have a tail behind me.

Like an acrobat on a tightrope, I walk a very thin line. One wrong move could send me crashing down. The horror of it is that I won't go down alone—that fall will bring my imprisoned husband down with me. I try not to let the weight of that thought paralyze me. Don't look down at the rope, I tell myself. Look ahead, always look ahead.

PART 1

1984

CHAPTER 1

A FOREIGNER IN HIS OWN LAND

It all began at my sister's wedding.

In preparation for the reception, my family's apartment had undergone a serious makeover. With the furniture rearranged, floors scrubbed, and silverware polished, it was now ready for the guests' arrival. The ceremony had already been conducted in the formal setting of city hall, with a humorless female fixture prompting quick "I do's." That was over with. Little by little, the guests—about thirty of them—trickled back to the apartment for a party. People gathered in the hallway, spilling into the only bedroom and the kitchen, leaving room for those busy setting a table in the living room. In typical Soviet-era fashion, friends and family were there to eat and drink each other under the table while toasting the newlyweds to no end. But for now, the table was still being worked on. While people were waiting to hear "Let's eat," introductions were being made, conversations were taking shape, and last-minute preparations were underway. The place was buzzing. The only person seemingly disengaged was *me*.

I wasn't quite there. I found myself distracted, paying too much attention to a stranger. A stranger to me, he turned out to be the groom's best man. He possessed an immense presence, enough to fill the whole room. He was tall, trim, and broad-shouldered. With a thick beard, classic Greek nose, and dark eyes, he looked like a mythical character. *He is almost too handsome,* I thought. *Who is he?* I was intrigued and weirdly affected by him.

The party was now in full swing, and people were loving it. But I felt flustered, for which I blamed the stranger. Quite often, in the course of the night, my eyes would zero in on him, blurring everyone else. There was just something about him! He exuded strength, maturity, and an abundance of personality, but also something else I couldn't quite express. What was it? It then occurred to me: There was an appealing animalistic quality to him. A fierce fighter, a wild thing—that's what it was!

I see him surrounded by a group of friends, talking, unaware of the fact that someone in the crowd—nineteen-year-old me—is watching him with awe. I hear his voice. It's deep, roaring. I hear his laughter and the laughter of people around him. I want to be a part of it, but I can't bring myself to approach him.

I never talked to him that night; I couldn't. My heart was beating too loudly. I was afraid he'd hear it.

For days after the wedding, I still couldn't get him out of my head. I found out who he was. His name was Zachar Zunshine, Zach for short. He was twenty-four years old, an avid chess player, and the quintessential bad boy. My sister, Lora—the bride—described him as someone highly intelligent, with a great sense of humor and an uncanny ability to turn his charm on and off. But what defined him at his core, she said, was his willpower and his distaste for conformity.

There was more.

He studied physics at university and planned for a career as a scientist. But after getting his degree and spending a few years in a lab, he completely reversed course. Something must have happened along the way—nobody knew what it was—but he traded the physics lab for a taxicab. After a short stint as a cab driver and another as a hospital worker, he took a shot at teaching physics at an evening school for adults. That was his job at the time of my sister's wedding.

Listening to all this, I was fascinated.

"But is he single?"

"No."

Over the next two years, I often bumped into Zach at Lora's apartment. He was a semi-permanent fixture there, spending nights in the spare room. His girlfriend, Tanya, was usually there as well. Life revolved around the kitchen in those days, and that's where we all hung out. In between the food and the conversations, the guys— Zach and Vladimir, Lora's husband—played endless chess games.

Spending time in that apartment, I learned more about Zach. I learned how complex he was. This was not your typical happy-go-lucky guy. Far from it, in fact. He was no stranger to the "misfortune of being clever"—a common malady among brilliant minds like his. He was what I would call "a puzzle of a man." The pure fantasy of being with him and being able to solve that puzzle, at least to some extent— that's what made him such a magnet for me. The crush I'd had on him since the wedding never fizzled, but even more, the moments I spent in his presence made my heart swell with something I had never felt before. I found myself under his spell, and the longer it went on, the clearer it became—I had fallen for him. In fact, I realized I had no choice but to fall for him. It was a force stronger than me.

I kept it a secret. Or so I thought.

Two years after Lora's wedding, Zach's relationship with Tanya ended. A few months later, out of nowhere, he asked me a question: "You are in love with me, aren't you?"

"Yes."

That's how it all began.

Zach knew that someday he would leave his country once and for all.

As early as the age of fifteen, he began to question Marxist dog-mas, challenging his teacher to admit their insolvency. In his twenties, Zach wanted nothing to do with Marxism or socialism. He dreamed of living in a society rooted in individualism, where independence and self-reliance were respected, encouraged, and nourished. "Imagine," he'd say, "a place where you can live in dignity, be who you are, and express yourself to the fullest. Better yet, imagine a place where there is no Big Brother, no state-owned media, no Communist Party, and no rulers clinging on to their positions until the day they die." The thought of living in such a society was so appealing that it drove him to realize that that was where he belonged. He was a foreigner in his own land. He knew he did not—and would not—fit the mold of a Soviet citizen, not at the age of fifteen when those thoughts first came to him, and not ever.

By his late twenties, he was ready; the time had come for him to leave. One question remained, however: whether or not we—two years into our relationship—would do it together. If I agreed to leave, we would marry. Otherwise, we'd go our separate ways.

"Are you with me?" Zach asked.

Am I with him? I was twenty-three years old, facing one of the most consequential decisions of my life. To be with him would come with a price. To be with him would mean abandoning my life as I knew it: to yank my roots from Russian soil and plant them in a for-eign land, hoping they would catch on; to tear myself away from my beloved family—my parents, my sister, my older brother; to run the risk of never seeing them again; to break their hearts, to break my heart. Just thinking about it filled my eyes with tears. But—

The truth is, there was no "but" for me.

Life without Zach seemed unimaginable. By then, he was my love, my life, my path, and I had to follow that path wherever it took me. With him by his side—that, at the moment, was the only path for me. Besides, his rebellious nature had rubbed off on me. I started questioning things I had previously taken for granted, such as the Soviets' lack of freedom and the contempt for human rights. Had I been blind, not seeing it before? Did I accept the Soviet way of life without giving it a thought? Like most people, I did. But not anymore. Little by little, I was gaining sight, and the more I saw, the less I wanted to be a part of it.

"Yes, I am with you," I answered.

CHAPTER 2

PROTEST IN MOSCOW

A few years later, I found myself thrown in jail.

When the door closed behind me with a metallic screech, I instinctively looked back for a split second—as if to make sure there was no escape—before turning my head to face the cell. About ten sets of eyes stared out at me. These, undoubtedly, were women of questionable behavior—prostitutes, petty thieves, bums. I was taken aback by their appearance, and I didn't know what to expect. Visibly shaking, I simply stood in front of them. One woman motioned for me to sit on her bench while she moved to the floor. I thanked her but demurred; she insisted. Her kind gesture pacified me a bit, and I took the seat. Slowly, I was regaining control of myself.

Except for a few exchanges, the women left me alone for the rest of the night. I spent that time observing, daydreaming, and reminiscing about the events that had led to this moment. My thoughts drifted back to the day Zach and I tied the knot.

We broke every rule there was: Zach put a wedding band on my finger in the cab on the way to city hall; there, in front of an officiant on duty, we suggested that she skip the "talk," heartfelt as it may be (not!), and get straight to the point.

"No speeches, please, just tell us where to sign!"

"Best of luck to you two," the woman said disapprovingly, "even though you don't seem to take this seriously."

We signed the papers and burst out of the building, laughing. We then went to a nearby restaurant to celebrate the night away. My sister, Lora, and her husband joined us.

With the formality of marriage behind us, it was time to get serious. We were about to embark on the journey of our lives, knowing all too well how hard the road ahead was. The timing was unfortunate. The chances of emigrating from the Soviet Union—a barometer of the Soviets' relationship with the West—had always fluctuated from bad to worse. At times, in hopes of getting some concessions in return, the Soviets would allow a random number of citizens to leave. Yet, more often than not, they'd tighten the screws, reducing emigration to a trickle. Then came December 1979, when, in the aftermath of the Soviets' invasion of Afghanistan and subsequent standoff between the Kremlin and the Western world, everything came to a screeching halt.

Having yet to apply for emigration, Zach and I were trapped.

Nobody knew how long the stalemate would last. A year, five, ten, an entire lifetime? The lack of an answer was an answer in and of itself. "We cannot just wait," we both said. "We cannot spend the best years of our lives in limbo, at the mercy of the Soviet apparatus."

Unwilling to put our exit on the back burner, we decided to go ahead and apply for emigration. After a short wait, a pre-typed cookie-cutter response arrived: "REQUEST DENIED." We were not surprised; in fact, we would have been surprised had the answer been any different. But there was still something tremendously exciting about this first step. We had put ourselves out there. We were now at the start of a whole new chapter in our lives. However challenging that chapter was going to be, we believed that one day—no matter how distant that day appeared—we would get a taste of freedom.

We spent hours talking about that day on our frequent walks along the shore of the Baltic Sea.

"How do you think it will feel to be set free?" I'd ask Zach.

"It will feel like home, finally."

There, by the sea, serenity was in full bloom. In the off-season months, the beaches were abandoned. A few people would pass by, but mostly, it was just the two of us in the company of the dunes. Pine trees stood proudly behind the line of white sand. It felt like they were listening, waving their branches approvingly. It felt like the sea was on our side, too, sending waves of support.

Once the Soviets *refused* to grant us permission to leave, Zach and I joined the ranks of people who called themselves *refuseniks*. Who were the refuseniks? To answer, let me take you back to the year 1975.

In 1975, thirty-five participating states, including the Soviet Union, signed a historic document known as the Helsinki Accords, with Article 13(2) stating, "Everyone has the right to leave any country, including his own." By signing this agreement, the Soviet government committed to opening its borders. But that did not stop them from issuing rejections to hundreds of thousands of hopeful émigrés. In response, armed with the articles of the Helsinki Accords, these newly named refuseniks initiated the fight of their lives—a fight with the authorities for the right to leave. For most, that fight took years; for some, decades.

The fight came with a high price. People were subjected to constant surveillance, physical assault, imprisonment, and exile to a faraway land. Careers were first to go. Barred from employment in their chosen field, these highly educated people had to settle for menial jobs. Quite a few PhDs found themselves painting apartments, working as night porters, or operating boilers.

A refusenik friend of mine, Dr. Evgeny Lein, was one of them. With a PhD in mathematics, he worked as a boiler room stoker. Another friend, Dr. Ari Volvovsky, worked as a plumber and handyman, while Dr. Vladimir Slepak, formerly the head of a scientific lab, considered himself lucky to have landed a job as an elevator operator.

Being an elevator operator became quite popular among refuseniks. Evgeny Abeshaus, a veteran refusenik, shared a funny story about his wife applying for that job. The interviewer asked her if she had a PhD, implying that it would be to her disadvantage not to have one as most of the people competing for the opening had doctorates.

To be fair, not every family of refuseniks endured the ire of the Russian apparatus. Some chose to exercise a safer approach: *Let's not rock the boat, let's just wait and see.* For them, there was a good chance life would not turn upside down. Others, however, wanted to take destiny into their own hands. Those brave souls were mapped on the radar and closely observed for signs of trouble. Zach and I belonged to that group. For us, endless wait was not an option.

Three long years passed after our request for emigration was rejected. We spent those years writing letters to Soviet officials, asking them to intervene on our behalf. We dispatched thousands of letters —to Communist Party officials, to the prosecutors' offices of the Latvian Republic and the entire USSR, and to anyone who appeared to wield influence—with no results. Determined to keep our campaign going until a positive resolution, we kept writing. We wrote to the deputies of the Supreme Soviet[1]—with no results. Frustrated, we nevertheless kept plugging away. Yet, there were still no results. Most of the letters likely ended up in a wastebasket. Some must have landed in a KGB file with our names attached.

---

1   "People's representatives," similar to members of Congress.

A lot more happened in those three years. Using the pretext of "staff reduction," Zach's school dismissed him from his job as a physics teacher. But worse, the KGB threatened him with a forced psychiatric evaluation. This is how it unfolded.

I came home from work one night to find Zach in a state of alarm.

"I found this in the mailbox," he said, handing me a note. It contained one line: "Could you please call Dr. Such-and-Such." (The name of the doctor escapes me.)

Zach said he had a funny feeling in his stomach about this, but he had called nonetheless. Indeed, it was the number of a psychiatric clinic. The voice on the other end of the line started cajoling him into showing up for an examination. "Many people who fight for permission to leave the Soviet Union," the man said, "become psychologically unbalanced." He acknowledged that the order for Zach's evaluation originated from the regional office of Interior Affairs. "Our hands are tied," the man added. "We will carry out the order. If you fail to show up voluntarily, we will bring you in by force."

Hearing those words, I forgot to breathe for a minute or so. This was by far the most terrifying prospect, as we knew all too well: There wasn't much anyone could do once they found themselves in the claws of KGB-backed "psychiatrists." Between daily torture and an occasional death sentence, one thing was indisputable—nobody escaped unscathed.

Putting fear aside, we needed to act swiftly and decisively. As a precaution against the police catching Zach on the street, he spent a few days at a friend's apartment. From there, he wrote numerous complaints, demanding answers from high-ranking officials. I spent the days pounding the pavement, delivering letters to party apparatchiks, and discussing the incident in detail. One of them—the chairman of the Central Committee of the Communist Party of Latvia—could not believe the lack of discretion behind this whole charade. He was outraged. Did he object to the act itself? Or to the lack of secrecy around it? It was not clear. Nevertheless, he said, "Go home, and don't you worry. I will stop that." Shockingly, and thankfully, he kept his word. We dodged the bullet.

In times like these, support is paramount. Without it, you expose your vulnerability and open yourself up to potential persecution. In other words, you need friends around you. Having met many refuse-niks in Riga, we had a small—but tight—group of friends. Our group consisted of two families blended into one. A family of friends rather than a blood one, we shared a common goal: to free ourselves from the claws of the Soviet regime. Besides Zach and me, these were Svetlana Balter, a mother of two in her mid-forties; her older son, Alexander "Sasha" Balter, in his early twenties; and Svetlana's younger brother, Leonid Umansky. We called ourselves the "Group of Five."

By the summer of 1983, tensions with the KGB had escalated. We found ourselves hounded, unable to break away. The tails no longer cared to blend in with the crowd. In fact, they stalked us openly, bla-tantly, as if trying to send a message. Zach and I, Svetlana, Leonid, and Sasha made several attempts to board a train for Moscow. But a certain scenario unfolded on the platform every single time. Plainclothes men stood on each side of the carriage door, watching people climb the short stairway onto the train, their luggage in tow. One after another, the passengers would board. The minute *we* ap-proached the door, the men closed ranks. They stood there, arms folded on their chests, legs spread at shoulders' width. Total silence. That silence was loud and clear. Not willing to waste words, we would turn around and leave.

The tension was palpable. It came to a climax on December 26, 1983, when the KGB staged a provocation on the streets of Riga. I re-ceived a phone call that day from Sasha Balter. His call found me in the office. Sasha sounded a bit distressed. "Tan'ka," he said, calling me by my nickname, "don't panic, but Zach just got arrested."

"*Arrested?*" I cried out. "What do you mean, arrested? What for?"

"For nothing. This was a provocation."

He assured me that the arrest was not permanent. It was a stunt the KGB often pulled, throwing refuseniks in jail for fifteen days. "Pure intimidation tactics," Sasha said. I hung up the phone, excused myself, and rushed out of the office to see Sasha. He told me exactly what happened.

Zach and Sasha met earlier that afternoon. Walking along the street, engrossed in conversation, the two of them were oblivious to what had been cooked up for them. In the most primitive scenario, an "ordinary citizen" walked toward them carrying an unlocked brief-case, holding it shut with his fingers. As he crossed paths with Zach, the man pushed him with his shoulder while releasing his fingers. The briefcase contents flew out, spreading all over the sidewalk. Pointing at Zach, the man screamed, "He pushed me!" Police burst out of a car that had been waiting at the curb. They grabbed Zach and shoved him into the car. As this was unfolding, Sasha tried to get into the car with Zach, loudly proclaiming to the police that he had witnessed precise-ly what had happened. They muscled him away, and the car took off. Sasha went to the police headquarters, where he insisted that they take his witness testimony. They showed him the door.

"There was nothing else I could do," Sasha said.

I knew that. There was nothing any of us could do. This had been a poorly orchestrated and shamelessly indiscreet bit of business, and yet, it had fulfilled its function: Zach ended up in jail. They accused him of "disorderly conduct" (a.k.a. "hooliganism") and slapped him with fifteen days of confinement.

In response, in a letter to the highest-ranking Soviet officials, our group made a statement renouncing our Soviet citizenship.

Nobody cared.

Frustrated but undeterred, we decided to put more pressure on the authorities. Since nothing we had done so far bore fruit—neither years of letter writing nor demands to renounce our Soviet citizenship—we decided to stage a protest in Moscow. Peaceful protests were legal, guaranteed by Article 50 of the Soviet Constitution of 1977, which promised "freedom of speech, of the press, and of assembly, meetings, street processions and demonstrations." Yet again, when it came to civil rights in the Soviet Union, there were laws, and there was reality, and one had nothing to do with the other. This was a gamble, and we knew it. Yes, this was a legal protest, but what would the consequences be? That we didn't know. It was out of our control.

We chose a special location, in front of the Karl Marx monument in Moscow (the irony of which was not lost on anybody). We chose a special date, March 4, 1984, the day of elections to the Supreme Soviet and, therefore, a day of tremendous significance in the Soviet Union. Our intention was to put ourselves on the radar of the newly elected deputies of the Supreme Soviet. Our message was abundantly clear: *We have had it with arbitrary rule. Enough. We are not asking for favors. We are asking for our right to leave this country—the right to be free.*

Having been stopped on the platform too many times in our attempt to reach Moscow, we now created a careful plan. Three people would participate in the protest—Zach, me, and Sasha. A fourth person—Leonid Umansky, another group member—volunteered to be a decoy. Leonid would write a letter to the prosecutors general of the Latvian Republic and the entire USSR, announcing the date—March 3, 1984—the time, and number of the train he intended to take from Riga to Moscow to submit a petition for renunciation of Soviet citizenship on behalf of our group's two families, the Balters and the Zunshines. That letter was nothing more than bait designed to steer the KGB directly to Leonid. It ensured they would closely monitor him before his departure—and, more importantly, upon his arrival in Moscow—therefore deflecting their attention from us.

Meanwhile, the three of us had to escape the surveillance in Riga and travel to Moscow independently of each other.

Zach was the first to leave for Moscow. He went a week before March 4, using a chance gap in surveillance. That day, surprisingly and unpredictably, he was left alone. Counting his stars, he went home to leave me a quick note, grab a bag, and get out in a hurry. There was no chance to say goodbye. When I discovered the note, I held it to my heart. I knew I wouldn't hear from Zach until the day we met in Moscow. That is, *if* we were able to meet in Moscow! I was worrying, wondering: *Where is he going to hide for an entire week?* I found out later that he spent the week couch-surfing at friends' apartments, worrying about *me* and wondering whether or not I had been able to escape. The lack of communication was unsettling for both of us.

Sasha and I were due to leave later in the week. By then, however, the surveillance resumed. It picked up where it left off the morning following Zach's departure, and I felt it on my back the minute I stepped out of the door. This was how it always happened: I felt their presence first, without seeing them. It manifested as a tiny sensation, a shudder in my spine, not from fear but from the pure presence of something vile. When I finally saw them minutes later, it would give me a silly feeling of satisfaction that I was, without fail, able to *feel* their presence. That was the case the morning the surveillance resumed. I felt it first. Then I saw them.

I assumed the same was happening to Sasha. He and I were facing a nearly impossible task: to escape, we both needed to lose our tails.

Before Zach left, he helped concoct the plan for my escape, and I was now ready to execute it. First, to ascertain how many agents were tracking me that day, I led them to Riga's central department store. There, with crowds bustling and numerous exits on each floor, they flocked so close that I felt their breath on the nape of my neck. Then I took them on a stroll from store to store, and I was able to count: *those three right behind me, the two on each side, a couple by the elevators, plus the one in the corner.* To top it off, I grabbed a piece of clothing and went into a dressing room. Coming out, I found some agents standing in front of my booth as if they were about to ask, "Well, how did it look? Did it work out?" It worked out great! It allowed me to learn how many of them were after me and what they looked like.

From there, I went to the apartment where Sasha's mother, Svetlana, lived. Located on one of Riga's central streets, Svetlana's building had a few residential entrances—one of which led to her apartment—and a large but cozy circular interior courtyard. A narrow opening led from the street into the courtyard, which you then crossed to get into one entrance or another.

In all my previous visits to Svetlana's, my tail contingent stayed behind in that narrow alleyway leading into the courtyard. And there they stayed again, settling in for a long wait.

Unbeknownst to my trackers, the building entrance about ten yards from Svetlana's served a dual purpose: besides leading to residential apartments, it also opened onto a store's back door. The storefront faced a different street.

That building entrance, the store's back door, and the store itself were the key to my escape.

Next step—change of clothes. "Wear something with a splash of color for a big part of the day," Zach suggested, "and then change to a muted palette." *Why?* you might ask. It's simple. By wearing bright colors the whole day long, I was leading the agents on, practically assisting them in stalking me. Follow the bright spot—that's all they had to do. Changing the colors midstream, we thought, could possibly throw them off. Would it help? Who knows. It couldn't hurt.

I had brought the change of clothes to Svetlana's a few days earlier. Now it was time to change. Shortly after, a friend who had offered his help as a human shield showed up at the apartment. He was a sweetheart, a Pierre Bezukhov[2] type, who, just like Pierre, happened to possess a substantially large frame. Laughingly, he suggested that we put that frame to use.

After a few hours passed, I was ready to get out. Dressed in pastels from head to toe, I went downstairs accompanied by "Pierre." Together, we walked into the courtyard, my five-foot-four, 110-pound body fitting perfectly behind my human shield. With him blocking me, we covered the distance between the two entrances.

Once inside the second entrance, I slipped through the back door into the store, crossed it, and exited on a different street. From there, I hurriedly walked tail-free to the train station and boarded the train to Moscow. The entire time, from the moment I left the apartment until the train started moving along the tracks, I was flying high, not feeling my hands and feet, but feeling one enormous rush that was hard to describe and even harder to calm.

Later that night, Svetlana went downstairs, and who do you think she found there? The agents, hanging out at the narrow courtyard opening, wearily awaiting my return. That cracked her up. Seeing them watch her building meant only one thing: they were oblivious to my escape. *Let them figure it out for themselves*, she thought, *whenever that happens*.

Unlike me, Sasha did not have an escape plan. He winged it.

In his mid-twenties and already married—to his wife, Polina—Sasha looked like a college kid. With his curly hair, eyeglasses, and reddish beard—which added a little age to his looks, but not much—he

---

2   A character in Tolstoy's *War and Peace*. A stout man with a big heart.

was a typical computer whiz. Sasha spent the day of the escape at the office. Although he appeared to be at work, work was the last thing on his mind—a group of KGB agents were camped outside the office building, monitoring his every move.

To find out who and how many, Sasha led them on a number of trips outside the office. He went for coffee at the nearby coffee shop. He went once, twice, and eventually six times. By the time he was done, he knew exactly how many were on his surveillance team, what they looked like, and where they positioned themselves. All but one were watching the main entrance of the building from the outside; a single agent hung out by the back door.

Sasha's behavior was so bizarre it must have baffled the agents. *Who drinks that much coffee in one afternoon?* they must have wondered. He did. He had to! To make the outings look legitimate, with KGB inside the store watching him, he had no choice but to drink every single cup. At some point, on his way back to the office, Sasha noticed that all the agents were with him, including the backdoor guy. He walked slowly and leisurely toward his office building. Once inside, he shot out the rear of the building so fast that he was through the back door before the agent could get there. Out on the street, he ran around the corner and into the building next door.

He hitchhiked about a quarter of the way to Moscow, caught the train he initially had tickets for, and exited one stop short of his final destination. There, on the platform, he spotted a few men who looked suspicious. Not having enough time to analyze—is it *them* or is it not?—he hopped back on the train once it started moving again. A few hours later, as the train approached Moscow, Sasha simply jumped off. Luckily, the March snow was still on the ground, cushioning what would otherwise have been a harsh fall. He emerged unscathed and hitchhiked the rest of the way into the city.

Standing on a street corner in central Moscow, Zach, Sasha, and I could not believe our eyes. *We did it, didn't we? We all made it! How utterly remarkable!* We were jubilant to see each other. Not having had any contact for the entire week out of fear of being tapped, we had no idea who would manage to show up in Moscow. What were the odds all three of us would slip through the cracks in surveillance? Slim to none. And yet, that's exactly what happened. Having outwitted the KGB at every turn, we had each found our way to Moscow.

Meanwhile, our friend Leonid Umansky traveled to Moscow "officially." What happened to Leonid?

While attempting to submit a petition at the office of emigration, he was detained by the KGB and taken to their headquarters. By then, they already knew we had escaped Riga. They placed him in a situation room to demonstrate their mighty efforts to locate us and convince him to do a good deed by assisting them. Sitting in a situation room, he got a chance to witness how the KGB operated: information came into a control panel about the two quick calls we had made from pay phones—one to Riga, another to Leningrad; our photographs handed out to police officers patrolling the center of Moscow, especially around the area where the calls came from. But the truth is that even if Leonid were inclined to help them, he wouldn't have been able to. Not wanting to put him in a bind, we deliberately kept our whereabouts to ourselves.

That day, March 4, 1984, Zach, Sasha, and I walked up to the Karl Marx monument in the heart of Moscow. It was three in the afternoon. There was truly no time to waste; it was now or never. We raised two signs. One read: WE DEMAND OUR RIGHT TO RENOUNCE OUR SOVIET CITIZENSHIP; the other: STOP TYRANNY.

We stood there for five minutes. These were five odd minutes. They were a little scary, yet exhilarating and liberating. My heart was in overdrive, beating loudly and furiously; I could hear it. These were five long minutes, too. The three of us did not talk much; we just stood there, holding signs, knowing that the cars would arrive at any moment. They finally did, and from there, things escalated very quickly. Two Volgas[3] with no official markings leaped the curb onto the sidewalk, ending up a yard or so away from us. A few men jumped out, knocked down our signs, and rounded us up. They pushed us inside the cars and drove off.

"Where are you taking us?" I asked, realizing it was a rhetorical question.

"Where you belong," one of the men answered.

At the county jail, they ushered us into a guarded room. We expected to be interrogated, but that didn't happen. They just kept us there for the remainder of the day. Later that evening, they sent me to the women's section of the jail while Zach and Sasha went to the men's.

And so I spent that night behind bars, surrounded by women of questionable behavior. Prostitutes, petty thieves, bums—you name it, they were there. There were about ten of them in the cell. The moment I set foot in there, I was taken aback by their appearance. They looked a bit scary: thin, crepey skin caused by lack of care and overexposure to the sun, missing teeth, ragged clothes, and unkempt hair. But in contrast to what their looks suggested, these women turned out to be quite good-natured. They were respectful and, for the most part, indifferent. They asked a few questions—what brought me there and the like—but did not dwell on my answers. *A protest? Okay, whatever.* They left me alone for the rest of the night.

The cell was small—no more than 150 square feet. No windows. No beds, just backless benches to sit on. Sitting on a bench for a long time was as painful as lying on the hard floor. Most women preferred the floor. Crunched up on a bench, I spent the night with

---

3   Volga was the most commonly used KGB car.

my eyes wide open. I was dead tired but couldn't sleep, reminiscing about the events that had led to that night and wondering if and when I would be able to reunite with the boys.

CHAPTER 3

WAKING UP A DIFFERENT PERSON

The following day, to my relief, I was escorted from the jail to the train station. Zach and Sasha were already there, surrounded by a few plainclothes agents. We were elated to see each other, but the celebration quickly soured when we learned that Riga's KGB agents had flown to Moscow for the sole purpose of escorting us back. That was unsettling enough, but to make things worse, Zach happened to catch the flu and was running a high fever.

The train arrived in Riga early the next morning. More agents were waiting for us on the platform. They put Zach and me in one car and Sasha in another. From there, a small procession of cars drove us home. I wanted the ordeal to be over so that I could give my attention to Zach; by then, he could barely stand on his feet. Once we got home, however, the situation escalated.

We knew something was cooking when the agents followed us upstairs, treading on our heels up to the third floor. There, in front of the apartment door, we stalled. "Now open the door," they said. Immediately, I felt a punch in the gut, and I am sure Zach did, too. Once the key turned, they took over the whole place. Zach's flu grew progressively worse, and I, too, was in a haze. I felt violated, sick to my stomach, but more than anything, I felt sick with worry about Zach. I had an excruciatingly bad feeling that he was in imminent danger.

Soon, a small battalion of men turned the place into a war zone. Some men targeted the desk, sifting through the stacks of documents in their relentless search for incriminating materials. They cherry-picked papers for the dossier, tossing the rest on the floor as garbage. Others ransacked the rest of the house, yanking every drawer open and examining its contents with meticulous scrutiny. They left no corner unexplored, not a single object untouched.

As the hours dragged on, I asked them to let me make a quick trip to the pharmacy to pick up some aspirin for Zach's raging fever.

"No," came the answer.

"Can we open the windows, please? We're suffocating."

"No."

It became increasingly clear that this was not going to end well.

"Just out of curiosity, what kind of charges have you cooked up for me?" Zach asked, not really expecting an answer.

Surprisingly, he got one: "Article 183."

Every refusenik in Riga knew what Article 183 stood for: "Systemic dissemination in oral and written form of deliberately false insinuations, defaming the Soviet state and social system." It carried a maximum sentence of three years in the Gulag.[4]

"That means three years guaranteed, doesn't it?" Zach asked.

"You're a smart guy, Zunshine. You've figured that one out," an agent replied.

The moment I heard the agent's words, my world collapsed. I don't remember much of what happened afterward. All I remember is saying to myself, rather deliriously: *Somebody please stop them. Don't let them take him away. They have no right. Somebody, pleeease!*

Then it happened. The front door closed on the agents escorting Zach out of the apartment. I rushed to the window.

---

4   GULAG is an acronym for Glavnoye Upravleniye Ispravitelno-Trudovykh Lagerey, or "Chief Administration of Corrective Labor Camps," the system of forced labor camps established by Joseph Stalin and made infamous by author Aleksandr Solzhenitsyn's three-volume exposé, The Gulag Archipelago, circulated underground in Russia and first published in the West in 1973.

I see a black car with him in the back seat, his face turned back, turned to me. I am horrified by our parting, not believing yet what is happening. Beyond the glass of the car windows, plainclothes men are on both sides of him. The car is moving away, and I can't see him anymore.

For the rest of the night, I submitted to tears. I cried, I wailed, I railed from side to side as if trying to release the pain that overwhelmed my heart. It worked. The pain was now running through my veins. It was everywhere, and everything hurt. By early morning, I had no tears left; I was spent. My eyes were burning. I couldn't keep them open. I fell asleep.

And woke up a different person.

The day after Zach's arrest was a blur. I remember going to work to submit my resignation. It didn't occur to me to question how I would support myself from now on. That, in time, would work itself out. For the moment, having a job was not an option. My job was to get Zach out of jail—alive. That was going to take all my strength, all my courage, all my creativity—everything I had. Nothing else mattered.

I boarded a train to Leningrad[5] that very night. I was going to get in touch with a man named Yakov Gorodetsky. He was a former mathematician who, having joined the ranks of refuseniks, established some powerful contacts in the West. I needed his expertise in obtaining such contacts, and, more importantly, I needed the contacts he already had.

Yakov, his wife, Lina, his infant daughter, and his mother-in-law occupied two rooms in a centrally located communal apartment. A rather large living room, by Russian standards, slept all four of

---

5   The city was called Saint Petersburg from its founding in 1703 until 1924 when it was renamed Leningrad. When the Soviet Union collapsed in 1991, the name reverted to Saint Petersburg.

them. A tiny den, with books wall-to-wall and a beaten-up couch, was reserved for visitors (if you lived in Moscow or Leningrad, you could count on having visitors all year round).

In his mid-thirties, short, solid, never without his signature leather jacket and a French beret, Yakov was wickedly smart and somewhat unpredictable. You never knew quite how he was going to react. When, choking with tears, I told him what had happened, he surprised me by asking, "So why are you crying?"

Did I need to explain?

But Yakov favored a no-nonsense approach. "We are going to the post office," he said matter-of-factly, "where I am expecting a phone call from a very influential woman in Chicago named Pamela Cohen. We'll tell her what happened, and we'll go from there."

Yakov and I went to a nearby post office for a messenger call from Chicago.

What was a messenger call?

For those lacking a phone in their home—as many did—the only way to connect with the outside world was by messenger call. It worked like this: The person initiating the call would contact a post office near the recipient. The post office would summon the recipient for a particular time slot; he or she would then be guided into a phone booth where the two parties would connect.

On our way to the post office, I told Yakov that I hadn't spoken a word of English in ten years. Before college, I attended a specialized school where English was the main subject. We studied British English, memorizing information about the city of London, Big Ben, the river Thames, and on and on. We studied Chaucer, Shakespeare, and Thackeray, among other literary greats. But did they teach us conversational English? Unfortunately, not so much. That, combined with the fact that I had not practiced English in a decade, left me with a big challenge: a communication barrier that made me think I could barely utter a word. Yakov agreed to talk to Pamela Cohen on my behalf.

The clerk directed us to a booth where an operator announced that our party was on the line. "Pam, hi, Yakov speaking."

They exchanged pleasantries for a few minutes, and he told her my story. Then he said, "Okay," and handed me the phone. "Pam wants to talk to you."

"Oh, no, no, no, I can't." I shook my head vigorously. "I just can't!"

Yakov just kept nodding. "Yes . . . you . . . can."

I took the phone. "Hi, Pam, my name is Tatiana Zunshine," I began in halting English. Then we proceeded to talk for what felt like an eternity. I don't know where the words came from. I don't think I found *them*—somehow, they found *me*.

Talking to Pam was comforting, even with my broken words and distraught state of mind. She kept repeating, "I understand. I understand," and also, "We've got you." Her voice was calming and reassuring while projecting confidence. When she said, "Within half an hour, the governments of the United States, Canada, France, and the United Kingdom will start working on this case," I knew we were in the right hands. I continued telling her our story. She kept reassuring me that things would be okay. At the end of the conversation, I felt I was saying goodbye to a new friend.

Back home, I kept myself busy. "Go! Go! Go!" was my mantra. I missed Zach dreadfully and needed to fill every minute of the day. Like a runner in a relay race, I took over letter writing for him. I sat in front of the typewriter for hours, punching the keys, typing, and retyping what amounted to hundreds of letters. I demanded that the authorities order Zach's immediate release. I demanded answers regarding his health. Having been arrested while sick with the flu, was he receiving adequate medical care? I sat at my typewriter until the wee hours, tiring myself into a zombie. Then I would crash in bed. For what it was worth, I forbade myself from having dreams about Zach. Those would have been too heartbreaking to wake up from. Miraculously, my mind listened.

My mission was clear: Every minute of every day was to be spent fighting for Zach's release, calling attention to his case, engaging human rights organizations, world leaders, celebrities—anybody and everybody who was willing to listen. Connecting with Pam Cohen was the first crucial step in establishing the beginning of an international campaign. But to sustain itself, that campaign needed a constant flow of information. What kind of information? Any information about Zach leaked from prison and put into the hands of our supporters would be golden. Who could provide that information? *I* had to. It was on me.

This was no easy task, considering the fact that those awaiting trial in the Soviet Union were imprisoned and denied contact with the outside world. The option of being released on bail didn't exist, nor did prisoners' meetings with their families. After the moment of arrest, the next time a family was allowed to see their loved one was in the courtroom on the day of the trial.

The only person who could have shed light on Zach's situation would have been a lawyer. However, I was stunned to discover that, between the time of the arrest and the end of the investigation, the right to legal representation was not guaranteed (except for defendants who were physically or mentally impaired). Whether a lawyer was allowed on the case was strictly at the discretion of the prosecutor's office. As expected, the prosecution denied Zach the right to a lawyer pending the end of the investigation.

Back from my trip to Leningrad, I sorted through the piles of paper discarded by the KGB agents during their raid of our apartment. It turned out they had left behind some important evidence: the letters Zach had sent openly to Soviet officials arguing against their denial of our exit visas. Having come across multiple copies of such letters, the agents took the top copy and tossed the others. Now they've become my prize possessions. If the KGB were going to use those letters as incriminating evidence against Zach, I decided, I would use the same letters as proof of his innocence.

And that's what I did. I photographed everything of value in the remaining paper copies and then destroyed them. All documents were now in the form of a filmstrip. With the help of my refusenik friends, I contacted a reporter from the Associated Press, an Englishwoman named Alison Smale. I asked her to meet me in Moscow so that I could pass along the film. Sasha, who'd become my right-hand man ever since Zach was taken away, would accompany me on the trip.

Another overnight train ride took us to Moscow. We found the agreed-upon meeting place not far from the AP bureau and spotted a woman whose appearance matched Alison's description. We knew we could get intercepted any moment, so there was no time to waste. Sasha and I approached her. Her native British English proved we were with the right person. I handed her a copy of the filmstrip, and she disappeared into the crowd.

We were jubilant. *It worked! What do you know?* Our first little mission went so smoothly that there was hardly anything to it. We could now spend the rest of the day hanging out in the city before catching an evening train home.

Having heard of Zach's arrest, my older brother, Gennady ("Gena"), insisted on visiting me. At the time, he and I lived thousands of miles apart, but that didn't stop him. I, on the other hand, did try to stop him. As much as I wanted to see my brother—and I wanted to more than anything—I did not want him to step into my world. I was afraid for him. It was one thing for Zach and me to risk endangering ourselves—something we felt was necessary to achieve our goal. But risking our families' well-being? The thought was unbearable.

I begged my brother not to come. He didn't listen.

Gena arrived the same day Sasha and I returned to Riga from our mission in Moscow. Sasha went home to be with his wife, Polina, and I spent the day with Gena. We dissected the Moscow affair—how Sasha and I had passed the film loaded with documents to the Associated Press correspondent—and celebrated the fact that there wasn't much to it. "If all my future missions went as smoothly as this one," I said to Gena, "I'd be happy."

At about 11:00 p.m. that same night, I began to get antsy. It was just an intuition, but I sensed that something might have happened to Sasha. I needed to hear that he was all right. Lacking a phone in my apartment, I asked Gena to come with me to a nearby phone booth so that I could give Sasha a quick call.

The phone booth was across the street. Sasha answered my call immediately. There had been an attempt to assault him and Polina that very night. *Oh, my god, so I was right!*

"What did they do?" I asked anxiously. It turned out that upon arriving home, Sasha and Polina encountered several KGB agents waiting at the entrance of their building. The men tried to start a fight, but Polina ran into the building first, then Sasha, and they began banging on every door, making lots of noise, alerting neighbors. That racket made the men withdraw, but not without a threat: "Stop supporting Zach, or we'll cut your legs off!" one of them shouted. By the time I called, Sasha and Polina had calmed down. "That was close," Sasha said.

Under the spell of this conversation, Gena and I walked back to my apartment. The street was almost deserted. Just two neighbors were walking toward us, probably taking an evening stroll. As they approached us, the pair separated to give us space to pass. But as soon as we walked between them, the moment the four of us formed a horizontal line, each "neighbor" grabbed one of us by the arm and threw us over their body—me to the right and Gena to the left.

I am in the air. I am suspended, and so is time. I wonder what is coming next—a kick in the stomach or a fist to the face? Or both? Curl up, protect yourself! my mind screamed.

Baaam!

Landing hard on the cobblestones, I curled up in a ball and instinctively closed my eyes, anticipating a kick or two. But that didn't happen. Instead, I heard the sound of running feet. I opened my eyes and saw the shadows of two men running away. About four yards to my left, my brother was trying to get himself off the ground. His hand was bleeding. By the time we picked ourselves up, the men were gone. I looked around for my purse. It was gone too.

"Run!" Gena shouted. Adrenaline still surging, we raced for the building entrance, ran up the stairs to the third floor, and burst into my apartment. We were home, safe. Breathing hard, my brother and I were unable to speak, both of us visibly shaken. Gena's hand was still bleeding slightly, and I felt bruised. My heart was pounding hard. It took a few minutes for us to calm down.

That calm didn't last for long. There came a loud knock on the door. "Open up! Police. We understand you've been assaulted. We need to interview you." I looked out the window. There was no police car anywhere on the street.

"How do you know about it?" I asked through the closed door. "We never reported it."

"Open up, I said!" someone shouted.

I looked at the door and then at Gena, shaking my head. We were not letting them in. If they broke down the door, so be it; we were not going to open it.

Gena and I stopped responding. But that didn't keep them from banging on the door over and over and over again. We stepped away from the hallway, into the living room, and closed the door behind us. That muffled the sound a bit, but not much. We stayed in there for hours, waiting for the terror to end. With only a few intervals of quiet, it went on all night.

This assault was clearly retaliation for our meeting with the journalist in Moscow. That's why it happened to Sasha and me on the same night. The KGB was sending us a message. But there was more to it.

My stolen purse presented a problem. *Why?* you ask. The law required anyone approached by law enforcement to hand over their Soviet passport. Failure to do so could result in a thirty-day detention. Unwilling to give the KGB ammunition to detain me, I made sure I always had my passport in my purse. And now it was gone.

By 5:00 a.m., the banging stopped. The door withstood the pressure. So did we.

CHAPTER 4

PAM MACHINE

Pamela Cohen treated us refuseniks as if we were her adopted children. I don't know how she did it. In her early forties, a mother of three and wife of a business executive, she found the time and the heart for all of us.

At the time of my first telephone conversation with Pam, in a post office in Leningrad, she was co-chair of Chicago Action for Soviet Jewry, a branch of a national organization called the Union of Councils for Soviet Jews (UCSJ). Two years later, in 1986, Pam was named UCSJ's president.

Her network was vast. She had numerous contacts in major cities in the Soviet Union, including Moscow, Leningrad, Kyiv, Odessa, Riga, Tallinn, and Vilnius. Glued to the phone for hours at a time, Pam wanted to make sure everyone in her orbit was okay. *What's happening to you? Your family? What are your needs? Here is what we are doing to help your case. And now, how is so-and-so?* She would steer the conversation to another refusenik or a prisoner—whoever needed help at the time.

Separated by the ocean, none of us refuseniks had the opportunity to meet her in person (that would not happen until we escaped the Iron Curtain), and yet we all felt incredibly close to her. So close that neither I nor any of my refusenik friends would hesitate to call her at home, day or night. Pam told me her day started at 6:00 a.m. and seemingly never ended. "Call me any time," she'd say, and I did. Once, while visiting Siberia during Zach's incarceration, I needed

Pam to call the prosecutor's office at a certain hour. Never mind the time difference of fourteen hours and the fact that my "certain hour" coincided with her "middle of the night." Pam was always there when I needed her, and she got up to place the call.

The Union of Councils for Soviet Jews had numerous branches in the United States. Once Pam received information—say, concerning a refusenik who had been arrested, detained, or interrogated—she would telegraph it to other branches, initiating a whirlwind of activity all over the United States. Every branch would get involved, from Chicago to San Francisco to Des Moines to Miami and everywhere in between. Pam's partner in crime was her co-chair at the time, the equally tireless Marillyn Tallman. I never dealt directly with Marillyn, but by all accounts, she was quick-witted, energetic, and brilliant. Together, they traveled the world as champions for Soviet Jewry. Their most frequent stop was Washington, DC, where they advocated for us on Capitol Hill. Pam and Marillyn provided information to US government representatives, forming the basis for official statements made by members of Congress on our behalf.

The "Pam Machine" was set in motion within days of our very first phone conversation. Pam's principal contact on the Hill was Congressman John Edward Porter (R-IL). Representative Porter was the founder and co-chairman of the Congressional Human Rights Caucus, an association of more than 250 members dedicated to improving human rights worldwide. He had an exceptionally close relationship with Pam and was the first congressman she'd contacted after Zach's arrest on March 6.

On March 15, I received a messenger phone call from Congressman Porter. He told me that Pam and Marillyn had just called, and that he was very concerned about what happened to Zach. He was also concerned that my brother and I had been assaulted by the KGB and wanted to know if we were all right. At the end of the conversation, he said, "I am going to make a protest in regards to this case to the Soviet embassy in the United States." He did more than that. Following our conversation, he went to the floor of the US House of Representatives and made his first statement on our behalf. From that day onward, Congressman Porter, in effect, adopted us and became one of our most ardent supporters.

On the Floor of the US House of Representatives—John E. Porter (R-IL).

March 15, 1984

Mr. Speaker, I went to the Soviet Union in 1982 to help refuseniks and saw 45 families at that time, and I suffered some of the harassment that the KGB has to offer, but, of course, nothing compared to that suffered every day by people who desire to emigrate and apply for exit visas from the Soviet Union . . .

I wish to report also [that] I placed a call to Tatiana Zunshine, whose husband has recently been arrested in the Soviet Union for his desire to emigrate and for his renouncing of his citizenship in furtherance of his cause and her cause to emigrate. I called her to talk to her and to give her assurances that we care about them and that we are watching what happens. And she told me today . . . that they have been hounded by KGB agents, that most recently she and a brother who was trying to help her were knocked to the ground violently, . . . that they took away all of their [her] papers, including their [her] right to travel in the Soviet Union, and that she has not heard what has happened to her husband, where he is being held . . . that no information is forthcoming, and that the harassment is severe indeed . . .

I will certainly bring this matter up with the Soviet Embassy on Monday. I hope that we can get some action in regard to it to stop these outrageous actions by the Soviet Government against their own citizens, people who simply want to exert basic human rights and human freedoms in a society that has far, far too few of them.

We are going to have to work day after day, week after week, month after month, and probably year after year, in order to provide the kinds of pressures to open up the gates of Soviet immigration and to allow people to escape to freedom.[6]

In the meantime, I deployed another tactic. Back in 1983, about a year before his arrest, Zach came up with a very creative idea. Frustrated by the lack of results from our letter-writing campaigns, he decided to ditch envelopes. "Let's start writing on postcards," he said. "Let's describe what's been happening to us—dismissals from work, charges of disorderly conduct, fifteen-day jailings, threats of psychiatric evaluation, constant surveillance—let's write it all down on a postcard, and send it out, without envelopes, for all to see."

Simple move, right?

Simple but aggravating to our opponents. Flying around the postal channels, accessible for anyone to read, those little three-by-five cards contained bombshells of information. It turned out that sending those postcards was like stepping on the regime's collective toes. By airing our grievances on postcards, we turned them into open letters (literally). Yet sending them out was perfectly legal, and there was nothing *they* could do about it.

When Zach first hatched this idea, we sent postcards to every single deputy of the Supreme Soviet of the Latvian Republic—all 360 of them. Unlike their counterparts in the US House of Representatives, the deputies of the Supreme Soviet typically kept their day jobs (on top of their perk-laden appointments), and their companies' names and addresses were publicly available. We used this opportunity to send the cards to each deputy's place of work.

---

6   *Congressional Record—House* (Washington, DC: US Government Printing Office, 1984), pp. 5647–5648.

That created quite a stir. Some deputies would show up at our door, card in hand. Glancing around fearfully, they asked why we had singled them out and how we knew their work address. We calmly explained that the addresses were public knowledge and that they were by no means singled out—all 360 deputies received a postcard. That served to pacify them a bit, but one female deputy complained: "What are you doing? How would you like it if something like that landed at your place of work? People in the mailroom saw it, and word spread around. Everybody was talking about this."

That was precisely our intention. We knew the postcards were effective when a KGB officer threatened Zach: "If you, Zunshine, do not stop contacting the deputies by postcards, we will begin to doubt the state of your mental health." When that happened, I went to see the same official who had shielded us from a psychiatric examination back in 1983. "There is nothing else I can do for you," he said. "Please stop contacting me." Clearly, he had reached the limit of his ability (or desire) to help.

Well, we decided, *we'll continue sending the postcards, but they will no longer come from Zach.* The next batch of postcards had *my* name on the return address. What were they going to do now? Doubt the state of *my* mental health?

They didn't. The threat fizzled out on its own.

Knowing how effective the postcards could be, shortly after Zach's arrest, I sent another 360 postcards to the deputies of the Supreme Soviet of the Latvian Republic. Describing his unlawful arrest, the trumped-up charges, and his poor state of physical health at the time of the arrest, I sent these postcards to the deputies' places of work and asked them to intervene on our behalf.

I continued using these cards as my weapon for the rest of Zach's incarceration.

CHAPTER 5

THE LADY IN THE CAR WITH GLASSES AND A GUN

Walking along the sidewalk, the last thing one wants to hear is the sound of screeching tires. And yet, that was the sound I had heard from just a few feet away.

It happened so fast—the squeal of the tires, the doors flying open before the car came to a complete stop, men jumping out of it in an alarmingly coordinated way, then shoving me inside and driving off in a roar of exhaust, the tires unspooling a cloud of burning rubber.

"What is going on?" I cried out, grabbing on to the front seat as the car jolted forward.

"Don't pretend you don't know," the guy in the front passenger seat said. He didn't bother to turn his head. "You are going to the KGB headquarters for an official warning."

This was not hard to imagine: In a textbook Jekyll and Hyde scenario, a KGB officer plays the classic good cop, bad cop routine, taking you on a wild roller-coaster ride packed with gruesome threats, psychological abuse, and brutality, alternating with bouts of pretend compassion—up and down, down and up. By the end of the ride, he presents a document containing a long list of outrageous deeds you have supposedly committed, coupled with a warning: *We, the KGB, have been patiently tolerating you so far, but no more; we've had it with you. Should you engage in any of these appalling acts ever again, be assured you will feel the fury of the power apparatus. Sign here. Date here.*

Barely recovered from the initial shock, I gave myself some strict rules to follow: *Once inside the building, don't talk. Don't respond to "How are you?" or "What is your name, address, and date of birth?" None of that. Once the conversation starts, you won't be able to end it. They know how to weave a basket out of you, so don't talk!*

I told the agents that I wasn't going to talk.

"Sure," they said mockingly.

I said it again: "Tell your boss, or whomever you are taking me to, that I won't talk and will not answer any of his questions." To my surprise, they did. They told the officer who met us upstairs what I'd said. It cracked him up.

That man was KGB Major Gailis. He started on a conciliatory note.

"How are you?"

Silence.

"Do you know what you're here for?"

Silence.

Genuinely annoyed, he quickly abandoned his "good cop" persona and went straight to the bad one. "By now," he said harshly, "you've exceeded your husband's record. Not only did you participate in the same protest that he did, but you also brazenly supplied a foreign correspondent with materials right in front of our noses. You've been defaming the Soviet state in your conversations with the West, with Pam—your Pam—while repeatedly supplying her with information."

The list of my misdeeds continued. He brought up the postcards I had sent to the deputies of the Supreme Soviet. "This," he said, "is the last straw. You and your husband were warned not to do it. This we will not tolerate."

By now, he was all worked up. "How many years is your husband facing? Three? Well, you're asking for more! You'll get seven years in prison and five in exile." He went on to paint a vivid portrait of

Siberia's brutal climate, then seamlessly steered to a different kind of climate, the climate of anti-Semitism inside the forced labor camps.

"Wanna see what it's like in there, eh? Well, you're *that* close." He held two fingers so close together they were almost touching. "And how long do you think it will be before your dear friend Pam abandons you? Once you're in jail? Let me tell you: exactly one second!"

On and on it went until he had to switch.

Back to the good cop. "Hey, we understand. You're fighting for your husband. Anybody would understand that. But you've gotta stop, for your own sake. And for his sake, as well. 'Cause you know what we're going to do to *him* if you don't stop?"

In a quick switch, his tone—his whole demeanor—changed. Now it was Mr. Hyde again, recounting all the horrible things they were going to do to Zach if I didn't stop defending him. He took the time to describe it in excruciating detail. He spoke of wild scenes in the men's cells: how newcomers would find themselves thrown to a veritable pack of wolves; how other inmates would strip them of their clothes and subject them to the most humiliating acts; how rape and brutal beatings would occur on a regular basis. "Stop what you are doing," he demanded, "and maybe we can shield him from that. Otherwise, he is on his own. Is that what you want?" By this point, he had worked himself into such a state that his eyes were popping out with rage.

Silence.

While he sat behind his fancy executive desk, I sat in front of it, against the opposite wall. About two yards separated us. He reached across the desk with a document—that official warning they had brought me in for.

"Here," he said. "Read it and sign."

I locked my arms behind my back. He got up, came around the desk, and stuck the document in my face. I turned my head away.

Now he was back behind the desk, the paper still in his hand. Things were not working out for Major Gailis. Time for another code switch. He decided to resort to humor. "Never in my life," he declared jovially, "have I *not* been able to make a woman talk! What's going on here?"

Silence.

"Hey, listen. Now it's getting personal. Can you please say something? It doesn't have to be related to *this*. Say a word, any word!"

Silence.

He waited a few seconds. "Okay, you don't want to talk. But did you hear what I said? I know you didn't listen, but did you *hear*? Blink your eyes if you did." I turned my eyes away to make sure I didn't blink accidentally.

Now, let me tell you what I was doing during the entire ordeal. While he was busy running his mouth, *I* was busy inside my head repeating a single random phrase over and over again. That phrase had popped into my mind the moment I walked into the room, and it wouldn't leave. It was the title of a mystery novel I'd read a while ago by the French writer Sébastien Japrisot: *The Lady in the Car with Glasses and a Gun*. It burrowed into my brain like a mind worm, and I found myself repeating it a thousand times. "The lady in the car with glasses and a gun . . . The lady in the car with glasses and a gun . . . The lady in the car with glasses and a gun." Why this phrase? I don't know. But I do know that it helped me stay silent. By repeating it endlessly and tirelessly, I *was* talking—talking inside my head. And that kept me from responding to my interrogator. But more, by repeating it endlessly and tirelessly, I subconsciously transformed myself into that very lady in the car with glasses and a gun.

By now, the major had grown very frustrated indeed. His pupils darted around as if searching for an answer. He looked bewildered. He knew that he'd used up his arsenal and was going in circles. He also knew this tape-recorded conversation would label him within the agency as powerless and inept, earn him ridicule, and tarnish his reputation. At that point, he lost all patience. He yelled, he roared, he thundered. He'd wipe me off the face of the earth, he promised, leaving nothing of me behind. He, Major Gailis, would personally make sure of that.

Three hours into it, he seemed to have had enough. He rose and motioned me to the door. Standing by the doorway, he said, "I'm letting you go. I just want one word out of you. Any word."

I walked through the doorway like he wasn't there.

Outside the building, I threw my hands up in the air and let out a jubilant "YESSS!"

I was happy to have escaped the trap of KGB interrogation, and yet I soon found myself trapped in a cell. Again. Let me explain.

If you didn't know any better, you might assume that Russian refuseniks were nothing more than a bunch of hoodlums simply because so many of them had *this* written in their record: "Arrested for disorderly conduct and served a fifteen-day term in a county jail."

What was *that* all about? It was about the fact that the KGB liked to give a little preview of what was in store for anyone who didn't obey them. A little tour of the inside of a prison, perhaps? And a small but potent taste of how it would feel to be locked in there.

A fifteen-day jail term for so-called disorderly conduct became a convenient tool in the KGB's arsenal. No disorderly conduct was actually needed as no proof was required to prosecute for the "crime." Just walking down the street, a refusenik could be apprehended, taken to the courthouse, and put in front of a judge. Given that the directive came from the KGB, no judge would ever object to it. He or she would sign you off for a fifteen-day jail term, no questions asked.

Many refuseniks—Zach included—received this treatment at one time or another. Now, it seemed, it was Sasha's turn. He was picked up on the street and sent to a county jail for his fifteen-day term. His wife, Polina, told me about it, and I went to see her to offer my support. Sasha's mother, Svetlana, was there as well.

We knew we had to do something. Throwing Sasha in jail was simply an act of retaliation, and we couldn't let it slide. We decided to stage another protest and use Sasha's lock-up to bring attention to the unlawful treatment of both him and Zach. We invited Zach's younger sister, Zhenya, to join us.

We believed that Zhenya would be safe no matter what happened. A mother of two young children under the age of three, she planned on bringing them with her, a tactic that would best ensure she avoided jail. As for the rest of us, who knew?

With the babies in strollers and signs hidden in our bags, the four of us proceeded to the attorney general's office in downtown Riga. We walked up the front steps, stopped at the entrance, and took out the signs. Mine read RELEASE MY HUSBAND, as did Polina's. Svetlana's read RELEASE MY SON, and Zhenya's, RELEASE MY BROTHER.

What happened next was what happened every time: police arrest, detainment, endless waiting. Our prediction for Zhenya came true—they let her go. Polina, Svetlana, and I, on the other hand, were sent to the county jail to serve *our* fifteen-day term for disorderly conduct.

In a minivan, accompanied by two policemen, we arrived at the county jail. We had heard story after story about that jail from friends and family who had the misfortune of staying there. We had heard about its dreadful, run-down conditions and stale, stinking, unhealthy air. Now it was time to see for ourselves.

The policemen handed us over to the guards, who took us downstairs to the basement. We walked along the corridor, passing cell doors on our left, with the canteen, the toilets, and a few offices on our right. The three of us formed one line, walking hand in hand, guards behind and guards in front. I caught myself thinking that I wasn't scared. Though I would have been horrified had my girlfriends not been next to me.

The guards stopped at a door in the middle of the corridor. It was made of heavy metal and had a small peekaboo window installed for observation. A lot of noise was coming from the other side. When the guards opened the door, the racket abruptly stopped. About fifteen women stared out at us. We stepped in, and the door clanged shut behind us.

The space that greeted us was about 200 square feet. Sitting two feet above the ground was a wooden platform divided into two sections—left and right. A passage on the floor between the platforms extended from the metal door to the opposite wall. Missing from the scene were beds, mattresses, and bedding—those were not allowed. The unyielding surface of the platform was your bed, your mattress, and your bedding.

Some women were sitting on the platforms; others lay around. There was little space left, but we found some in the left section and sat down. We said hi. Nobody answered. The group resumed their conversation, but we didn't understand a word they were saying. Why? It had something to do with the phenomenon of Russian cursing.

Russian cursing is a language in and of itself. Highly obscene, it is vast, complicated, and, some might even say, sophisticated. In that cell, combined with jailbird jargon, the cursing rose to a whole new level of obscenity. To our untrained ears, it sounded almost like a foreign language.

It took time to adjust, but we eventually got the gist of it. And the more we understood, the clearer it became that these women knew who we were. "Somebody" had told them about us, and they didn't like what they had heard. Not talking to us directly but pointing their fingers at us, the women discussed in their profanity-laced lingo the fact that we were protesting the arrests of our husbands and sons. *And who gave us the right to do so?* they wanted to know. How dare we? Oh, if only they were packing a gun right now. "Let me see," one said, "which of them would I take out first?"

This made no sense at all. Why were they so angry with us? And who exactly divulged our identities and reason for imprisonment? We didn't know all the answers, but one thing we knew for sure—it was going to be tough. And it was going to take a lot of discipline not to respond to a provocation, should it head our way. We would have to watch our backs day and night, night and day.

But the problem with night and day was that you couldn't tell one from the other. As part of the punishment, wearing a watch was not allowed. The guards took our watches away once the judge rubber-stamped our sentence. The cell had no window, and the glaring ceiling lights stayed on twenty-four hours a day. Under those conditions, how could you tell day from night? How could you tell what day it was or how many days had gone by? And how could you tell when to sleep and when to wake up?

Falling asleep, in any event, was nearly impossible. The lights glared right in your eyes, and the hard surface was unforgiving on your body. What's more, falling asleep was downright dangerous. The tension between us and the other women was palpable. Polina, Svetlana, and I took turns—one of us closed her eyes while the other two stood guard, then we switched.

The cell was always buzzing with chatter, but one incident left our cellmates speechless.

Among the guards was an infamous woman named Maria, a.k.a. "Mashka." Mashka was a legend. Any man or woman who had ever crossed paths with her in that jail knew her as an intimidating creature. When Zach came home after serving his fifteen-day term in December of 1983, he talked about Mashka, a permanent fixture of the jail. Tall and heavy—no less than 300 pounds—she had piercing eyes and didn't talk much. Yet, her very presence had a paralyzing effect on people. Nobody wanted to mess with her.

Who would have thought I would be the one to cross her?

The air barely circulated in the cell. More and more, I felt the air getting vacuumed out of the room. It was stuffy and hard to breathe. I complained to the guards, but they brushed me off. Then came a moment when I felt I was suffocating, about to pass out. Surprising myself, I ran to the door and began banging on it, yelling, "Open up! Open up!"

When the door opened, who do you think was there? None other than Mashka, with her arms crossed on her chest, her legs spread apart, taking up the entire space of the doorway. What happened next didn't just astound *her*; it astounded *me* as well—I pushed her. Amounting to one third of her weight, I pounced, pushing against her with all my might, making her take a step back.

Eyes wide in a state of shock, Mashka realized she had left a space for me to run out of the cell and into the corridor. Gasping for air, I ran into the nearest office and began telling the officers in the room how unbearable the atmosphere in the cell was. They must have been in shock, which is perhaps why they listened and promised to address the issue. I marched back to the cell. Shortly after, we all felt the air moving a bit better.

Incidentally, Mashka never retaliated. And for about five minutes, judging by a few approving glances, I thought I had gained the respect of our cellmates. But things quickly reverted to "normal."

The provocation that Svetlana, Polina, and I were wary of did not come from our fellow prisoners. It came from the guards. One day, they came in and abruptly ordered the three of us out of the cell.

"Where are we going?" we asked.

"You've been assigned to do some work."

"What kind of work?" The idea of getting out of the cell didn't sound so bad, but what exactly did they want us to do?

"Your job is to clean the bathrooms in the men's section of the jail," came the answer.

"Absolutely NOT!" we said in one voice. They knew we would never have agreed to such a humiliating task. They offered it to us, knowing we would refuse, thus giving them the pretext to punish us.

As it turned out, our punishment was losing the right to a daily hot meal. From now on, we would get a hot meal every *other* day. On off days, we would get a ration of rye bread and a mug of boiling water. But the truth is, what they called a "hot meal" was a muddy-looking liquid of a soup and a plate of something equally inedible. That food was hard to look at and even harder to stomach. To us, alternating it with a piece of bread was more of a relief than a punishment.

The hardest thing to stomach, however, was how badly those jailbirds treated us. For twelve days straight, they terrorized us, yelling, threatening, insulting, and fantasizing out loud about killing us. "This one, or maybe that one, what do you think?" was a constant refrain. Anti-Semitic slurs flew in the air like a swarm of flies. Jews, in these women's minds, were responsible for all the world's sins and needed to be eliminated, starting with the three of us. They never harmed us physically, but a few times, they came close. In the heat of the moment, one woman or another would charge at us only to stop inches away. On and on it went. The threat of violence was always hanging in the air, and at times, the threat felt worse than the violence itself.

On day thirteen, everything changed. An older woman was brought into the cell[7]. In her seventies, she was quite a character. Her face was deeply weathered, her voice was coarse, perhaps from smoking, and her entire demeanor was of someone who commanded respect. She was a career criminal. The women in the cell knew her well. And they knew not to mess with her.

She didn't say much at first, just sat there quietly, watching, observing the situation in the room. As the other women kept up their barrage of insults, she said, "Hold on." Then, "Did these three do something to you?"

Hesitantly, one woman replied, "No . . . not really."

The older woman's voice betrayed her slight irritation. "Then why are you treating them like this?"

That was all it took to transform the situation. The "hyenas" (as we referred to them between ourselves) started pointing fingers at each other: "She did it, not me!"

The scene that followed was surreal. As satisfying as it was to watch them turn on each other as viciously as they had turned on us, it was hard to watch, too. How could one sink so low? The women ended up telling her that the guards had instructed them before our arrival that we were people who had betrayed our country and suggested they treat us accordingly.

That explained everything. But in the older woman's mind, it excused nothing. "If I see you say one more word to them, you are gonna hear from *me*," she declared. The way she said that sent shivers down everyone's spine, ours included.

For the next two days, the tension evaporated, and once it did, the three of us let our guard down and fell soundly asleep. We slept through the bright lights, through the noise, through hot meals and bread-only meals. The harsh surface of the sleeping platform did not

---

7   The woman revealed the date upon arrival.

disturb us in the least. We slept through it all. We slept until the door opened, and the guards ordered us to leave.

When we said goodbye to our "good fairy," she just nodded.

We left the cell.

While my friends and I were still in jail, Representative John Porter was busy circulating the following letter among members of the US House of Representatives. Once he had collected 110 signatures, he sent the letter out, addressed to the investigator in charge of Zach's case, Guntis Grutup, with copies to the Prosecutor General of Latvia, Jānis Dzenitis, and the Secretary General of the Communist Party of the USSR, Konstantin Chernenko.

Congress of the United States
House of Representatives
Washington, D.C. 20515

April 19, 1984

Chief Procurator[8]
Rainis #9
RIGA Latvian USSR

Dear Sir:

I am enclosing a copy of a letter sent by 110 members of the U.S. House of Representatives to Secretary-General Chernenko expressing our concern over the treatment of Zachar and Tatiana[9] Zunshine of Riga.

---

8   Prosecutor General

9   In practically every official document included in this book (e.g., statements by members of Congress, pieces of correspondence, newspaper articles), my husband's and mine first and/or last names were misspelled. For clarity and readability, I corrected the names in the book's documents. The originals still contain misspelled names.

As you are aware, the Zunshines have applied for permission to emigrate to Israel and have been denied their request for exit visas. My colleagues and I are very concerned about the treatment the Zunshines and other Soviet "refuseniks" have been subjected to. We believe that Zachar Zunshine was arrested for appealing his denial of an exit visa. By easing the repression of Soviet Jews such as Zachar Zunshine your government would be sending a clear signal of a commitment to improving U.S.–Soviet relations.

We respectfully urge you to intervene on behalf of the Zunshines, drop the charges against Zachar and grant them exit visas.

I look forward to hearing from you regarding your intentions on this matter.

Sincerely,

John E. Porter,
Member of Congress[10]

For transparency, let me explain the letter's reference to Israel—it is not accidental. At the time, the only way to apply for emigration from the Soviet Union was to list Israel as the destination country. As for Zach and me, our goal was to leave the Soviet Union and settle in the free world, preferably in the United States. We were always open about this. But we could only apply for emigration to Israel. That was the game we were forced to play, and we played it, along with thousands and thousands of hopeful émigrés who, once outside Russia's borders, would clarify their true desired home, whether that was Israel, the United States, Canada, or Australia.

---

10   Tatiana Zunshine's personal archive.

CHAPTER 6

INTO THE WOODS

It had now been seven weeks since my passport was lost—or rather, stolen—during the assault in front of my house. Determined to get it back, I made numerous visits to Soviet officials. They dismissed me. One of the bureaucrats told me bluntly, "We will give you the passport when we feel like it."

Traveling without a passport meant taking a big chance, but I had no choice—I had to keep moving. I went back to Leningrad. As always, I stayed at Yakov Gorodetsky's apartment in the den designated for out-of-towners. On May 4, I spent the whole day moving around town, meeting fellow refuseniks, and gathering support for Zach. Later that day, I heard that while I was out, the KGB had carried out a search of Yakov's apartment; the search was initiated by the investigator in charge of Zach's case, Guntis Grutup. I also heard that the agents had picked the lock, forcibly entered the apartment, and restrained Yakov for no reason whatsoever.

I rushed back to Yakov's to offer support and hear more details. The search was over by then, and the KGB agents had departed. As with any search, they turned the place upside down. Yakov and Lina were busy cleaning it up; I joined in. When the doorbell rang at 9:00 p.m., we didn't hesitate to answer. *The KGB was just here*, we thought. *They wouldn't be coming back, would they?*

They did come back. This time, they came for me. In no time, a handful of agents formed a tight circle around me and forced me out of the apartment. Downstairs, three cars waited at the curb with more agents in them.

"Quite a waste of manpower, don't you think?" I taunted the agent standing next to me. He didn't respond, but once I was inside the car, he made sure to slam the door.

The procession of cars slowly made its way to the train station. There, the men arranged my ticket and put me on a train back to Riga with this warning: *Don't come back to Leningrad ever again.*

This was my first time ousted from a city, but it would certainly not be the last.

On the Floor of the US House of Representatives—Mario Biaggi (D-NY).

May 3, 1984

Mr. Speaker, I am proud to rise today as a cosponsor and advocate of House Resolution 450, a resolution expressing congressional support for Solidarity Sunday, a day when over 100,000 Americans rally in New York City to signify their unity with Soviet Jews . . .

Solidarity Sunday 1984 comes at a critical time for the more than 2,500,000 Soviet Jews, and it represents a unique public opportunity to demand that the new Soviet leadership reopen the gates of emigration and restore the basic human rights of the Soviet Jewish Prisoners of Conscience and refuseniks . . .

Particularly distressing are the considerable number of Soviet Jews who have been arrested, imprisoned, and denied freedom of religious expression in retaliation for requests to emigrate . . .

Tragically, Anatoly Shcharansky, who was arrested on March 15, 1977, on trumped up charges of treason, anti-Soviet agitation, and propaganda, remains imprisoned . . .

Other Soviet Jews, who have required special expressions of concern from myself and other Members of Congress this past year, include Rimma and Vladimir Bravve, Zachar Zunshine, and Vladimir Tsukerman, to name just a few . . .

Mr. Speaker, while it is difficult to assess the impact of any one of these actions in support of Soviet Jews, the message I have received both directly and indirectly from the Soviet Jewish population is that these efforts offer a great deal of much needed hope to the 2.5 million Soviet Jews who are denied any sense of hope by their own Government. As leaders of the free world it is our duty to ensure that these efforts in support of the Soviet Jewry cause continue. Solidarity Sunday is without question one of the most visible displays of our support for Soviet Jews. [11]

In mid-May, Sasha and I went back to Moscow. We planned to see a federal prosecutor in charge of our case. Reminiscent of Kafka's *The Trial*, the case was wrapped in complete secrecy. But knocking on the doors of those behind it still made a tiny bit of sense. Maybe, by meeting in person, some information would emerge through a slip of the tongue.

Getting off the train, we immediately spotted the group of KGB agents waiting for us by the tracks. (By then, Sasha and I had equally developed a radar for their mannerisms and behavior and could easily single them out in a crowd.) *Well, nothing new there*, we both said. From the train station, we went directly to the office of the prosecutor general of the USSR and requested a meeting with the prosecutor overseeing Latvia. Prosecutor Tihy made himself available right away.

"I don't know anything about the case," he said with a poker face.

---

11   *Congressional Record—House* (Washington, DC: US Government Printing Office, 1984), pp. 10973–74.

We then watched the art of evasion unfold before our very eyes. It was masterful. While we pressed him for answers regarding the unlawful charges against Zach, emphasizing that a person cannot be accused of slander for challenging a legal ruling, Prosecutor Tihy deflected. Again and again, he denied any knowledge of the case. By the end, however, he seemed to have "recalled" a little bit about it.

"Your husband's investigation is coming to an end," he said, putting the charade aside. "It will be over around June 10th, at which point the case will move to the courts for trial."

The following day, Sasha and I visited the so-called United Nations Association of the Soviet Union. It was a bogus organization, not to be confused with the UN itself. Using the same approach—knock on every door, and maybe one would open up—we decided to pay a visit.

Founded in 1956 as a nonprofit organization ostensibly "dedicated to building an understanding of and support for the ideals and work of the United Nations" in the USSR, it was, in reality, an arm of the Soviet government. Soviet citizens had no ability to appeal directly to the UN without going through this pseudo organization, whose primary purpose was to ensure that citizens' complaints to the UN never left the room.

I prepared an appeal to the UN Human Rights Commission regarding Zach's unlawful imprisonment. Sasha and I decided to hand-deliver the appeal and *demand* it be forwarded to the UN. An official, one Secretary Krepkov, agreed to meet us.

"Since you are advocating on behalf of someone under investigation, we can't do anything about it," Secretary Krepkov told us. "Let the prosecution run its course." Then he added, "This doesn't belong to us anyway. We only deal with human rights abuses."

I looked at Sasha, shaking my head. This guy must be kidding! How was this not a human rights abuse? We jumped on him. "That

is exactly why we are here! Because of the blatant human rights violations in the case of Zach Zunshine."

Krepkov's response was robotic. "I cannot act unless I get an order of inquiry from the UN Center for Human Rights . . . We do not
deal with violations of the human rights of a single individual . . . We
only deal with violations of colossal proportions," and so on.

It was exhausting talking to that guy. We ended the conversation with a declaration: "What is happening to Zach Zunshine is
also happening to thousands of other people in the Soviet Union,
people just like him—refuseniks, dissidents, religious believers. If
you want us to, we will bring you thousands of appeals like this one.
Together, they will make a claim of colossal proportions."

What a colossal waste of time that was!

On our third and last day, I called a French correspondent from
Agence France-Presse, whom I knew by the first name of Pierre. We
made plans to meet him by Moscow's famous Puppet Theater later
in the afternoon, before our planned departure for Riga that night.

Before the meeting, Sasha and I went to the train station to buy
return tickets to Riga, only to discover they were sold out for the
day. *What should we do?*

One member of our tail team was hanging out just a few yards
from us, pretending to be somebody he was not—an ordinary citizen. I looked at him, and a daring thought crossed my mind. *Why not
ask the KGB to help us get tickets? They're all connected, aren't they? Let
them be useful for once in their lives instead of tagging along after us like
sheep for three days straight!*

I told Sasha what I was about to do. He thought I was kidding,
and that I wouldn't dare, but I said, "Wait for me," and walked up to
the guy. For some reason, he didn't retreat. I said, "Listen, can you

help us get tickets back to Riga? They are currently sold out, but we know you guys have some sway. So can you please?"

A long moment passed as he stared at me in shocked silence. Then he shocked *me* by saying, "Okay, I'll ask."

I was dying inside, laughing, but I didn't dare show it. He trotted over to the area of the station where the rest of the agents were hanging out. After a few minutes, a different agent showed up. "Nobody asked you to come here," he snarled. "You can leave the same way you came. It's on you."

"Aren't you better off if we leave?" I asked.

"No," he smirked. "*You're* better off if you leave."

We lingered at the train station a while longer, trying to decide what to do. Suddenly, a third agent approached us and said matter-of-factly, "We hear you're having trouble getting tickets. It just so happens—purely by chance, you understand—that two tickets are waiting for you at the ticket office."

We waited until he was out of earshot to burst into laughter. Then we went to get the tickets.

From the train station, Sasha and I headed to the Puppet Theater for our anticipated meeting with the French correspondent. We showed up early and hung around near the theater's entrance, awaiting his arrival. Then we spotted Pierre's Citroën and started walking toward it.

Suddenly, a far too familiar scenario unfolded at lightning speed. Two gray Volgas jumped the curb and surrounded us front and back. In one well-synchronized movement, three men jumped out of the car in front of us and pushed us inside. Before we could blink, the three of them were back in the car with us, driving off. Besides the driver, there was an agent in the front passenger seat. The third agent sat by the window in the back seat. Sasha landed in the middle, next to him, while I ended up on Sasha's other side. Once our car took off, the second car followed.

Pierre attempted to follow us in his car, but one of the men said to the driver, "Lose him." He repeated the same instruction into the radio, and the two cars squeezed Pierre tight, letting him know he was pushing his luck. He was forced to back off.

We asked the men where we were going, but they weren't talking. Suddenly, the car began speeding. It accelerated so fast that Sasha and I had to grab onto each other. The second car stayed neck and neck with ours. Neither car had sirens to alert the crossing traffic, which made plowing through intersections at top speed a terrifying experience. Sometimes, they stopped for a red light, but other times, they flew right through.

What is going on? They are going to kill us all!

"Who are we chasing? Can we please slow down?" I asked anxiously.

They ignored the question and continued with reckless speeding.

"Hey, listen, we know your lives are worthless, everybody knows that," one of us said rather daringly (I can't remember who that was), "but we're still young, and we'd prefer to stay alive—so could you pleeease slow down?"

The agent in the front passenger seat said, "Shut your mouth."

We left Moscow's historic center, passed through an unending succession of Stalinist neighborhoods, and continued on to the newer developments. By then, we knew they weren't taking us to KGB headquarters (we had left that building in the dust). We sped through the outskirts of Moscow, then blasted through a series of townships before turning onto a narrow road leading into the woods. There, finally, they had to slow down. The two cars—ours and the one that followed—wobbled on a bumpy road bordered by trees on both sides. Then they turned off the road into the woods and navigated between the trees. Ten minutes into this joyride, our car stopped, and the men got out.

"Sasha, get out." All three men stood by the open door.

I dug my fingers into Sasha's arm. "He is not going anywhere by himself," I said. "Either we go together, or we don't get out at all."

A series of heated exchanges followed.

The men yelled, "Get the hell out!" "Out—now!" "You are testing our patience!"

And I repeated over and over, "He's not going anywhere! If you need to pull us apart physically, you can, but we are not parting voluntarily."

Sasha kept saying, "I'm not leaving her behind!"

The agents did nothing. They looked frustrated. My fingers dug deeper into Sasha's arm, and my mind raced. *Why in the world are they listening to us?* We must have tapped into some gray area. For some reason, these men seemed unwilling to use force.

The other car was about a hundred feet behind us. We noticed it had no license plates. A man stood by each of its open doors. They looked puzzled as if thinking, *What's the deal? Why the delay?*

Then the two agents from our car walked back toward these other men. We watched as the half dozen strangers argued, animated and visibly annoyed.

Coming back, the two agents showered us with threats, but they still hadn't touched either of us. For whatever reason, our line of defense was still working. We just needed to hang on.

By then, we'd been in the woods for over an hour. The two men walked back to the others a few more times, then returned to assail us. Finally, they spoke to someone via radio, and after that consultation, things changed dramatically. Speaking in a conciliatory tone, one of the men said, "We didn't bring you here to hurt you. We brought you here to talk to you, to tell you that making so much noise in support of Zach is making things worse for *him*."

It was almost comical. They had brought us to the woods to talk? How did one respond to something like that? We responded accordingly: "We gotta do what we gotta do."

They got back into the car, turned it around, and we drove off.

In the car, it was quiet for a while, and then Sasha said, "Didn't go all that well for you, did it?"

"Shut your trap, or we'll do it for you," one of them said. We exchanged a few more insults, and then the conversation, such as it was, died out.

Out of the woods, out of the townships, out of the suburbs—

Back to the city.

So, what had just happened? How could we make any sense of it? Why hadn't those men forcibly separated us? With no way of knowing, we could only speculate. Later, when I had time to process our abduction, I conceived a possible scenario.

There was no way to explain that restraint but for the publicity we were building in the United States and the wider world. *Maybe it is starting to protect us*, I thought. *Maybe it is starting to fulfill its purpose.* Thanks to the publicity, in my mind, our captors must have been instructed not to lay their hands on me. But because I glued myself to Sasha, tearing us apart would have required just that—laying their hands on me. If Sasha had gotten out, as ordered, they most likely would have driven off, taking me away and leaving him to face the men from the second car. Those guys were undoubtedly there to teach Sasha a valuable lesson about why he shouldn't be helping people like me. That lesson could have easily included breaking a bone or two.

As for *my* lesson, the most probable scenario was this: driving to another part of the woods, ordering me out of the car, and leaving me there. *Get back to the city on your own if you can.*

If my theory was correct, there were valuable lessons to take away, mainly these: publicity is golden; the KGB, however lawless, still lives by some rules; and, if thrown off script, lower-level agents don't improvise. Something to keep in mind for the future!

Back in the city, the car pulled up to the train station. This time, when the men said, "Get out," we did. Our train was about to depart, and we ran to board it, eager to leave the KGB behind.

Once the train was moving and we were out of the danger zone, I felt the weight of the day's heavy, surreal events crashing down on me. I was exhausted and needed to lie down. Of the four berths in the compartment—two lower and two upper—ours were the upper ones, and we climbed onto them. We were quiet for a while, and then Sasha said, "I'll be back. Need to use the restroom." He climbed down from his berth and left the compartment.

I stayed deep in my thoughts for a while, but then I noticed Sasha hadn't returned. Five minutes passed, then ten, then fifteen.

Suddenly, it hit me: *What if they had boarded the train, too? What if they'd finally got him?* I felt nauseated. *What if they'd thrown him off the train?*

I flew off my berth and ran to the end of the car, then through the door leading to the area where the toilets were. I pounded on the toilet door. "Sasha, you there?"

He opened the door. That's when I burst into tears. "What did you do in there for so long?"

"You mean the number?" he asked, trying to make a joke.

I started laughing through my tears. "I thought they had thrown you off the train, you idiot!"

It was just the release I needed. It made me cry; it made us laugh. We stayed there a little longer, talking.

"Let's not get paranoid," Sasha said. "Promise?"

I promised. We went back to the compartment to rest.

Back in Riga, I didn't waste time. Since my appeal to the UN Commission on Human Rights had not left the United Nations Association of the Soviet Union, I decided to use a back door. I dictated it to Pam over the telephone and asked her to give it a go. This prompted an exchange of communications between the Union of Councils for Soviet Jews and the Centre for Human Rights, United Nations Office in Geneva.

May 22, 1984

To: Mr. Jacob Moller
Centre for Human Rights, United Nations Office at Geneva
1211 Geneva, Switzerland

Dear Mr. Moller,

Thank you for being so immediately responsive to our plea on behalf of the Zachar Zunshine family of Riga, Latvia.

As you requested, I have enclosed a transcript of the telephone conversation between Tatiana Zunshine and Pamela Cohen, Vice President, Union of Councils for Soviet Jews, of May 20, 1984, 8:30 a.m. EST.

The Zunshine case is extremely critical at this time of stepped up "anti-Zionist" activities. (Mr. Zachar Zunshine has been imprisoned since March 5.) It represents a possible Soviet test case that would prevent legal appeals to be made to Soviet authorities for purposes of emigration and repatriation.

Mrs. (Tatiana) Zunshine went to the U.N. office in Moscow on May 19 and met with Mr. Krepkov in the office of the assistant to the U.N. representative. He informed her that he could only act if he had an order of inquiry from the U.N. Centre for Human Rights.

Mr. Moller, I appreciate your attention to this vital human rights matter and look forward to hearing from you soon.

Sincerely,

Robert Arsenault
Associate Director for Congressional Affairs

Soon after, I found out that a televised town hall would be broadcast on Riga's central TV station. The town hall would feature the prosecutor general of Latvia, the minister of justice, and the minister of internal affairs. The citizens of Latvia were offered an opportunity to call and ask questions. As with any town hall, the organizers would select the questions in real time and present them to the panelists for answers.

I organized a little campaign among my refusenik friends in Riga, Moscow, and Leningrad. I asked everyone to call and ask questions about Zach—his imprisonment, his trumped-up charges, and the state of his health. I gave the numbers to Pam, too, and asked for her people to call.

Every phone call, including mine, was interrupted multiple times. Operators on the other side would hang up, only to get another call from one of us. Our questions were never aired. I can't say I counted on it; I just wanted to bring awareness to Zach's case.

A few days later, I secured a meeting with the chief Latvian prosecutor, Jānis Dzenitis. Calling this a meeting would be a stretch because it turned out to be a rather terrifying freak show. "Your husband," he yelled, clenching his fists, "committed a heinous crime. I will personally come to court and do everything in my power to ensure he gets the maximum sentence. Your husband will be jailed . . . even if the court declares him innocent. I will make sure of that!" He then pivoted. "Your husband committed a crime, yes, but the person who is truly responsible for all this is *you!*" he growled, pointing his finger at me. "You are guilty more than he is. You ought to be in jail in the first place! You can tell the West what I've just said."

Oh, yes, I will, I thought. *I will tell the West what you've just said, you freak.*

I passed his words on to Pam and asked her to quote him every chance she got. Not only did she do so, she also tasked a Chicago-based attorney, Michael J. Freed—who happened to be in Moscow for business—with seeking a meeting with the federal prosecutor to express concern about Dzenitis' prejudicial statements. Back in Chicago, Attorney Freed reported to Pam and Marillyn with the following written statement:

To: Pamela Cohen and Marillyn Tallman

From: Michel J. Freed, Much Shelist Freed Denenberg Ament & Eiger, P.C.

Re: Meeting with Deputy Prosecutor Maslov re Zachar Zunshine case

On May 25, 1984 I met with Deputy Prosecutor Maslov in Moscow to discuss the Zachar Zunshine case . . .

Maslov started the meeting by asking why I was there. I advised him that I represented a group of attorneys involved in human rights cases throughout the world and that, as their representative, I wanted to discuss the Zunshine case since I was in Moscow. Maslov asked me how I was familiar with the Zunshine case and I advised him that I heard about it through Tatiana Zunshine . . .

Maslov then inquired about my interest in the case. I informed him that I had heard that Zunshine was being investigated for anti-Soviet slander and that the Latvian prosecutor had made a number of prejudicial statements prior to the completion of the investigation . . . I further said that the prosecutor had expressed a belief in Zunshine's guilt and stated that he would appeal a verdict of innocence. Maslov inquired how I had heard about the prosecutor's statements and I told him that I had heard about them from Tatiana Zunshine, to whom the statements were made . . .

I then took the opportunity to restate the identity of the attorneys who I represented and our concern for the violations of law and human rights violations of the Zunshine case . . . I again restated the position of our group that an appeal to the authorities could not be anti-Soviet slander or anti-Soviet propaganda and that, in fact, any fair legal system would encourage an individual to petition authorities with his grievances and not punish him for doing so . . .

I then advised Maslov that there was extreme concern for the health of Zunshine and that his wife had been absolutely unable to communicate with him. Maslov said that while a person is being investigated it is the standard procedure in the Soviet Union for him not to be contacted by his family. Maslov then volunteered that Zunshine's hunger strike (which had never been previously mentioned in the conversation) would not jeopardize his health because "no prisoner has ever died from a hunger strike in the Soviet jail." Maslov said that Zunshine would either be force fed or fed intravenously if his hunger strike became life-threatening . . .

I took the opportunity to thank Maslov for his courtesies in visiting with me and hearing my position on behalf of my group . . . At this point the meeting adjourned after about 45 minutes.[12]

Around the same time, the New York-based Jewish Telegraphic Press Agency published the following report:

MOSCOW, LENINGRAD REFUSENIKS PLEA FOR RELEASE
OF PHYSICIST HELD AFTER WRITING
LETTER SEEKING EXIT VISAS[13]

NEW YORK, June 7 (JTA)—Scores of refuseniks in Moscow and Leningrad have appealed to Soviet authorities for the release of Zachar Zunshine, a Jewish physicist from Riga who was arrested there last March 6 and charged with the

---

12   Archives, Center for Jewish History, New York, NY.

13   This article originally appeared on the Jewish Telegraphic Agency website. http://pdfs.jta.org/1984/1984-06-08_108.pdf?_ga=2.137396080. 1775847909.1715174440-1737578818.1715174439. The articles may not be reproduced without JTA's permission. More information available at https://www.jta.org/

"circulation of fabrications known to be false which defame the Soviet state and social system."

The appeal and an accompanying statement, dated March 19 and April 5 respectively, were released here by the National Conference on Soviet Jewry and the National Lawyers Committee for Soviet Jewry. The documents point out that the charges of "circulation" and defamation against the 33 year-old Riga refusenik stemmed solely from the content of letters he addressed to the Soviet authorities in increasingly desperate efforts to obtain exit permits for himself and his wife, Tatiana, which have been denied them since 1980 [1981].

Zunshine, who is being held incommunicado in a Riga prison, faces up to three years in a labor camp if convicted. He and his wife have suffered persistent harassment, according to the NCSJ. He has repeatedly asked to renounce his Soviet citizenship and emigrate to Israel to join relatives there.

The appeal on behalf of Zunshine was addressed to the Soviet Procurator [Prosecutor] General, Aleksandr Rekunkov and the Latvian Procurator, Janis Dzenitis. It points out that Zunshine's efforts to get permission to emigrate resulted in the charges against him . . .

The appeal cited "the peculiarity of the judicial investigation at hand" in as much as the alleged defamation of the Soviet State was contained in his letters pressing his case for emigration under Soviet law, the addressees of which were the same authorities who ordered his arrest.

CHAPTER 7

EVERYTHING THAT IS SUPPOSED TO HAPPEN WILL HAPPEN

I am in big trouble. I don't exactly want to admit it, but I've developed a certain phobia. I know where it came from: the assault on my brother and me a few months earlier in the courtyard of my building. The dread of that episode repeating itself now makes me wary of courtyards, entrances, and stairways.

My fear manifested at night, and night only. *How do you know,* whispered my mind, *somebody isn't waiting for you in that dark stairwell?* Stairs were unavoidable—I lived on the third floor of a building with no elevator.

More and more, I found myself reluctant to leave my apartment after sunset. I solicited help from my friends without telling them what was going on. "Come pick me up," I'd say, or, "Can you keep me company going home?" The longer it lasted, the more I realized I had to address it. *I can't let myself be in that kind of a bind,* I kept thinking. I needed help. But the problem was, there wasn't anyone I could ask for help. It was all on me.

The solution came one summer night in early June.

I was returning late at night by train from the nearby town of Jurmala, kicking myself for losing track of time and coming home past midnight. I got off the train and exited the station to catch a cab. There were none in sight. Something must have been going on in the city that night. I decided to walk a few blocks, hoping to catch a cab on the way, but not a single one passed by. When I reached the edge of the central park, a short distance from the train station, I stopped. This park—Riga's oldest—was established in 1814. Stretching across twelve acres of land, it featured exotic trees, flower beds, a rose garden, and a fountain.

As beautiful as the park was in the light of day, at night, it spelled danger. The dark paths winding through old trees looked like sinister alleys. The trees were monstrous. The wind blew, making their leaves murmur, creating a feeling that all of them—the exotic trees, the flower beds, the rose garden, and the fountain—were whispering, conspiring to scare me away. I stood anxiously at the park's edge, not knowing what to do. I could go back to the train station and stay there till morning. Or I could call my friends and ask them to come and get me. Or—

As I stood there, contemplating what to do, I was fully aware of the fact that I was not alone. The agents, standing just a few yards away, were waiting for my decision; they, too, were wondering what I was going to do. I hated for them to see me in this moment of weakness. I began to reason: *What if I went across the park?* There, on the other side, the nightlife was still going strong, and my house was not far away. *What if this was my chance to conquer my fears?* I was afraid of somebody waiting for me in the dark. *What if I took that somebody into the darkness of the alley with me?* By doing so, I could possibly conquer my fears once and for all, couldn't I?

That was quite a thought. But another, bigger one followed on its heels, the most consequential thought of all. If it turned out to be right, I realized, it would free me of my fears and sustain me for the rest of my journey.

Everything that is supposed to happen will happen, and nothing will happen by chance. Remember, I said to myself, *the low-level agents don't improvise. Having received an order to attack, they will carry it out no matter what, no matter where, whether it is in this park, a dark stairwell, the courtyard, or broad daylight. There is nothing you can do to stop them. On the other hand, without such an order, they can't possibly touch you. You can find yourself in the darkest alley, with them only steps away, and you will see that nothing—absolutely nothing—will happen to you.*

Holding on hard to that thought, I started moving toward the park. I went in. I took the first steps cautiously, as if dipping my toes in water, then picked up speed with every step. Walking through the maze of alleys in the darkness of the night, I was riddled with fear. I didn't hear the murmur of the trees; all I heard was my heart pounding. At times, the scrape of the agents' footsteps broke through the sound of my pounding heart. They were behind me, somewhere close, but I didn't dare turn around and look. I kept walking, my knees buckling from time to time.

I don't know how I made it, but I did. Once I made it to the other side of the park, I was cured.

Meanwhile, with Zach's trial looming, it was time to escalate the search for a lawyer.

In political cases, the defendant's family had to go out of their way to find a trustworthy lawyer. This was no easy task, considering how few of them were willing to represent political dissent. Once you did hire one, you had to watch them closely. There was a good chance the lawyer would flip—if they hadn't already—and start double-dealing.

In early June, four weeks before Zach's trial, I hired a lawyer. He was Jewish and a Riga Ghetto survivor. That alone gave me comfort, and I offered him the job. He soon informed me that the investigation had wrapped up ahead of schedule, and the case had moved to the courts for trial. Most importantly, he had met with Zach. According to him, Zach was in good spirits despite conducting numerous hunger strikes, losing forty pounds, and spending 40 percent of his time in a punishment cell (a.k.a. solitary confinement).

"Numerous hunger strikes? Lost forty pounds?[14] Spent half his time in solitary confinement?" I was horrified. "What are they trying to do to him?"

The lawyer ignored my questions but commented on Zach's appearance: very thin. I showed him a photo of Zach, pre-arrest. "Clearly," he said, "Zach looks quite different now."

The closer we got to the trial date, the less the lawyer was willing to talk. He would visit Zach in prison and come back empty-handed. "How is he?" I demanded, eager to hear every little detail. "Tell me everything!" I got no straight answers. That left me plagued by doubts. *Why is this lawyer so evasive? What if he—? Has he . . . flipped? Is he a lawyer or a liar?*

I would never know the answer. The fact was, it didn't matter. The seeds of doubt had been sown, and I had to let him go. Two weeks before the trial, I found myself in a state of pure panic. *How can I find somebody on such short notice?* I lamented. *And even if I do, how will I ever know who is trustworthy and who is not?*

What sounded like a disaster, however, turned out to be a godsend.

In an act of pure desperation, trying to find a solution to the attorney fiasco, I picked up a brochure summarizing the Code of Criminal Procedure. I skimmed it, looking for . . . I didn't know what. Then something caught my eye. Something so bizarre it gave me pause. It was an obscure little clause that stated, "In addition to a licensed attorney, the persons who can represent a defendant in a criminal court

---

14   In dialogues and personal letters, measurements were initially referred to in the metric system; for clarity and readability, I have converted them to the US Standard system.

are . . . among others . . . close family members." A list followed that included a spouse.

Wait, WHAT?

I reread this clause repeatedly but still didn't know what to make of it. *Is this for real?* I wasn't aware of a single political case where a spouse, a non-lawyer, had served as defense counsel. *There has to be a catch somewhere, no? Otherwise, how could this opportunity have been overlooked? Why hasn't anybody tried it before?*

I was losing my mind, and I didn't have an answer, but I knew what I was about to do. *Let me be the first one to try it*, I thought. *I'll never know until I do.* That same day, citing the clause, I submitted a petition asking the court to allow me to serve as my husband's defense counsel.

After a short wait, the response came back. And it read: "APPROVED."

This was truly one of those pinch-me moments.

Stunned, I stared at the paper. I thought I was dreaming. Otherwise, what had just happened? Did they have any idea what they were doing? Was I missing something? Had they missed something? Becoming Zach's defense counsel gave me the right to access the file of his criminal proceedings: his trumped-up charges, the protocols of interrogations, witness testimony, internal communications, and other materials therein. Obtaining these documents would grant me a rare glimpse into the lawless and arbitrary world that ruled political cases like ours—and provide the rarest opportunity to expose it.

If this wasn't surreal enough, there was more: becoming Zach's defense counsel gave me the right to see him—my client—prior to the court hearing for an unsupervised, uninterrupted meeting inside the prison, lasting up to seven hours.

For the wife of a political prisoner, all this was unheard of and unprecedented.

Somebody pinch me!

Armed with the document approving my role as defense counsel, along with lots of pencils and paper, I headed to the prosecutor's office to gain access to Zach's file. My document had been signed by the judge assigned to Zach's case, but somehow, I still wasn't convinced. Could it be a joke? I imagined handing my paper to the official in charge only to see him or her laugh devilishly in my face.

I had been working myself up for nothing because the opposite happened. I was greeted at the door and led to an office. Others in the room were doing their daily work. The person in charge offered me an empty desk and a chair and explained the rules. I could be in the office eight hours a day for a total of three days. I could copy the originals; I could not, however, take any originals outside the office.

He brought me three fat volumes of the criminal proceedings. They included a bill of indictment, Zach's letters to Soviet officials written before his arrest, his letters to the prison administration demanding they stop their inhumane treatment of him, the witness interrogation reports, the experts' conclusions, the chief investigator's requests, and all the other nuts and bolts of the case.

I opened the first volume, and there it was, on the top page: a shamelessly fabricated Bill of Indictment. This document, in particular, would have never seen the light of the day had I not assumed the role of Zach's defense counsel.

Bill of Indictment N81200184

Zachar Zunshine, born in 1951, of Jewish nationality, residing permanently in Riga, previously not convicted, married, highly educated, is accused of systemic dissemination in oral and written form of deliberately false insinuations, defaming the Soviet state and social system after refusal by the emigration officials of the Ministry of Internal Affairs of the Latvian Republic to grant him and his wife permission to leave the Soviet Union.

With this goal, he manufactured, with the aid of a typewriter, epistolary works in the form of letters, complaints, and applications, in which he expounded actions of the emigration officials and other authorities in a distorted way, asserting—with reference to refusal to grant permission for exit—that there is no observation of law in the Soviet Union, designing to show under a negative light some aspects of the state and social system as a whole and the work of specific state organs in particular. Zunshine sent these manufactured works by mail to various state and social organs.

To show in a negative light some aspects of the state and social system, Zunshine, on occasions of important political events in the USSR—namely, during a Session of the Supreme Soviet of the USSR—walked out on the streets of the capital, Moscow, with posters, on which were inscriptions defaming the Soviet state and social system.

By the actions mentioned above intended to discredit Soviet power and Soviet democracy, Zunshine committed a crime stipulated by Clause 183 of the Criminal Code of the Latvian Republic.

Next, I reached for Zach's letters. These hurriedly scribbled lines were handwritten on torn-off pieces of heavy brown stock paper. My eyes filled with tears as I read them while copying their contents into my notebook as fast as I could. The whole time, I was terribly anxious that a random tear might escape—much as I tried to prevent it—land on the paper and smudge it, causing blame to fall on me and denial of further access to the documents.

March 14, 1984

To: The Prosecutor's Office of the Latvian Republic
From: Zachar Zunshine

On March 13, I was summoned to see Investigator Grutup. I informed him that from March 6—that is, from the date of my arrest—till March 12, I was in the prison hospital. From March 8, they stopped giving me medication, and an orderly threatened me with a punishment cell when I asked him to be more civilized and to refrain from unnecessary insults directed at me.

On March 12, I was discharged from the hospital with a fever well over 100°F. Furthermore, I get nothing but denials from the administration when I request a pen and paper to write a complaint about their illegal actions.

In addition, on March 12, I was thrown into a "common" cell, as it was later revealed, "by mistake." There were sixty men in the cell. I asked Investigator Grutup to inform the officials of the shadow organization which stood behind this frame-up. If their plans don't go as far as to murder me, I request that they don't repeat such "mistakes" in the future. To put you into the common cell, where "fresh fish"[15] are stripped of their clothes while being subjected to a process of initiation—the most devastating procedure, designed to squeeze a person out of their dignity—where people from the Sonderkommando[16] beat you to the ground, damaging your kidneys and liver for refusing to accept the "Law of the Wolf Pack"—this can mean dooming you to inevitable death.

It has become increasingly clear that life does not constitute a primary value in itself. There are more important things in the world than life itself, and in some cases, it is not worth a damn to cling to it very strongly. Or is somebody out there proposing that jailbirds will straighten me out? And I, following their wishes, will catch flies[17] or get down on my knees just to stay alive?

On March 14, Investigator Grutup summoned me back. I informed him that, as of that day, I was declaring a hunger strike to protest the lack of medical treatment. Since the day of my arrest, I have had a constant fever, and an inflammation in my throat has

---

15   Newcomers.

16   Prisoners appointed by prison officials to run the common cell; not by accident were they given this Nazi label.

17   A bizarre form of inmate initiation for newcomers.

been rapidly developing to the extent that when I drink, the water comes out of my nose. I asked Investigator Grutup to get me some aspirin. Nothing more than damned ASPIRIN!

How do you think Investigator Grutup responded to my request? Very simply. He doesn't have any aspirin. He cannot influence the prison administration. As for common cells, they are not that bad; nobody is being killed there, and order there— thanks to the Sonderkommando— is being maintained pretty well.

Z. Zunshine

Halfway through the letter, I had to stop. This was too much to bear. I sat there, my hands covering my face, catching my tears. I kept saying to myself, *I can't read this, I just can't. This is horrid, and I can't imagine Zach going through this.* I ached for him. It took time to pull myself together, but I knew I had to. Still rattled by the vivid picture Zach painted of the jungle of prison life, I read on. It took a lot out of me. I copied the letter with trembling hands and turned to his next one.

March 21, 1984

To: The Prosecutor's Office of the Latvian Republic
From: Zachar Zunshine

In some very elaborate and crafty manner, the investigator has led me to consider the fact that the court makes generous allowances for those—and my case would not be an exception—who accept their guilt, understand the fallacy of their delusions, and cease to persist in defending them.

One who said "A" should say "B." The investigator uttered his own "B." It was as absurd and meaningless as everything that has been happening here, and it came down to this: if I were to accept my guilt, the court might be so generous as to sentence me to one year of probation instead of imprisonment in a labor camp.

The office in which the questioning took place was small and windowless. The only light bulb shed its banal light. The investigator—a corpulent, stout person aged about fifty who habitually repositioned his glasses on his nose—leafed through the pages of the examination form. From time to time, he stood up to vent his feelings and began to walk back and forth, making the office seem even smaller.

Every day, every hour, every moment, nature creates and observes its sacraments. Isn't it a sacrament, a miracle, that if the investigator were in my shoes, he would be content, or rather, happy, to sell his soul for a year of probation, but as for me . . . why the hell would I take this bait?

Z. Zunshine

That was quite a scene he had transported me into. I could see the windowless room with a dim light, Zach sitting in front of that corpulent investigator, laughing off his offer. I wondered how little they knew Zach to offer him freedom in exchange for his admission of guilt for something he hadn't done. *They've got themselves the wrong man*, I thought. I was proud of him. I knew he couldn't have lived with himself had he accepted the deal.

Then a single-page witness testimony caught my eye. It caught my attention because it had nothing to do with the actions Zach was accused of. Instead, it had to do with his attitude. This little piece of paper truly gave me pause. The person providing this testimony could have easily stepped off the pages written by absurdists like Franz Kafka or Albert Camus.

From teacher V. V. Korobtsov, Evening School #4

May 17, 1984

I have known Zachar Zunshine, the physics teacher from evening school #4, since December 1982. In June 1983, he was laid off from his job. Zunshine's attitude toward our ideological and political development was quite negative, and he didn't try to conceal it. In particular, it came to light when Zunshine was asked to report to one of our regular meetings; there, he announced that he planned to leave the country and, therefore, should be spared of participating in meetings of that kind. His answers to our questions were rude and tactless. For example, answering the question of why he didn't attend a seminar on Soviet politics and Soviet ideology, Zunshine said, "Because Marxism-Leninism is horseshit." After the meeting, I, together with the chairman of the committee, decided to talk to Zunshine to convince him that he was greatly mistaken in regard to our Soviet ideology and our Soviet way of life. As soon as I started talking to him, he suggested for me not to speak to him about those seminars ever again and repeated, "Marxism-Leninism is horseshit." Then he left. Therefore, I have twice heard him being aggressive toward our Soviet ideology.

Signed,
V. V. Korobtsov

On June 26, two days before the trial, I stood outside Riga's Central Prison. It was a formidable complex. The two-story administrative building faced an abandoned street with a metal fence separating it from some train tracks. A barbed-wired wall stretching hundreds of yards in each direction enclosed the entire campus, including the several four-story buildings where prisoners were kept. Observation towers set a short distance apart encircled the perimeter. Both the outer wall and the buildings inside it, their worn camel paint dotted with patches of white, black, or gray, looked dreadful.

I was about to see Zach. As I waited, I recalled the night he was taken away and how, at that moment, I was unable to move, unable to breathe. *How long has it been?* I asked myself. *Only a few months. A* few months that felt like an eternity. A few months when I'd never stopped moving and never had a chance to catch my breath.

Many more months were going to pass, I knew, too many to count. But for now—

I was about to see Zach. If you had asked me just a few weeks before if that was possible, I would have said you were dreaming. Was *I* dreaming?

I showed the guards the paper authorizing my access, and they let me in.

And now let me tell you something.

I saw the inside of the prison. Unlike the county jail, bad as it was, this was the real thing, a spine-chilling human construction I was permitted to see from a unique angle. Not in a visitors' meeting room, divided into two compartments by a glass partition—one side for the family, the other for the inmate—where the best policy for an inmate having a one- or two-hour conversation (with a prison warden listening in on the phone line) is to tell the family: *Don't worry. I'm holding up fine.*

No, I saw a different prison. The one where barred gates rise up with a metallic screech right in front of you like gnashing teeth, and as you pass through, one after another, they crash down again behind your back with the same nerve-shattering squeal, making you shiver with the inescapable fear that you yourself may be trapped forever.

I ran into escorts leading inmates to interrogations. The inmates, their shoulders bent and arms tied behind their backs (in compliance with prison regulations), looked like they were trying to become more invisible than they already were. But walking through the long, dimly lit corridor, I thought of one thing and one thing only: *I'm about to see him.*

The guards placed me in the office designated for interrogations and told me to hold on while they brought him in.

The door opened. Zach was standing in the doorway.

We stood there locked in what might have been the world's longest embrace.

Once he regained his ability to talk—which took a while—we looked around for a place to sit. The room was small, poorly lit, with a desk and two chairs—one for an interrogator, the other for an inmate—both bolted to the floor. We spotted a bench in the corner. Trying to avoid a situation where one of us had to sit in the interrogator's chair, we landed on the bench. It was just big enough to fit the two of us.

I took a closer look at Zach, and oh, my god! Thin, so thin, pale from lack of sunlight and fresh air, with long, uncut hair. *What miracle had made him even more handsome?*

At first, all he could do was stammer, "How? How is this possible?" He was still in shock and disbelief. It was a surreal moment, not just for him but for me, too. We both thought we were dreaming.

I told Zach how I had gotten there. He found it remarkable. The guards didn't warn him he was going to see his wife. All they said was, "Zunshine, out, you're meeting your lawyer." And what a shock I gave him, being there!

We spent seven hours in that room.

I told him about Pam Cohen, Congressman John Porter, Sasha Balter, Yakov Gorodetsky, our new friends all over Moscow and Leningrad, and the mounting support we'd been getting. I told him about the woods, the trains, the automobiles, the assault, the official warning, the protest, my jail time, and everything else that had brought me to this point. We talked about the night in the park and my fears—all quashed by a simple thought: *Everything that is supposed to happen will happen, but nothing will happen by chance.*

He told me about his life in prison, and I listened in horror, shivering inside, trying not to miss a single word. As it turned out, on the very first day, the prison administrators made their intentions clear. "We are going to let you rot in the punishment cell," they said, and they delivered on their promise.

Here is the punishment cell in Zach's description: Known formally as the "special isolation cell," it had a few nicknames—box, sack, coffin, dungeon. Designed to make a prisoner's life a living hell, it measured all of forty square feet. The tiny room was always semi-dark, with no window and one meager light bulb encased in metal gratings to dim its glow. "When you step out of there," Zach said, "daylight cuts into your eyes like a sharp knife." He went on: The air was stale. Concrete walls, floor, and ceiling made the inside temperature unbearably cold in the winter and too hot in the summer. A hot meal was served only every other day, alternating with a ration of bread and a mug of boiling water. Drinking water was not easily accessible—the water pump outside the cell was at the guards' disposal; some would turn it on, while others refused. In this environment, time stood still. You learned the day was over when a guard showed up to lower a wooden cot bracketed to the wall. The bare planks of the cot were all you've got; no mattress or bedding allowed. At 6:00 a.m., the guard would return to fasten up the cot. Climbing off, you felt the pain spreading over your body, overwhelming it. Caused by pressing against the harsh, unyielding surface of the cot, the pain, it seemed, accumulated in the night, waiting for the morning to show up. It then showed up with a bang. Groaning, you would move your achy self onto a wall-mounted bench, but not for long. That bench just wasn't big enough to seat a grown man. Between the pulled-up cot and the too-small bench, you would end up on your feet for most of the day. At times, water crept through the concrete cracks, threatening to keep you off the floor (as a workaround, the guards provided a pair of old galoshes[18]). After hours of pacing the tiny cell, exacerbated by hunger, darkness, thirst, wet

18   Rubber shoes worn on top of regular shoes

floor, and stale air, by nightfall, your head would be spinning, and your legs ready to give way.

For one manufactured reason or another, Zach spent almost half the time of his pre-trial imprisonment—58 days out of 144—in the hellish environment of punishment cells. Including now. Two days before our meeting, he had been thrown in there yet again. The most probable reason was to weaken him before the trial, scheduled just a few days out, and keep him there for its duration. The special uniform and those infamous galoshes he wore reflected the fact that he had come straight from the punishment cell. Once our meeting was over, the guards were going to take him back.

"When you get out of there," Zach said, "the regular cell feels like paradise."

Every word felt like a dagger in the heart. "Animals!" I cried. "What animals! How can we stop them from torturing you?"

"Just keep doing what you are doing," Zach assured me. "That international campaign you're building, all that support, the maximum exposure, and publicity—that's what will keep me alive."

We both agreed it was the only way. We would expose every instance of their rotten treatment of him. We would find out who was responsible and call them out by name. Let them hear their names broadcast in the foreign media and spoken by political and public figures from the United States, Europe, and elsewhere. Let them know they couldn't make a single move without having it echoed from across the ocean. We would air their dirty laundry for all to see. We would expose every detail of the inhumane conditions in their prisons and camps. Using the avenues of publicity we'd established, we would elevate the case so the guards no longer had discretion in their treatment of Zach—no, that would be too volatile and unpredictable. Thanks to the spotlight of international attention, those decisions would now rest with Moscow. Then, and only then, we could confidently repeat my fear-canceling mantra: *Everything that is supposed to happen will happen, but nothing will happen by chance.*

The guards showed up as we were saying goodbye. It was a devastatingly crushing moment. As Zach was led out of the room with a guard on either side, he turned his head and smiled at me with his eyes. "I'll be okay," he said.

And then he was gone.

Locked in prison, Zach didn't waste time. He came up with a secret code. It was designed for future use: to smuggle information via letters in and out of the labor camp—information that would otherwise have been prohibited. He masterminded writing letters with messages hidden between the lines, ensuring the content sounded intelligible, reasonable, and utterly inconspicuous.

To hide a message within our letters, we would place every letter of every secret word in predetermined positions scattered throughout the text. Those positions were based on an algorithm Zach created, which served as the key to retrieving the message. The starting point of the message would correspond with the day of the month the letter was written, thus creating about thirty different ways to hide the message within the text.

Zach told me about his code the day I spent with him in prison. Afraid to talk about it out loud for fear of the room being bugged, he whispered it in my ear.

"How brilliant, and what a lifesaver!" I whispered back.

Using the code, he could leak vital information from the labor camp: his health, conditions in the camp, how they were treating him—everything they didn't want him to tell. I, in turn, could tell him what was happening at home and how much support we were getting. I would now be able to provide all the encouragement I possibly could.

Before I left the prison, I had to memorize his algorithm. We kept whispering in each other's ear until we were both sure I'd gotten it. On the way home, I was anxious about remembering the code. Even though I thought I'd learned it, what if I messed it up before I'd have a chance to write it down? One mistake would break our whole line of communication. Once at home, I found a group of friends waiting for me in my apartment, eager to hear the details of the meeting. Before I said a word to anybody, however, I wrote down the algorithm and hid it in a safe place.

The very first letter I received from Zach from the labor camp would prove my memory had served me right. Within the maze of words, I would find his message.

CHAPTER 8

A SATIRICAL HORROR SHOW

On June 28, 1984, the long-awaited court trial of my husband, Zachar Zunshine, took place.

Let me rephrase that: On June 28, 1984, a satirical horror show called *The Trial of Zachar Zunshine* premiered. A prime specimen of absurdist drama, this play featured the KGB in the leading role, a judge in a supporting role, and a defendant, played by Zachar Zunshine, in a bit part.

The trial, indeed, had all the elements of a staged theatrical performance. Its artistic director—the all too familiar KGB Major Gailis—strolled the courthouse hallways in dark glasses, putting on the airs of a celebrity and making it known that the place belonged to him. (It did!) The stage manager, Major Zhukov, wearing an armband that read STEWARD, was busy giving last-minute instructions to the stagehands and ushers—all KGB agents.

It would have been funny had it not been so tragic.

In the days leading up to the trial, family and friends from various parts of the country flocked to Riga, some despite the danger it posed. Once again, rejecting the idea of staying put, my brother, Gena, flew in to be there for Zach and me. Others made attempts to travel to Riga but were forced off the trains. Whoever made it there wanted to be a part of it and, most importantly, wanted to show their support for Zach. Nothing was surprising about that. In general, loyalty and friendships among fellow refuseniks ran solid and deep. We were more than friends; we were "partners in crime," in the best sense of the term.

Our two families, mine and Zach's, arrived at the courthouse an hour early on the day of the trial. Zach's parents, in their sixties, anxiously awaited the chance to catch a glimpse of their son for the first time in months. One by one, each of our friends and supporters checked in. We gathered in front of the courtroom, waiting for the doors to open and for a bailiff to allow us to take our seats. I was there both as Zach's wife and as his defense counsel. In the normal course of events, I would have taken a seat at the counsel table.

But that's not what happened.

Three buses arrived and unloaded a large group of people in the courtyard. *Who are they?* We wondered. We were stunned to realize that these were the extras in this drama, recruited to play the role of an audience. Employees of an anonymous organization, they'd been promised a fun day outside the office, fully paid. The KGB agents directed the imposters upstairs and ushered them into the courtroom. Meanwhile, another group of agents pushed us from where we stood in front of the courtroom to the far corner of the hallway, forming a human shield and bulldozing us with their bodies.

It was madness. A scuffle erupted. A young agent twisted the arms of Zach's father, Mikhail, a sixty-two-year-old college professor and World War II veteran wearing military medals on his jacket. "Who do you think you're assaulting, you punk?" Mikhail cried out. "A war veteran! A participant in the Battle of Stalingrad!"

Zach's mother pleaded, "What are you doing? Stop it!"

Suddenly, we spotted Zach being escorted by guards into the courthouse. We began to chant, "Zach, we're with you!" A man with an armband ordered the person who started the chanting detained.

As Zach's defense counsel, I demanded answers. I went straight to Major Gailis because he was clearly running the show. But apparently, Major Gailis had not recovered from the embarrassment I caused him by keeping silent for three hours straight and making him look like a fool during our "official warning" session a few months back. He was still mad, so mad he wouldn't look at me.

"What's with all these strangers, and why aren't Zach's friends and family allowed in the courtroom?" I protested.

"The courtroom is full," he answered through gritted teeth. "There are three seats left—for the defendant's father, mother, and sister. You may take your seat at the counsel table."

Now it was my turn to get angry. "Shame on you! You've packed the room with strangers so that Zach's supporters can't get in." He didn't respond, making it clear the conversation was over.

Back with my friends, I hurriedly wrote a petition to the judge asking for a meeting with my client. He allowed it—limited to fifteen minutes—and the guards led me to the courthouse basement, where Zach was held.

I described to Zach how the situation was unraveling upstairs. They packed the courtroom with strangers and KGB agents, I told him. They staged a freak show, and all they were waiting for was our participation. I mentioned that I had submitted a list of witnesses for the court's approval, which the judge ignored. At the moment, we had no way of presenting witnesses. *What should we do?*

The decision came fast. What do you do when you don't like the show? You walk out! In our case, that meant we wouldn't walk *in*. We would demand that the court open up the trial by letting the defendant's friends and supporters into the courtroom. Just as important, the court had to allow the defense to present witnesses. If these demands were not met, we would not participate.

We scribbled all this on paper before the guards came to take me back upstairs. I gave the paper to the bailiff, asking him to pass it on to the judge. Then I waited for the judge to rule, but that didn't happen. Instead, a KGB officer, the stage manager with the armband, came to me and asked, "Are you no longer interested in serving as defense counsel?"

"As interested as I've ever been!" I exclaimed. "I'm interested in representing my husband at trial—you're making a mockery of it."

He then announced that our requests were denied. "The room is full," he said. "There are only three seats left—for the immediate family. No place for friends and supporters. No witnesses allowed. Take it or leave it. Now, are you going in or not?"

"No," I answered emphatically.

"In that case," he said flatly, "your permission to serve as counsel has been revoked."

I was angry, but I wasn't surprised. I knew we had done the right thing by standing our ground. No supporters and no witnesses? Then no participation from our side. Zach and I were in total agreement when we discussed it during our fifteen-minute talk in the basement.

And that is how it all went down: None of the family, including myself, stepped inside the room. Having revoked my permission to serve as counsel, the court did not bother to appoint another. At this point, none of it mattered. The sentence was predetermined, and the rest was a pure charade. Zach declared that he did not intend to co-operate with this court. Truly in keeping with his bit-part role, he uttered a single phrase: "This audience is not for me."

He kept silent and smiled from time to time when the judge asked him questions, when the witnesses for the prosecution gave their mumbling testimony, when the prosecutor made his closing argument, when they offered him a chance to make a statement, and when the judge announced a guilty verdict with a maximum term of three years in the Gulag.

The entire show lasted two and a half hours, with one intermission.

It's hard for me to recall the night following the court trial. I remember being utterly exhausted, almost hollowed out. After so much preparation and anticipation, was this how it had to end? No trial, just a complete travesty of one? Many people gathered in my apartment, where a somber mood prevailed. I remember friends telling me that they had already contacted Pam and that she had passed the information along.

An immediate response from John Porter followed.

On the Floor of the US House of Representatives—John E. Porter (R-IL).

SOVIETS RAILROAD REFUSENIK ZUNSHINE TO LABOR CAMP

June 29, 1984

Mr. Speaker, for several months I have been actively following the plight of Zachar and Tatiana Zunshine. On March 15, 1984, I had the opportunity to speak with Tatiana Zunshine on the telephone from my Washington office. During our telephone conversation Tatiana described to me the persecution she and her husband had suffered as a result of applying for emigration visas.

In early March Zachar Zunshine was arrested following his attempt to appeal a government decision to refuse him and his wife permission to emigrate. Out of concern over his arrest, over 100 House Members joined me in writing Secretary General Chernenko to express our views on the treatment Zachar and Tatiana Zunshine had been subjected to.

Following his arrest Mr. Zunshine was charged with spreading anti-Soviet slander. Since his arrest a widespread effort mounted to protest his unjust arrest. However, I am sorry to have to report today that Zachar Zunshine was sentenced to 3 years in a labor camp as punishment for his so-called criminal acts.

CHAPTER 8: A SATIRICAL HORROR SHOW

In the free world, we know that Zachar Zunshine is not a criminal. He and his wife are guilty only of having expressed a desire to live in Israel.

And the Soviet authorities know that Zachar Zunshine is not really a criminal. They resorted to a mock trial with no semblance of justice in their attempt to prove Zachar's guilt. A week ago the authorities agreed to allow Tatiana to serve as counsel to her husband during his trial. Yesterday, they reversed their decision and denied her permission to represent her husband. At the trial, the authorities refused to allow the defense to present witnesses. Following his unbalanced trial, it comes as no surprise that Zachar was found guilty. In protest against his unfair trial and unjust sentence, Zachar Zunshine has announced his plan to begin a hunger strike.

Mr. Speaker, I know that my concern over the treatment of Zachar Zunshine and other Soviet refuseniks is shared by many Members of the Congress, by our constituents, and others living in the free world. I urge my colleagues to raise their voices in protest against the treatment of Zachar Zunshine. We must continue to call attention to the abuses of the Soviet Union and their continued harassment of Soviet Jews and other minorities who are denied their fundamental freedoms.[19]

The White House
Washington

The Honorable John Edward Porter
House of Representatives
Washington, D.C. 20515

June 28, 1984

Dear John:

Thank you for your June 19 letter to the President in which you quoted from a telephone conversation between Tatiana

---

19   *Congressional Record—House* (Washington, DC: US Government Printing Office, 1984), p. 20461.

Zunshine, a Soviet Jew, and a representative of Chicago Action for Soviet Jewry [Pamela Cohen].

We appreciated hearing from you and receiving this account of the problems which Zachar Zunshine has encountered in his attempt to emigrate from the Soviet Union. In addition to conveying your concern to the President, I have asked his foreign policy advisers to review the information in your letter and in the letter which you and a number of your colleagues sent to Mr. Chernenko on April 6. In the interim, let me assure you that this Administration shares your concern over the human rights situation in the Soviet Union and will continue to take every appropriate opportunity to keep the Soviets aware of our deep concern for this matter.

With best wishes,

Sincerely,

M.B. Oglesby, Jr.
Assistant to the President[20]

United States Department of State
Washington, D.C. 20520

July 6, 1984

The Honorable John E. Porter
U.S. House of Representatives

Dear Mr. Porter:

Thank you for your recent enquiry enclosing correspondence concerning the Zunshine family, which has long sought to emigrate from the Soviet Union.

The United States Government has followed with concern the case of Zachar and Tatiana Zunshine. Zachar Zunshine was arrested March 4 in Moscow when he and several other refuseniks from Riga, Latvia, staged a brief demonstration

---

20 Tatiana Zunshine's personal archive.

to renounce their Soviet citizenship and demand permission to emigrate. On March 31, Tatiana Zunshine met with Americans outside the Moscow synagogue. She subsequently returned to Riga, and in early April was reportedly taken into custody for a period of fifteen days. There is as yet no confirmation of what charges Zachar Zunshine might face, or when he might come to trial.

The United States Government has consistently encouraged Soviet authorities to adopt a more favorable attitude toward Soviet Jews who wish to emigrate. We have included the Zunshine family on the Department of State's list of Soviet Jews who have been denied emigration to Israel despite repeated applications. We present this list periodically to high Soviet officials to emphasize the deeply felt beliefs of the American people and government that Soviet Jews should not be forced to stay in the Soviet Union against their will. The Zunshine family will remain on this list until their case is resolved favorably.

Unfortunately, the Soviets have not been responsive to our efforts, labeling them as "interference" in their internal affairs. U.S. influence on Soviet emigration practices and decisions remains extremely limited. We will not give up, however, and intend to persist in our attempts to exercise what influence we have.

Sincerely,

Robert F. Turner, Acting Assistant Secretary
Legislative and Intergovernmental Affairs

Back in his punishment cell, Zach declared a hunger strike, protesting his absurd trial without legal defense and witnesses.

During our brief talk in the basement before the trial, he told me about his intention to go on a hunger strike.

"Not only will I not participate in that sham of a trial," Zach said, "I'll stage a hunger strike, too."

"And so will I!" I chimed in.

As it turned out, we were not the only ones willing to declare hunger strikes. In a show of solidarity, over a hundred refuseniks in Riga and Leningrad announced a series of hunger strikes that started on July 10 and lasted for a hundred days. According to the Union of Councils for Soviet Jews, this was "the first time in years that activists in Leningrad and Riga dared, in spite of the difficult situation, to choose a highly demonstrative means of protest . . . This means was chosen to demonstrate solidarity with Zachar Zunshine and to express their protest against the pressure by the authorities in a highly organized way."

On July 23, 1984, in the article "Zunshine in Solitary Confinement," the Jewish Telegraphic Agency detailed the protest hunger strikes. Describing them as a "dramatic and unprecedented show of support," it went on to report that the hunger strikes publicizing Zach's plight were being conducted on a rotating basis, with several fellow refuseniks striking for two or three days followed by another group, and another until all one hundred protesters had participated.

Meanwhile, on July 3, the *New York Times* reported a stunning development: Ephraim Katzir, former president of Israel, was arrested in front of Yakov Gorodetsky's apartment in Leningrad, where a number of Jewish activists had gathered to discuss protesting Zach's imprisonment.

The Jewish Telegraphic Agency published a more detailed account. In a story dated July 5, the wire service reported that Katzir, a biochemist by trade, who had come to Leningrad to attend a scientific conference, recounted that he and his wife had been detained "courteously but very firmly" for ninety minutes:

"We entered the building, and even before we entered the elevator, three men in civilian clothing barred our way. One of them who looked non-Jewish but spoke Hebrew, showed us their KGB cards and asked us to accompany them to police headquarters for interrogation," Katzir said.

He said he clearly identified himself as Israel's ex-President, but this made no impression. He and his wife were driven in a military jeep accompanied by the three KGB agents and several armed soldiers to an official building, about 10 minutes' drive from the building where they were arrested.

They were asked to empty their pockets and Mrs. Katzir had to show the contents of her handbag. The Hebrew-speaking KGB man acted as interpreter during their interrogation. The KGB wanted to know what they had been doing and with whom they met since their arrival in the USSR two weeks earlier.

After nearly 90 minutes they were told they could return to their hotel and that same evening they boarded the night train to Moscow.[21]

I was one of the people planning to attend the meeting with Mr. Katzir. Days after Zach's trial, I went back to Leningrad with hopes of meeting him. Yakov Gorodetsky and I were heading to the house where the gathering was about to occur. The *New York Times*' report that it was held at Yakov's apartment was inaccurate; the meeting was about to take place in the home of a different Yakov, Yakov Rabinovich. But they were correct in stating that a number of Jewish activists had gathered to discuss protesting Zach's imprisonment. And that's what I was there for.

We weren't too far from Yakov Rabinovich's building—about 300 yards—when Yakov Gorodetsky and I were intercepted. The KGB

---

21   This article originally appeared on the Jewish Telegraphic Agency website. The articles may not be reproduced without JTA's permission. More information available at https://www.jta.org/.

agents separated the two of us, whisking us away from each other. They shoved me into a car and drove off. After a short ride in the back seat, I was at the police headquarters, where they put me in an empty office with an agent standing guard on the other side of the door. A KGB officer soon showed up to lecture me on the fact that—not too long ago—I'd been ousted from Leningrad and was told never to come back. And here I was again.

"How many times do we need to tell you not to come here?" he exclaimed irately. "You are testing our patience. We have enough trouble with our own people, for god's sake! We don't need you here, so stay in your lane."

On and on he droned. Tuning him out, I was wondering if my friend Yakov was all right. *I hope they let him go. I hope nobody else was detained on the way to the meeting.*

"Are you listening?" the officer's voice broke in.

No, I wasn't listening.

Later that night, the Leningrad KGB passed me on to two agents who had flown in from Riga to escort me back home. Another ride, this time to the train station, and the three of us boarded an overnight train to Riga. I wanted them to leave me alone for the night and stay in the next compartment, but that wasn't the plan. I was stuck with them for the entire trip.

A few hours into the train ride, the two agents let their guard down. They started mocking their boss, Major Gailis, for failing to make me talk a few months back. (Apparently, rumors flew around KGB headquarters just like everywhere else.) *Why are they putting down their boss in front of me?* I wondered. *Are they baiting me?* Not knowing what to make of it, I ignored it. I ignored them as well.

On the phone with Yakov the next day, I found out that—unlike me—he had not been detained. The KGB let him go right away. He told me not to worry about missing the meeting because it had not taken place. "Katzir and his wife were arrested on the way to the meeting," he said, "just like you were." He told me that the Katzirs and I were arrested five minutes apart.

"Who went down first?" I asked jokingly.

"You did."

Luckily, nobody else did.

Immediately after the court trial on June 28, I filed an appeal asking the higher court to overturn Zach's conviction. Given that the courts played second fiddle to the KGB, there was no hope for any change in the ruling. Applying for an appeal, however, would let the process take its course through all legal avenues. Most importantly, it would postpone the horror of what was coming next. The appeal court granted a hearing, but not without a caveat: neither Zach nor I would be permitted to attend.

Having learned that family members could request a meeting with anyone newly convicted of a crime, I immediately petitioned for such a meeting. The prison administration approved the request but limited the meeting to an excruciatingly short half an hour. On July 5, full of anticipation for seeing Zach, we—his parents, his sister, Zhenya, and I—arrived at the prison. After a short wait, the guards took us into a room divided by a glass partition.

We waited anxiously for the guards to bring Zach in, and when they did, we gasped. He looked dreadful, simply dreadful. The hunger strike he declared a week earlier, post-trial, had taken its toll on him. Even though he was no longer on strike, he looked dangerously thin. That, combined with the newly shaved head—shaved in accordance with prison regulations in the aftermath of the trial—made him look utterly exhausted. It seemed he had no energy to carry himself through the meeting. He was struggling. Watching him, I struggled to contain my tears. The half hour flew by as he told us what happened in the courtroom while we were shut out. We told him about the historic hundred-person rotating hunger strike in solidarity with him. Then the guards got up, signaling that the meeting was over. Choking back tears, we said goodbye, not knowing when we would see him again.

A few weeks later, on July 24, the appeal trial took place, presided over by three justices. It lasted a grand total of nine minutes, resulting in a ruling: "APPEAL DENIED."

Just days after Zach's three-year sentence of forced labor was upheld, US Congressman Ted Weiss (D-NY) circulated a letter among his colleagues. Representative Weiss was an immigrant himself. Born in Hungary, he immigrated to the United States with his family at the age of eleven. Known for civil rights advocacy, he became one of our outspoken supporters. The letter read as follows:

Congress of the United States House of Representatives
Washington, D.C.

August 1, 1984

Dear Colleague:

I am writing to ask you to join me in sending a letter to President Konstantin Chernenko concerning Zachar Zunshine and his wife. Mr. Zunshine, a 33 year old math [physics] teacher, has been unjustly sentenced to three years in a Soviet labor camp and has been denied permission to emigrate to Israel.

Mr. Zunshine was arrested on March 4 after he, his wife and a relative stood on a street in Moscow bearing a simple sign that read: "Please give us exit visas." Mr. Zunshine was brought to trial and convicted for "anti- Soviet slander." The incriminating evidence used against him were letters he had written requesting an exit visa. Mr. Zunshine's case came up on appeal on July 24, but his sentence was upheld.

Zachar Zunshine's case has attracted widespread attention in the Soviet Union and in the United States. One hundred Jews in Riga and Leningrad have taken the bold and dangerous step of engaging in a 100-day hunger strike to demonstrate their outrage at Zunshine's conviction and their sympathy for his plight. In Washington, students recently began a hunger strike outside the Soviet Embassy.

Cases such as Zachar Zunshine's have become all too common in the Soviet Union where Jews are imprisoned for the "crime" of wanting to emigrate. Mr. Zunshine and his wife ask only that they be granted permission to leave the Soviet Union.

I urge you to join me in sending the attached letter to President Chernenko.

Sincerely,

Ted Weiss, Member of Congress[22]

Congressman Weiss's appeal was successful. The letter below, signed by members of the House of Representatives, followed closely on its heels. In general, US policy was to pressure the Soviets on human rights, constantly reminding them about cases of political prisoners while hoping for cumulative results.

His Excellency Konstantine U. Chernenko
Secretary General of the Communist Party
Kremlin, Moscow, USSR

Dear President Chernenko:

We, the undersigned members of the United States House of Representatives, are writing to request your intervention on behalf of Zachar Zunshine and his wife. We are deeply concerned by the fact that he has been sentenced to three years

---

22   Tatiana Zunshine's personal archive.

in a labor camp without just cause and that he has not been permitted to emigrate to Israel.

Zachar Zunshine was arrested on March 4 after he, his wife, and a relative stood on a street in Moscow bearing a simple sign that read: "Please give us exit visas." On June 28, he was convicted of "anti-Soviet slander." The only evidence against him were letters he had written requesting an exit visa. Mr. Zunshine's appeal was heard on July 24, but his three-year sentence was upheld.

To imprison Mr. Zunshine would be a grave injustice for he has been convicted only because he asked permission to leave the Soviet Union. To free Zachar Zunshine and allow him and his wife to emigrate to Israel would be a significant humanitarian gesture on your part, and would contribute to improved relations between our two countries.

We therefore urge you on humanitarian grounds to overturn the conviction of Zachar Zunshine and to grant him and his wife permission to leave the Soviet Union.[23]

---

23   Tatiana Zunshine's personal archive.

CHAPTER 9

ETAP

Derived from the French *étape*, the Russian word этап (pronounced *etap*) means, variously: forced transportation of prisoners and/or exiles; the route of the prisoners and/or exiles to the place of detention, and/or exile.

Etap is a strictly Russian phenomenon closely associated with another Russian phenomenon, Stolypin carriages. First built in 1908, these train cars were named after Pyotr Stolypin, an interior minister and prime minister of the Russian empire from 1906 to 1911. He initiated an agricultural policy known as the Stolypin reform, designed to entice the Russian peasantry to relocate from European regions of the country to Siberia. An offer of private property ownership in the vast Siberian lands stimulated the resettlement of landless serfs. To facilitate the ensuing influx of peasants and their families moving east, a special type of railroad car was built—the Stolypin carriage. On the outside, it looked like a standard railroad car. Inside, a passenger compartment in the middle of the car housed a peasant and his family for the long journey. On either side of the compartment were two larger spaces for transporting the family's livestock and agricultural tools.

After the October Revolution of 1917, the Bolshevik government began using Stolypin carriages for a less benign purpose: transporting prisoners to forced labor camps in Siberia and other destinations. The passenger compartments would now house the guards escorting the prisoners, while the cattle spaces housed the prisoners themselves. They were treated accordingly—like cattle.

Times changed. The *etap* of the 1980s was different from the *etap* of the 1920s. But its essential nature did not change; those in power continued to treat people like livestock in gruesome violation of international norms of human rights and human decency.

Let me describe the *etap* Zach was subjected to.

Strict procedures governed the way prisoners were taken on and off a Stolypin carriage. A special van brought the prisoners from a transit jail to the vicinity of the carriage. "Once your name is called, grab your belongings and jump out of the van," the commander shouted at them. "Squat immediately, hands on the back of your head. Head down! State your name and date of birth. Keep your head down at all times. Try to escape, and we'll gun you down, no warnings given!" Once everybody was out of the van and squatting, the commander would order the whole group off the ground. Soldiers carrying Kalashnikovs restrained wildly barking German shepherds on their leashes as they marched the procession toward the Stolypin carriage. At the carriage entrance, the prisoners were ordered to squat again. "Hands on the back of your head! Don't get up until your name is called. Then get up and jump on the train. Fast!"

Once inside, they were herded into what had formerly been the livestock compartments. The Stolypin carriage of the 1980s differed from the original in that its cattle spaces were divided into nine chambers instead of two. The five "large" chambers, all of 36.5 square feet, each had a maximum capacity of twelve people; the four smaller chambers, 21.5 square feet, were meant to hold five people. The reality was different. More often than not, the larger chambers were crammed with as many as fourteen to sixteen people.

How, you might ask, could sixteen people fit into 36.5 square feet? Not easily! There were six berths in a chamber—three on each side.

Ten people could sit on the two lower berths, all squeezed together. A set of planks connected the two middle berths and became a berth of its own. With limited space between the middle and upper berths, one could only stay there in a horizontal position. Thus, three people could occupy the middle berths, and two could lie on the two upper ones. That made fifteen. *And what about the sixteenth person?* you ask. Well, that person was just out of luck.

If you find this unimaginable, consider this: every inch not occupied by human bodies was occupied by their belongings, as each prisoner was allowed to bring along a trunk weighing up to 110 pounds.

A Stolypin carriage moved at a snail's pace. Most of the time, it traveled at night, hitched to a regular train for part of the journey, unhitched and parked on a siding for hours at a stretch, then resuming the journey hitched to yet another train. Every man in the carriage had his own destination, which meant endless getting on and off of one carriage, then switching to another, and another, and another. In between were numerous stays in transit prisons notorious for their unsanitary conditions, such as filth, moldy walls, and mice and roach infestation. Crammed in a cell with other transient prisoners, one had to wait for the next leg of the journey, whether it happened the following day, the following week, or the following month.

Before each leg of the trip, prisoners were given dry rations of crackers, instant cereals, packaged soup, and tea. With no additional food served on the train, these rations were to last the entire leg. But prisoners used them wisely. Some abstained from having food or drink for twenty-four hours before the train ride and kept their consumption to a minimum while on board. Why? The guards were notorious for not providing adequate access to toilets. By law, transit prisoners were allowed access to the toilets every five to six hours, which may have been painful enough, but out of pure spite, some guards would let them out as rarely as twice a day. Worse, when the carriage was parked on sidings for many hours at a time, prisoners had no access to the toilets at all.

A windowless car, the Stolypin carriage provided no natural light. A side corridor extended past the entrances to each chamber, with gratings installed in lieu of doors. The guards strolled back and forth along the corridor, peeking through the gratings, keeping a watchful eye on their subjects. Out of the chambers and through the gratings came perpetual streams of cigarette smoke. With no ventilation, the air in the chambers was saturated with it. Between the dense clouds of smoke and other foul smells, hunger, thirst, insufficient access to toilets, the absence of fresh air and natural light, and the lack of space, the situation was utterly unbearable.

For the entire duration of the *etap*, the prisoners did not know which camp they were being transported to; nor did their families. Dragged thousands of miles across Mother Russia, with no idea of their whereabouts and no contact with the outside world, the prisoners seemed to have vanished from the face of the earth.

Zach spent sixty horrific days in *etap*.

On the Floor of the US Senate—Al D'Amato (R-NY).

August 1, 1984

Mr. President, today, August 1, 1984, marks the ninth anniversary of the signing of the 1975 Helsinki accord. This international agreement, endorsed by the Soviet Union, guarantees certain fundamental human rights to all peoples in the Soviet Union. Under the Helsinki accord, the Soviet Union is obligated to respect the freedom of thought, conscience, religion and belief of all human beings . . .

The USSR also agreed to "deal in a positive and humanitarian spirit with the applications of persons who wish to be reunited with members of their family." Yet, the Soviet Union has flagrantly violated every one of these provisions . . .

Most disturbing of all, practically every Jew who requests permission to emigrate to Israel or to the United States is refused a visa. Those who apply for visas risk losing their jobs, their social status, their civil rights, their communication with the outside world and their hopes of living in a world free of persecution . . .

These people are being denied the most basic human rights and many of them are serving jail or prison terms. In a recent development, Zachar Zunshine of Riga, was tried and sentenced in July [June] for pursuing a legal course of action. He was jailed because he made formal, legal appeals to the authorities for permission to emigrate to Israel and then protested the refusal . . .

When the Helsinki accord was signed by the Soviet Government, hope for a more humane future was instilled in the citizens of the Soviet Union. We must persevere in our efforts to ensure that those hopes are realized. The Soviet Union must be pressured to recognize its international commitments and guarantee the human rights so vital to the lives of its Jewish people and, indeed, to all people.[24]

---

24   *Congressional Record—House* (Washington, DC: US Government Printing Office, 1984), p. 21821.

CHAPTER 10

GROWING UP

Considering how long Zach's journey was taking, I concluded that he was undoubtedly being transported to Siberia. This meant his *etap* was destined to pass through Sverdlovsk,[25] the largest city in the Ural Mountains, the city he and I grew up in, the city of my child-hood memories.

The most vivid memory of all was the perpetual presence of snow.

Where I grew up, snow stayed on the ground for five months straight, from November to the end of March. Then the spring thaw began and lasted for weeks and weeks, turning the city into a sea of puddles. Located 1,100 miles east of Moscow, Sverdlovsk was the capital of the Urals, the mountainous region sitting squarely on the dividing line between Europe and Asia.

The city was rather large but largely unremarkable. Its main claim to fame (or infamy) was the 1918 murder of the last emperor of Russia, Tsar Nicholas II, along with his wife, Empress Alexandra, their five children, the family doctor, the children's nanny, and oth-er members of his staff. They were slaughtered, execution style, in the basement of a centrally located house that belonged to an engi-neer named Nikolai Ipatiev. The execution of the Romanov family

---

25   The city was called Yekaterinburg from the time it was founded in 1723 until 1924, when it was renamed Sverdlovsk. When the Soviet Union collapsed in 1991, the name reverted to Yekaterinburg.

and their attendants marked the end of a Russian monarchy that spanned over eleven centuries.

The Soviets had systematically engaged in a cover-up, first outright denying that the Romanovs were dead, then suggesting that perhaps they had been murdered by left-wing anarchists. When they finally acknowledged the murders, they took no responsibility for them. In 1977, the city demolished the notorious Ipatiev house and, in 2003, eighty-five years after the execution of the former royal family, built a lavish church on top of it. Ironic, isn't it?

Neither one of my parents was originally from Sverdlovsk.

Born Abram Disik in 1912, my father grew up in Kryve Ozero, a settlement near Pervomaisk, in Ukraine. He was only five years old when he lost his mother and a younger sister to a pogrom.[26] Shortly thereafter, his father died from smallpox. My dad, aged six, was taken into an orphanage, where he befriended a teacher named Mr. Kremnev. That teacher became his best friend, mentor, and father figure. It lasted a few years, but sadly, my father lost his mentor just the same.

In the early 1920s, there was a wave of emigration out of the country. Mr. Kremnev was among those eager to leave their newly Bolshevik homeland. He decided to go to America and asked my father to join him. And what did this ten-year-old say? He said no. Why? Because of a red scarf. Let me explain: 1922 marked the birthday of the All-Union Pioneer Organization—a scout-like youth organization of the Soviet Union. Back then, for my father, at the age of ten, the biggest attraction of being a pioneer was the red scarf they wore around their necks. That's all he wanted—a scarf. And so he stayed.

---

26   Anti-Jewish massacres ravaging Ukraine between 1917 and 1921.

At eighteen, upon leaving the orphanage, my father went to study in Odessa. The country was ravaged with hunger, and Odessa was no exception. As a student, he received a minuscule amount of bread (the exact amount is unknown) supplied by a rationing system. He had to make it last, eating it crumb by crumb. But that piece of bread had stiff competition. *Another red scarf?* you ask. No. This time, it was opera.

My father happened to be a passionate opera lover, and Odessa happened to have a legendary opera house. With no money in his pocket, torn between the hunger for bread and the one for music, he chose to satisfy both by sacrificing a portion of that bread. He would slice the piece of bread in half, keep half for himself, sell the other at the market, buy a ticket, and go to the opera.

Sometime after leaving the orphanage, he changed his name to Alexander Kremnev in honor of his teacher. That last name—Kremneva—was my maiden name until I married Zach.

My mother, Frieda Pertsovskaya, had a story of her own, a story of remarkable courage, resilience, and survival. She was an eighteen-year-old finishing her freshman year of college at the Institute of Foreign Languages in Minsk, Belarus, when Hitler declared war on the Soviet Union on June 22, 1941.

Two years earlier, in August 1939, Stalin's Russia and Hitler's Nazi Germany signed a short-lived nonaggression pact, forming a shameful alliance at the expense of neighboring countries. It allowed the Russians to land-grab Eastern Poland, a part of Finland, and three Baltic countries—Latvia, Lithuania, and Estonia. This pact did not last. On June 22, 1941, Hitler invaded the Soviet Union by launching Operation Barbarossa, sending three million German soldiers over its western border.

Two days later, on June 24, German bombs fell on my mother's city, Minsk. Before the attack started that fateful day, she and her fellow students had come to school to take a final exam. Hearing the sounds of explosions and fearing their school might get blown up at any moment, a group of students, including my mother, ran out into the open only to find that the city had turned into hell on earth. There were bodies and body parts scattered everywhere, buildings collapsing under the constant rain of bombs, and the horrifying sounds of explosions all around them.

Zigzagging their way through what remained of Minsk, the students managed to escape the bombs and found themselves at the city's edge. That was the beginning of an arduous journey lasting many weeks. They each wanted to return to their hometowns, and the only way to do this was on foot. And that is precisely what they set off to do. They walked through the woods, crossing roads and bridges, all the while dodging more bombs along the way; by then, the whole of Belarus was in flames.

At some point in their odyssey, the students were able to climb onto an east-bound train. My mother recalled riding on that train as one of the happiest moments of her life. I used to wonder: *Happiest? How did you find happiness in moments like that?* She was simply happy that something other than her own bloody feet was taking her away from the most hellish experience of her life. On the train, she kept praying that this blissful interlude would never end. But it did. The train was bombed, and the kids had to jump off, one after another, while the train was still moving at full tilt.

Back to walking. Early on, the boys helped rip the high heels off the girls' shoes. Eventually, there wasn't much of a shoe left, causing the kids to walk on their bloody bare feet. The soles of my mother's feet were open wounds.

She described an encounter with Russian soldiers that almost cost her and her friends their lives. They approached a bridge guarded by Russian soldiers. After running away from the Nazis for days and weeks, the students were happy to run into their compatriots. What they didn't know was that the soldiers had been given orders to shoot anybody who approached the bridge, no questions asked. And they almost did, aiming their guns at this group of kids who were yelling, "Don't shoot, we are Russians!" at the top of their lungs. Luckily, common sense prevailed; the soldiers put down the guns and allowed the kids to cross the bridge.

There were other bridges, other trains, and hundreds of miles to cross before my mother, gravely ill with dysentery—the result of drinking water from creeks—reached her uncle's residence. Thank god, they were able to nurse her back to health. A few years later, she found her immediate family.

My mother did not return to Belarus after the war. She finished her schooling elsewhere and moved to the city of Sverdlovsk to teach. There, she met my father, married, and had a family.

My family occupied an apartment in a five-story building far from the city center. When we first moved in in 1956, it was a communal apartment. Our family of five—my parents, my four-year-old brother, my twin sister and I, both newborns—all moved into one room of the apartment, which measured 200 square feet. There was one more room in the apartment. The smaller of the two, it measured 150 square feet and housed another family of five. They, too, had three young children. All ten of us shared one bathroom and a kitchen with a four-burner gas stove—two burners per family. A long, narrow hallway connected the entrance and the kitchen, extending past the doors to both rooms—ours and theirs. One of my most vivid childhood memories centers on that hallway: all six kids taking turns riding a tricycle from one end of the hallway to another.

My father worked two jobs. By day, he was a supervisor at a plant that manufactured heavy machinery. On nights and weekends, he volunteered at a construction site for a residential building. He toiled there for free so that we would get a chance to expand our quarters. The deal was that once construction finished, one of the two families would get an apartment in the brand-new building; the family that stayed in the old one would get the entire place to themselves.

When the promised day came, my family chose to stay, while our neighbors were happy to move on. We couldn't believe our good fortune to have inherited this virtual "palace" all for ourselves, with two rooms, the hallway, the bathroom, and the kitchen, with its stove and all four burners! We were also happy to get our father back; from now on, he would only work one job. All this we celebrated joyfully.

The larger room was now a living room by day and my parents' bedroom by night. We three children moved into a smaller room. We shared that room until my brother was nineteen and my sister and I were fifteen years old.

My mother taught English at an evening school for adults. She left home before we came back from school and didn't return until ten or eleven at night. Another vivid memory of my childhood:

It's late at night. Outside, it's pitch-dark. Stray dogs are running around the neighborhood, barking. Seven years old, I am glued to the window, anxiously awaiting my mother's return. I'm worried about her being out there alone, running into a pack of dogs or a pack of drunks. Finally, I hear the turn of the key—she is back, thank god—and I run to greet her.

Our school was forty-five minutes away. Unlike the neighborhood schools, this one offered a better education with an emphasis on English. To get there, you'd walk fifteen minutes on city streets, crossing busy intersections and navigating through the succession of traffic lights until you reached the hub, where a multitude of streets converged into one big, noisy traffic circle. Trams, buses, trolleys, and cars surged through the hub, crisscrossing it in all directions. During rush hour at the tram stop—buried within this mad circle— you'd join a crowd waiting to jump onto an incoming tram. Counting your lucky stars, you'd squeeze yourself in while others stayed behind or resorted to hanging onto the outer steps, holding on by the handles while riding in the open air. After fifteen minutes of that joyride, you'd force your way out. One final stretch wading through heavy traffic, and you'd arrive at school.

My sister and I were ten years old when we started going to school on our own. In the company of two other classmates, with no adult supervision, we four munchkins had to cross all those roads and find the way to get on and off the trams to arrive safely at school. Maybe, in a small way, navigating the hurdles of traffic at this young age helped prepare us for the future, which is all about navigating the biggest hurdle of all—life itself.

Let me assure you, there was nothing unusual in the way we lived. Neither the apartment nor the lack of space, shared burners, working parents, children taking themselves to school—none of it was out of the ordinary. It was simply the norm.

After high school, I studied economics at the Institute of National Economy in Sverdlovsk. While in college, I worked in IT, which I continued to pursue upon graduation. Life was predictable. Until I met Zach.

Meeting Zach disrupted my life in the best way possible; it changed everything. Together, we were no longer at home in our own country. We dreamed of leaving it, but first, we needed to leave our hometown, Sverdlovsk. The reason was simple: Given the potential for the KGB's retaliation, we wanted to protect our families from the fire we were about to ignite. Distancing ourselves, we thought, would shield them from getting inadvertently drawn into our fight; the farther away we were, the safer they would be.

After considering a few options, we zeroed in on Riga, the capital of Latvia. Located on the Baltic Sea, this historic city dating back to the thirteenth century was an enticing destination. Besides its attractive seashore and dunes, it boasted European architecture, a medieval town center, and narrow, winding streets with bookstores and coffee shops on every corner. More importantly, Riga had experienced a small but steady flow of emigration. We thought we'd go there, apply to emigrate, and leave within a year.

We made it to Riga, but not beyond. Instead, we found ourselves caught up in the biggest fight of our lives—the fight with the Soviet apparatus. In the background of it all was our beautiful city. We still loved it. We would lose ourselves in the labyrinth of the streets and alleys of the old town, letting our feet take us wherever they could. We would lose ourselves in conversation, too, and the only reminder of time passing was the recurring sound of church bells.

Back in Sverdlovsk, my mother didn't take our departure lightly. The day I announced that Zach and I decided to leave the country was one of the saddest days of her life. She was devastated. "How could you possibly leave?" she asked me, her voice filled with tears. "Doesn't it mean we may never see you again?" Yet, much as she hated for us to leave, when Zach was arrested, everything changed for her. Now she wished we were gone. Although apart from her, we'd be safe.

When, in April of 1984, my two girlfriends and I were thrown in jail for a fifteen-day term, my mother traveled to Riga to greet me at the time of my release. Outside the prison, friends cheered us as we emerged from the door. With them stood a tiny woman, a proud woman—my mother. No more than five feet tall, she stood in the front row, holding a bouquet of flowers. Inevitably, she started crying when she saw me. We both cried. Those were happy tears, and it was a moment I will never forget.

CHAPTER 11

IN THE LION'S DEN

It had been two months since Zach vanished into a no-man's land, transported to an anonymous penal colony in an anonymous part of a country.

This process of forced transportation of prisoners, the *etap*, was truly an evil invention, utterly dangerous and inhumane. Dragged across Mother Russia, jammed into a tiny chamber with over a dozen humans whose most primitive physical needs were shamefully denied and, therefore, whose fuse was shorter and shorter with every passing mile, spending weeks at a time in the rotten cells of transit prisons with rampant roach and mice infestations, surrounded by prisoners of volatile behavior—all this spelled danger. It opened the door to violence, disease, and accidents; god knew what else could spiral out of control. Thinking about it made me sick, but that was all I could think about. *How is Zach? How is he holding up? Where is he? Why is his journey taking so long?*

Any number of trips to the mailbox, day after day, produced no answers. No letters, no telegrams, no word about his whereabouts. My letters to the Gulag administration demanding information bounced back with a single line: "You will be informed of your husband's placement once he arrives at the penal colony of his destination." Maddening, to say the least.

The wait ended in late September. I found a letter in my mailbox, and I tore into it. I had a hunch this was the news I'd been waiting for, and I was right. It was *the* letter. In a couple of short paragraphs, it informed me that my husband, Zachar Zunshine, had arrived at his destination, Penal Colony UK 272/40, located in the township of Bozoy in the Irkutsk region. I gasped, "That's the other side of the world!" Located in the heart of Siberia, the region's capital, Irkutsk, lies nearly 4,000 miles from Riga.

The last paragraph of the letter, though, held a consolation prize. It read: "Upon arrival in the camp, Zunshine is entitled to have his first twenty-four-hour conjugal meeting with his spouse and/or other family members." The Gulag administration rarely disallowed a first meeting upon prisoners' arrival. Thank god nobody had tried to mess with ours! I had my meeting approved. I was going to see Zach! Even the thought of it made me smile.

As soon as I got the letter, I passed the information about Zach's whereabouts to his parents, Pam Cohen, and all our family and friends. Pam, in turn, telegraphed it to other branches and sister organizations, asking our supporters to mail letters and postcards to the camp. This initiated the beginning of a worldwide campaign designed to send a strong message to the camp administration: *Hands off prisoner of conscience Zachar Zunshine. We are watching your every move.*

Plans were made at once for my mother-in-law, Dora, and myself to travel to Siberia together for our first meeting with Zach. I would fly from Riga to our hometown of Sverdlovsk, where both sets of parents lived, and from there, Dora and I would go on to Siberia. Dora would be with us in the daytime but would check into the visitors' dorms at night. That was the plan.

But things don't always go as planned.

While Dora and I were busy making arrangements, Zach's father, Mikhail, was on a business trip in a town near Irkutsk. Hearing the news, he realized he wasn't far from the camp where his son had just arrived. Into Mikhail's mind came the idea: *Why not swing by and check it out?* Whatever his thinking was, it didn't seem to him like much of a big deal. *I'll go, and maybe I'll find out something about Zach. It won't hurt to try*, he must have thought.

I wish that he had talked to me about it. With all my heart, I wish he had given me a chance. I would have tried to dissuade him from going. I would have told him that, being new to this and unfamiliar with KGB tactics, he would be sticking his head into the lion's mouth, hoping it wasn't chewed off. At any rate, he went.

The lion's name was Kofel. He was head of the Men's Division of Penal Colony UK 272/40. Happy to receive a visitor, the father of the first political prisoner they had ever had (the rest of the camp's population was strictly criminal), he sat Mikhail down for a talk. Because he had come there on his own initiative, Mikhail's actions were perceived as a willingness to cooperate. *That's even better*, Kofel must have thought, *a cake already half baked.*

He congratulated Mikhail on the arrival of his son but proceeded to tell him that Zach had not endured *etap* well. "Your son lost forty pounds," he said. "And I am sorry to have to inform you that he's lost his marbles. You know what I mean? He's no longer mentally all there. A shell of a man, he arrived here deranged, a madman of sorts. You wanna know what he did? He attacked one of the inmates with a razor blade. We have signed testimony from the victim. He is a crazed, broken man, your son!"

Looking Zach's father in the eye, Kofel went on: "You are gonna have to tell him to get down on his knees for the rest of his term. No more resistance. Enough! If he keeps on being defiant, we'll finish him off. We'll let him rot to death here!" The threats escalated. "If we choose to, we can transfer him to another camp surrounded by chemical factories, or better yet, send him to work in Siberia's numerous radioactive mines. He won't get out of there alive, nor will you ever find his grave." The sadist carried on by vividly describing the burials deceased inmates received in the camp. Then, in his most predictable move, he connected Zach's survival with my attempts to defend him. "Tell your daughter-in-law if she doesn't change her ways, she will never see her husband again. Tell her to cease all her activities. No more fuss! No more protests! Tell her to be quiet. That, and only that, might turn things around."

Shell-shocked and overwhelmed by fear, Zach's father left the camp and flew home with a heavy heart and a heavy sense of duty to reverse the course of our actions. Not only did Zach have to "get down on his knees for the rest of his term," but all of us had to follow suit. Full stop, starting *now*! In Mikhail's mind, if that's what Kofel wanted, that's what was going to help his son survive, and hell, that's what we were going to deliver.

Unaware of what had transpired only a day earlier and how our lives had just taken another unexpected turn, I was on my way to Bozoy. I first had to fly to Moscow, which took an hour and a half. My next leg was a two-and-a-half-hour flight from Moscow to Sverdlovsk. After spending a night there, I would join Dora for a four-hour flight to Irkutsk. And finally, upon arrival, we had to find our way to Bozoy, a township located sixty miles northeast of the city.

Having Dora with me was going to be a huge help. We had lots to carry—everything Zach might need or want. One item in particular was of the highest importance. I consulted with other wives of political prisoners, asking them about their husbands' needs, and they all said the same thing: warm underwear. For those who did hard labor in Siberia's harsh climate, that was a lifesaver. Following their advice, I asked Pam to send me the warmest long johns, long-sleeved undershirts, and socks she could find. Pam knew exactly what I needed (unfortunately, I was not the first wife to request these items) and sent me state-of-the-art Canadian underwear made of pure wool—the type they wore in Canada's Northwest Territories. It warmed my heart to think how much of a difference it would make in Zach's life. Of all things—underwear! Who would have thought?

Just as with underwear, there was a shared knowledge among families of political prisoners about the food one should bring to the camp. A homemade meal was every prisoner's dream, yet bringing it to the camp presented an enormous challenge. If you opt to make it, I was told, select your husband's favorite, most nutritious dishes and choose them wisely. Cooked a day or two ahead, packed in ice, they would travel with you on planes, trains, buses, or whatever your means of transportation were. They had to last the entire journey, however long that might be.

I settled on Zach's favorite, gefilte fish. I made that and a few other dishes. I also brought caviar, bread, butter, and scores of other delicacies. Regardless of the situation—or despite it—we were going to have a feast.

On the plane, I was able to relax, tune out the chatter, and settle into my thoughts. From now on, I reflected, this was how it would be: me crossing six time zones to see my husband, food and warm underwear in tow. From now on, my focus would be on Bozoy and everything that took place there. I would watch that camp like a hawk, looking for signs of trouble. I pictured myself as a bird flying over Zach's camp, swooping down to pick up every crumb of information I could possibly find, then flying away to a safe place where I could share that precious crumb with my fellow birds, the ones who lived on the other side of the pond. That thought entertained me quite a bit. I was flying high, anticipating my meeting with Zach, us spending a night together for the first time in seven months. I imagined a room with shabby state-owned furniture and barred window, the stark opposite of a romantic setting. Yet, in the moment, that room sounded like the most romantic place on earth. We would be there together; that was all that mattered, and nobody would dare to separate us.

At Sverdlovsk airport, my brother, Gena, met me at the gate. I asked him to drive me to my in-laws. I would spend the night there, and Dora and I would get an early start the following day.

Happy about the upcoming meeting with Zach, full of hope and anticipation, I arrived at Zach's parents' apartment building. Gena helped me drag the luggage up the flights of stairs, wanting to make sure I got in safely. We rang the bell, and the door opened. Dora and Mikhail were both at the door. Seeing them there, I knew at once something had happened. I signaled Gena to come in with me. "What happened?" I asked, worried.

They told us about Mikhail's trip to the camp. "They informed me," Mikhail said, his voice cracking, "that two months of *etap* pushed Zach over the edge. He had a mental breakdown and is now a broken man, a crazy man. They described him as a village idiot running around with a razor blade. They have signed testimony from an inmate whom Zach had attacked with that blade."

Thunderstruck, I refused to believe what I was hearing. "This is impossible!" I cried. "Impossible!" I shook my head, repeating the word over and over. Gena was by my side, trying to calm me down.

Mikhail went on, detailing his whole conversation with Kofel. He spoke of chemical factories, radioactive mines, and grotesque burial practices and ended with a message from Kofel to all of us: *Though a madman, Zach is still alive. But that could easily change. We* [the administration] *could finish him off. If you ever want to see him again, tell him to be quiet, and just as important, tell his wife to do the same.*

My first reaction was pure, unadulterated horror that paralyzed me. But slowly, reason returned. The more I heard of all this, the less sense it made. *A madman . . . chemical factories . . . a deranged person* .

. . *radioactive mines . . . This doesn't add up*, I thought to myself. By the time Mikhail finished, I had a clear picture in my mind. Then I stated it flatly, out loud:

"This can't be true."

"What do you mean it's not true?" Mikhail protested. "Kofel told me that's what had happened. He wouldn't lie; he's a grown man."

"This can't be true," I repeated, "and not because I refuse to believe it. It isn't true because there are holes in the story, and I can see them. There are too many inconsistencies. How can Zach be broken and defiant at the same time? If he's already a shell of a man, as they claim him to be, why would they need to do all those things to him? It just doesn't add up."

The conversation went on and on, but the argument remained unresolved. "If Kofel said it," Mikhail insisted, "it must be true. He gave me his word."

"Please listen to me," I begged. "They will tell you anything! Equally, their word doesn't mean anything!"

We were not getting through to each other. Mikhail demanded that we accept Kofel's ultimatum: cease all activism on Zach's behalf, or else. Meanwhile, I desperately tried to make him and Dora understand that to stop protesting would be suicidal. "That's when they *do* finish people off."

Mikhail was getting increasingly exasperated. Dora, although calmer than her husband, was fully in support of his position. We were all too exhausted and too upset to continue. I suggested I spend the night at Gena's, and we reconnect in the morning. "We will have clearer heads then," I said, and they agreed. Gena and I said goodbye, and we left.

In the car, on the way to Gena's apartment, I felt shaken and completely spent. *What a roller-coaster ride of a conversation*, I thought.

What they were asking me to do was impossible. I couldn't just quit. How could I convince them that it wasn't an option? The result would be devastating for their son. A sign of weakness would draw the knives out in earnest. But a sign of surrender? With that, Zach would never get out of prison! Not alive. The KGB would destroy him. Trust me on that!

I did realize how difficult it must have been for Zach's parents to entrust a twenty-eight-year-old with their son's life. How unsettling it must have been to accept the fact that I was the only one equipped to fight for him (as I was the only one who understood the rules of the game). But as hard as it was, they needed to accept that.

Zach's parents were no strangers to peril.

Mikhail was nineteen years old in 1941 when World War II began. A teenager serving in an artillery battalion, he found himself in the heart of the war's most consequential battle, the Battle of Stalingrad. The battle marked the turning point in the war and shifted the balance of power from the Nazis to the Russians. It lasted from August 1942 to February 1943 and was the deadliest, bloodiest battle in the history of warfare, with over a million Russian casualties. Mikhail's lucky stars saved him from being slaughtered. More so, they kept him from being severely wounded.

Zach's mother, Dora, was a radiologist. She, too, had a brush with danger. In 1953, she came face to face with the horrors of Stalin's purges.[27]

A few hours passed since we returned to Gena's apartment. My conversation with the in-laws had lodged deep in my mind, and I couldn't shake it off. I wondered if they knew their son the way I did. Did they know he was unbendable? That he would speak his mind no matter what? That he would never stop being himself? And that

---

27   https://www.britannica.com/event/Doctors-Plot.

prison or no prison, nobody would ever be able to tie his hands? That I was facing the nearly impossible task of tying the KGB's hands by exposing all the rotten things they were doing to him? That quitting would be suicide for both of us? That having smelled fear, the KGB *would* go after him relentlessly?

How did I explain all this to them?

Suddenly, the doorbell rang. It was Zach's cousin, Lev. "What happened? Why are you here?" I asked.

"Dora just died of a heart attack!" he shouted.

I fell to my knees.

NO NO NO NO NO NO . . . This could not have happened. This could not have happened. This could not have happened. I refuse to believe it. Tell me it didn't happen. Tell me! I am on the floor, wailing, unable to get up. Gena is helping me get on my feet, get my coat, get down the flights of stairs, get in the car, and get back to where it all happened.

I don't remember how we got back to my in-laws'. I was in a complete blackout. As we drove closer, through the fuzzy lens of my tear-filled eyes, I saw people gathered in a circle outside the building. Gena helped me out of the car. I then saw that people were surrounding the body—Dora's body. I pushed myself through them and collapsed on top of her.

On the Floor of the US House of Representatives—Edward F. Feighan (D-OH).

THE DEATH OF A REFUSENIK'S MOTHER

October 1, 1984

Mr. Speaker, I have just heard the terrible news that the mother of Jewish prisoner of conscience Zachar Zunshine, Dora Zunshine, died yesterday of a heart attack after hearing of the harsh treatment her son endured in a Soviet prison camp. Until yesterday, the whereabouts of Zachar Zunshine were unknown . . . A refusenik since 1980 [1981], Zachar Zunshine was most recently arrested in March of this year and tried Under Article 190-1 of the Soviet Criminal Code.[28] He was charged with disseminating anti-Soviet slander.

Dora Zunshine suffered her fatal heart attack when her husband brought her the news of the prison conditions endured by her son. Zachar's father is reported to have brought the news that the "camps where Zachar has been placed are near lead mines and chemical processing plants from which no one comes back alive." Further reports indicate that Zachar Zunshine suffers from repeated attempts of intimidation from the head of the prison camp.

The inhuman cruelty, the harsh conditions, and the brutal terror which Zachar Zunshine endures must be brought to the attention of the world. Lynn Singer, former president of the Union of Councils for Soviet Jews, has written eloquently on this subject. She has written that: "The crackdown of Jewish emigration is a part of a general drive toward inhuman discipline and regimentation in the Soviet Union. As the number of Jews who are allowed to emigrate continues to decline, as the persecution of Baptists, Seventh-day Adventists, and young Russian Orthodox believers continues apace, so will the number of men like Zachar Zunshine, willing to face the consequences of their pursuit of freedom, continue to rise."

The death of Dora Zunshine is a tragedy, not only for her family and her friends, but for all of us who are inspired by the courage and determination of her son. The struggle of Zachar Zunshine is not an easy one, and it will not be won without the commitment of brave men and women everywhere. I know that other members will join in my expression of sorrow at this tragic news.[29]

---

28   This is not entirely incorrect; Zach was charged with violating Article 183 of the Latvian Criminal Code, which is equivalent to Article 190 in the Criminal Code of the Russian Federation.

29   *Congressional Record—House* (Washington, DC: US Government Printing Office, 1984), pp. 28177–28178.

CHAPTER 12

THE ORWELLIAN YEAR

I lost myself to pain and wallowed in it incessantly. I didn't know how to go on.

Dora's heart attack, I learned, struck about an hour after Gena and I had left. It happened outside their building when she and Mikhail went out to get some air.

Dora was sixty years old.

The day after the funeral, in an altered, delirious state of mind, I left Sverdlovsk for Irkutsk for my meeting with Zach. As always, my brother was there for me. He accompanied me on the trip.

I truly didn't know how to go on. How would I go about breaking the news of Dora's death to her son? I didn't know how I could say the words or when to say them. That, combined with the idea of Zach being a broken man—if there was one iota of truth to the story— was simply unbearable. I fought off those thoughts, playing out the infamous conversation with Kofel in my head over and over, arriving each time at the same conclusion: no, it just wasn't possible. Was I free of doubts? I tried to be, but those insidious thoughts kept rising up, sweeping away all the logic behind them. Tangled into a hard knot, they settled in my stomach as a constant reminder that no matter how much I felt it couldn't have happened, I wouldn't know for sure until I saw him.

Arriving in Irkutsk, we went outside the airport to catch a bus to Bozoy. It turned out that the Bozoy bus left Irkutsk only three times a week. In between, you could only get there by hiring a cab and paying a double fare—the journey there and back—before a cab driver would agree to take you.

After an hour and a half in a cab, Gena and I arrived in Bozoy. *What a sad-looking place*, I thought to myself. Nothing but a penal colony surrounded by barbed wire, observation towers, and dilapidated one-story homes. Dirt roads everywhere. Everything—the houses, the bare tree trunks, people's clothes—was colored a uniform, dreary, asphalt gray. The day was relatively warm for early October, in the high thirties, but sunny, warmer than I expected. Yet seeing my breath hang in the air reminded me that winter was just around the corner. In a few more weeks, snow would cover the ground, blanketing the dirt roads and staying there for the rest of the winter.

Inside the camp headquarters, I presented a letter authorizing my first twenty-four-hour meeting with my husband. Once admitted, I said goodbye to Gena. He headed back to Irkutsk, where I would join him in a day or two.

The guards took me to a small barrack-like building designated for inmates' meetings with their families. Inside were a few bathroom-less rooms, each with a twin bed, a table, and a couple of chairs. A narrow hallway extended past the doors to each room, ending at the entrance to a bathroom shared by all.

While in the cab, I kept telling Gena that I was going to wait. I would wait until I saw Zach and would feel my way until I found the right moment to break the news to him. I wouldn't rush into it.

Inside the room, standing in front of the door, waiting for the guards to bring Zach in, I suddenly felt dizzy, about to faint. I propped myself up against the wall. The door opened, and there was Zach, smiling. I must have looked as pale as a ghost. "What's the matter?" he asked worriedly.

"DORA DIED!"

I almost shouted it out. I couldn't bear to hold it in any longer.

It took one look at him to confirm my conclusions: *They had lied to us.* Yes, he was thin—skin and bones—with signs of physical battery on his body, bruises and abrasions on his face and hands, and yet, this was not a broken man. Heartbroken, yes, but not broken.

We held each other tight, and we cried.

We shed a lot of tears that night, tears of overwhelming grief and sadness. We were rattled with anger, a seething anger at what had transpired over the past few days—the big lie that had been perpetrated and the toll it took. We came to a painful realization that no matter what happened in the end, nothing would ever be okay, and no matter how many battles we won, we had essentially lost the war. And yet, we were grateful for that night, for being there in that moment, together, consoling each other, helping each other, holding each other, grateful for the love that gave us the strength to go on.

We shared a lot of stories that night.

Zach had arrived at the camp on September 27. As a part of the admissions process, each newcomer was offered the chance to "voluntarily" sign a paper stating that he agreed to become a collaborator. Formally called "joining the Service of Internal Order," in reality, the signing of the paper meant becoming a stool pigeon, the eyes, ears, and, if necessary, fists of the camp administration. Once you signed the paper, you officially "put on an armband." This camp, in particular, was infamous for having 80 percent of its prisoners wear armbands.

It was common practice for new inmates to sign the paper on their first day. Zach arrived in a group of eleven, ten of whom did not give it a second thought. The holdout was Zach, who flatly refused.

When this happened, a higher-up summoned a group of collaborators and ordered: "Take him away!" The "armbands" knew what to do; this was a part of the contract, after all. They dragged Zach into a designated room, ironically called the "Crime Prevention Section," knocked him down on the floor, and kicked him with their boots all over his body. That ruthless pack of wolves delivered one blow after another and wouldn't stop until the door opened and someone said, "Enough." They dragged him back to where it all started. "Are you ready to sign the papers now?" the same higher-up asked. Writhing in pain, Zach laughed in his face.

Fighting off tears, I listened to him, trying not to miss a single word. Then I told him the razor blade story: how he had allegedly lost his mind and assaulted another inmate. This was the first Zach had heard of it.

"They claim to have signed testimony from the victim," I said.

He wasn't surprised. "They can get a collaborator to sign any paper they want; that's part of the deal. The poor bastards have no control over their own actions. But it's not about them. It's about the damned administration. To make up a gruesome lie like that and feed it to my father—for that, I hope they burn in HELL!"

The morning after the assault, with terrible chest pain, Zach was not able to get out of bed. He suspected broken ribs and asked for a doctor's slip. The doctor said no. Zach asked for an X-ray; another no. Unable to do manual work, he stayed in bed, earning a reprimand for being absent from work.

Seeing Zach in so much pain was gut-wrenching. Any movement he made, big or small, came with a wince and a groan. To get around, he covered his chest with one hand—as if trying to cushion the pain—and propped himself up with the other. But the physical suffering paled in comparison to what he was feeling inside. Dora's death, and the circumstances around it, was an emotional torture. He kept saying, "I cannot fathom it, I simply can't. Why did she have to die? Why?"

On his third day at the camp, Zach told me, he'd had no choice but to report to work. The ensign on duty, Ensign Averin, greeted him with an anti-Semitic rant: "Too bad Hitler didn't finish the job." He then turned to an armed guard and said, "If anything happens, shoot this Jew first and don't miss."

That was just the beginning, the first three days out of many more days, weeks, and months to come, and they had been brutal. Where would it go from here? We didn't know what the future held, but one thing was clear: we would continue to fight not only *despite* what happened but also *because* of what happened. From now on, all blades were out.

The twenty-four hours were coming to an end. The guards gave us a five-minute warning. We stood by the door, saying goodbye and holding each other close. Then the guards came and took him away.

Back at camp headquarters, I went looking for Kofel, but he was nowhere to be found. His deputy saw me for a brief meeting, and I let him have it. "Everything," I said, "*everything* that has happened here in the last few days will be aired in public. From the circumstances of the death of my husband's mother to the practice of forcing people into being collaborators, to the gangster tactics of breaking the bones of those who refuse to do it, to the anti-Semitic rants of Hitler-loving ensigns, and the lies, lies, nothing but lies."

He looked at me with a blank stare. "We're not keeping it a secret," he said. "We showed your husband to you, didn't we? We didn't have to, we chose to." *Oh, my god! So Zach was right!* One of the things he and I discussed was the timing of our meeting. Why would they show him to me all beaten up? Why not wait a few weeks until the bruises had healed? They might have done it on purpose, Zach suggested, to demonstrate what they could do to him if we didn't accept their offer.

Looking at this functionary, I realized that Zach was right—they had given us this meeting on purpose. I carried on. "Okay, if that's the case, here's what *we* choose," I said. "*We* choose to press charges against those who ordered the beating and those who executed it."

"Not so fast, Tatiana, not so fast!" The camp administrator was showing signs of agitation. "You want charges? No problem. The fact that your husband assaulted an inmate with a razor blade is well-documented on our part. So if you wish for charges, you'll get them! Except, they'll be pressed against your husband. Or, we have another territory to explore. How about Article 188-3 of the Soviet Criminal Code, which carries an additional three-year term for regime violation in places of confinement? You like that better? Is that what you choose, Tatiana?"

I stopped him right there. "Listen," I said, "I know what you're doing, and I'm not interested in playing this game. So keep your threats to yourself, and don't waste your time on me." On that note, I left.

Getting back to Irkutsk was challenging. There was no transportation out of Bozoy for the rest of the week. I went to a stand-alone barracks—a hostel of sorts—where the inmates' families stayed in anticipation of their meetings. I needed to talk to somebody about getting back to the city.

The hostel's focal point was a foyer with a furnace and half a dozen chairs grouped around it. People congregated by the furnace, talking, sharing their experiences with one another. On each side of the foyer, behind curtains, were two larger rooms, one for women, the other for men. Peeking behind the curtain into the women's room, I found that it looked like a field hospital, the stripped-down kind you see in World War II movies: long rows of metallic beds positioned only a few feet apart; no curtains between the beds, no privacy. The same for men, I assumed, on the other side of the furnace. One bathroom was to be shared by all.

Coming back to the foyer, I saw all eyes turning to me. Being new and dressed like a city girl, I clearly stuck out. I greeted the group and presented them with my dilemma: "How do I get back to Irkutsk?" They were friendly and eager to help. "You're gonna have to spend a night here. Tomorrow morning, you're gonna walk over to the crossroads, which is about a mile away. Make sure you're there by 7:00 a.m. A bus goes by that spot. If it's not packed, it will stop and let you on. If it doesn't stop, however, keep walking another four miles. You'll reach the next crossroads—the bigger one—where you're more likely to hitch a ride. They may not take you all the way to Irkutsk, but they will surely bring you somewhere closer to it. There is a village twenty-five miles away from here. They have a regular bus going to Irkutsk."

I found this information a bit overwhelming and needed some air, so I went out to explore the town. I saw a post office sign hanging on a shack the size of a one-car garage. Then I found a grocery store the size of a two-car garage. I went in. A one-stop convenience store, the only one in town, it offered a little of everything: a few items of clothing, a few pots and pans, some packaged foods, some pharmaceutical items, bread, milk, and other essentials. The store was unattended. It felt like the whole town was unattended. *Where is everybody?* I wondered. It then occurred to me that they must have all been at the camp. With nothing around but this camp, where else would they be? Most worked there as guards; others did the cooking, laundry, or bookkeeping, but one way or another, they were all part of that machine that runs you over and breaks your bones, the machine called Gulag. *And that's a sad state of affairs*, I thought. I was too exhausted to continue my "tour" and went back to the hostel. Tomorrow would be an early rise.

At the hostel, an attendant took me to my narrow cot in the women's room. I looked around. Of about twenty beds, only half were occupied. Hoping to get some company, I asked the women if anyone was going to the crossroads the next morning. Unfortunately, nobody was. I talked briefly with a few women sitting on the cots near mine. I told them my husband was "political"; that was something they had never heard before—their husbands were doing time for criminal offenses. Then I crawled into bed and fell sound asleep with the lights on and the women still chattering. I woke up in the middle of the night worrying about missing my 6:00 a.m. start. I couldn't sleep anymore.

Early the next morning, after walking a mile on a country road, I was lucky to be picked up by the bus. I was grateful. I was even more grateful to find my awesome brother waiting for me in the hotel in downtown Irkutsk, our designated meeting place. He was my rock and my shoulder to cry on. I felt so blessed to have him in my life.

On the plane back to Sverdlovsk with Gena by my side, I played out the past week's tragic events in my head. Dora's death continued to be devastating. But although I was still floundering in the sea of pain, I was no longer drowning—my time with Zach had given me enough strength to stay afloat. It reinforced what I knew all along—we had no choice but to ride the waves of this powerful storm, the storm of our lives. I remember Zach telling me, "Things have their own logic, their inherent internal logic, and we just have to follow it." Following inherent logic meant continuing to fight. It meant fighting more, not less. Fighting like our lives depended on it. And they did.

October and November were a whirlwind of letter writing. Our supporters worldwide wrote letters and complaints about Zach's treatment in the camp. We collected signatures from our refusenik friends in Moscow, Leningrad, Kyiv, and Odessa. We all demanded a criminal investigation of those who had ordered the beating as well as those who'd carried it out. We demanded that the Gulag administration form commissions to investigate the matter. We demanded that they send commissioners to the camp for witness testimonies. We demanded that they dismiss the Hitler-loving ensign from his post.

The most surprising thing was that commissions were actually formed. And commissioners were sent to the camp. The least surprising thing was that these functionaries admitted "no wrongdoing." Here are some examples from the commission reports:

> 11/23/84: This is to inform you that your husband has never been beaten up, which is well documented by testimonies of other inmates, as well as the camp's personnel.

> 11/28/84: This is to inform you that since your husband arrived at penal colony #UK 272/40, nobody has forced him to join the ranks of collaborators; nobody has ever beaten him up; nobody has seen him with any signs of a beating, neither on September 27 nor in the following days.

This cover-up would have passed muster had I not been there, had I not spent twenty-four hours with Zach, had I not seen the signs of the beating with my own eyes, had I not heard his moans of pain. How dare they! In moments like this, it was hard not to lose faith.

In the weeks after our meeting, Zach and I were able to exchange a few letters. Our secret code worked perfectly, hiding the information that we—and only we—knew how to retrieve. Because those letters looked innocent, they escaped administration's censorship. Concealed within, however, was a gold mine of information. That, combined with the official responses I received from the Gulag administration, painted a pretty grim picture:

September 28: reprimand for not reporting to work [Zach was unable to get out of bed due to the beating]

November 9: two days of punitive labor for delayed reveille

November 16–17: a hunger strike to protest the anti-Semitic rants of Ensign Averin

November 24: one day of punitive labor for being too close to restricted areas

December 4: three days in a punishment cell for refusing to work on an assignment regarded as humiliating[30]

December 13: seven days in a punishment cell for refusing to work on an assignment regarded as humiliating

December 17–25: hunger strike to protest provocation on the part of the administration, forcing him to work on an assignment regarded as humiliating

You can see how it escalated. At the same time, Zach told me (between the lines) that by dispatching commissions to the camp, we had put the camp administration on the defensive. Even though nobody admitted any wrongdoing, they preferred to live without the scrutiny, hype, and attention these commissions brought. That is exactly what we would continue doing: bringing as much scrutiny, hype, and attention to the camp as possible. And maybe, over time, things would change.

---

30   The "humiliating" assignment was building a fence in the restricted area near the camp perimeter. For unknown reasons, this job was deemed beyond the pale in Bozoy prison culture; it was usually assigned to prisoners with the lowest standing in the camp hierarchy. By assigning this job to Zach, the administration deliberately tried to lower his status among his fellow inmates, leaving him no option but to refuse.

In late December, I traveled back to Bozoy to request a short, supervised meeting with Zach.

The rules for granting such meetings left much room for manipulation. On one hand, the prisoners had a right to a certain number of meetings with their families. On the other hand, the administration could take away that right at any moment, depending on which side of the bed they woke up on that morning. On paper, they needed a legitimate reason to do so. In reality, they didn't. They used the meetings as leverage over prisoners' behavior and willingness to cooperate.

Zach was entitled to two long-term (twenty-four to seventy-two hours) and three short-term (two to four hours) meetings per year. We'd had our long meeting in October upon his arrival. Now it was time for a short one. Those take place in a partitioned room supervised by a guard.

To get to Bozoy this time around, I took an evening flight from Riga to Moscow. Then I switched to a red-eye, arriving in Irkutsk the following day. The flight itself took five and a half hours. With the six-hour time difference between Riga and Irkutsk, we landed there late morning.

Stepping out of the plane into the vast space surrounding the airport reminded me that I was in the bleak heart of Siberia. It was windy and bitterly cold, somewhere around -30°F. Outside the airport, people stood in line for a cab, but the cabs were few and far between. Everybody was dancing on their feet, clapping their mittened hands, trying not to let the cold get them. Even though I was well equipped—wearing a long mouton coat with a hood, hat, scarf, warm boots, and mittens—I, too, danced on my feet. The line moved at a snail's pace. Once at the front of it, I missed out on a few cabs as they had declined to go to Bozoy. Eventually, one kind soul agreed to take me.

We drove an hour and a half, talking on and off. In the quiet moments, I stared out the window, taking in my surroundings. Pine and deciduous forests gave way to the vast grasslands of the steppes dotted with thickets of shrubs. The Russian steppes possess an austere beauty, but I was in no mood to appreciate it. All I wanted was to get to my destination. We drove by sparsely populated villages and townships, then abandoned the interstate for a country road. It was well into the afternoon by the time we arrived in Bozoy.

I got out of the cab and looked around. Still a ghost town, it was now cloaked in snow, which softened its image a bit. But the barbed wire and observation towers quickly erased that first impression; no amount of white could cover the dark soul of this godforsaken place. Bozoy was ugly as sin. It was ugly for what it represented.

At the camp, the officer on duty informed me of the administration's decision to disallow the meeting. But worse, they disallowed the next three meetings as well. Why? In my interpretation, it was in retaliation for all the noise we had made about Zach's beating and anti-Semitic threats directed at him. Also, they didn't want to give us ammunition to make more noise; in their minds, the less I knew about Zach, the better. Last but not least, they did it just because they could. Formally, though, these were the reasons they gave:

> October 6: deprived of the right to a meeting for "showing bad attitude toward rehabilitation through hard labor by making an off-the-cuff remark: 'I don't intend to work for Bolsheviks'"
>
> October 9: deprived of the right to a subsequent meeting for "washing clothes during off time"
>
> December 17: deprived of the right to a subsequent meeting for conducting a hunger strike

The following morning, before daybreak, I walked to the central gates. I had heard it was a common practice among prisoners' wives to gather at the gates, hoping for a fleeting glimpse of their husbands while they were escorted out of the camp for work. Understanding their silent plea, the guards did not shoo the women away. They knew these women were there for nothing more than a wave. Not much to ask, was it? That was all I was hoping for, too. I stood there among the other women, our eyes fixed on the gates. The scene on the other side was a whirlwind of activity as the prisoners were sorted into various teams. One after another, the trucks arrived, and the prisoners, their movements hurried, climbed in. The escorts locked the back of each truck and took a special seat between the back area and the driver's cabin.

One by one, the trucks drove off. One by one, the women left, having caught a glimpse of their loved ones. I found myself alone, standing in front of the gates, shivering in the brutal cold. I tried to move my feet, but they wouldn't obey me—they were turning into glass. Soon, the last truck left, and now a line of those led to their work sites on foot came out of the gates. Zach, I knew, should be among them. The first group of prisoners passed, then the second and a third. He wasn't there. When the last group passed by me, I cried out, "I am the wife of Zach Zunshine! What happened to him? Why is he not here?"

One prisoner yelled back, "He was excused from work today! Don't know why."

I knew why. I knew perfectly well. I was standing at the gates — that's why. Me, attempting to see my husband at least for a moment —that's why. They wouldn't give us that moment. They would rather excuse him from work than give us a chance to see each other. What bastards!

On the bright side, it did buy him a day off.

I was leaving Bozoy. December was ending. 1984 was ending. The Orwellian year, it lived up to its name. What would the next one bring?

PART 2

1985

CHAPTER 13

INSIDE THE BLACK HOLE

One fundamental rule in dealing with the KGB is this: if you have skeletons in your closet, don't put yourself on their radar. It will cost you dearly.

It turned out that my best friend, Svetlana Balter, and her youngest son, Evgeny—Sasha's brother—had collective skeletons in the closet. This concerned Evgeny's run-in with the law and Svetlana covering for him. From the moment it happened, it was only a matter of time until the KGB engaged in the world's easiest case of blackmail. Soon, Svetlana found herself dangling from a hook, so to speak.

The rest was easy. Presented with a number of painful options for Evgeny's immediate future, each one worse than the last, Svetlana must have felt she had no choice but to agree to flip. And who did she flip against? You guessed it—me.

Unaware of all that had transpired, I suddenly found myself at odds with Svetlana. In a stark reversal, she started giving me advice that was quite contrary to my belief. To *our* belief! "You are hurting your husband," she'd say, echoing the KGB. "Stop what you are doing. You are only making things *worse* for him." The first time it happened, I was baffled yet willing to give my friend the benefit of the doubt. I wondered what was going on with her. One doesn't suddenly change one's mind about something as fundamental as this. Fighting was *the* only tactic we thought appropriate when dealing with the KGB.

Then she said it again. And again. Sadly, that was not the end of it.

A few months later, a bombshell arrived. Using our secret code, Zach informed me that he had received a letter from Svetlana in which she insinuated that her older son, Sasha, and I were having an affair.

The moment I read those lines, the light in my eyes went dark. It shook me like an earthquake. Never in my life had I experienced a betrayal of that magnitude. Alone in my apartment, with the letter in my hands, I felt a giant knot forming in my stomach, nauseating me. With that, the room started spinning. I let go of the letter, propped myself against the wall, and slid down on the floor. And that's when the waterfalls started. Burying my face into my knees, I cried inconsolably. I found myself chanting the same mantra I'd had the misfortune of using before: "This could not have happened. This could not have happened." Deeply wounded, I sat there on the floor until I ran out of tears, and even then I couldn't get up. Everything was blurry, and I felt thrown off. As I was sitting there wondering how I could recover from this, another question followed on its heels: *While I was learning to protect myself from the slings and arrows of the KGB, how could I protect my heart from the slings and arrows of my own friends?*

Zach was a bigger man. He knew me, he knew his friend Sasha, and he knew this was a lie, yet another lie perpetrated by the KGB and, this time around, delivered by a close friend. Zach's reaction was swift. In secret code, he told me that he had cut Svetlana off. He wrote back, telling her never to speak to him again. She never did.

Sasha was angry, so angry that he stopped communicating with his mother. It took several years for them to reconcile.

It took me years to reconcile with Svetlana in my heart. She had been given Sophie's choice and did what she felt necessary to shield her youngest son from the dangers he faced. I never talked to her after that incident, but I no longer judge her.

I debated whether or not to revisit this unfortunate event. I decided to do so for the sole purpose of telling the truth. I wanted to show the lengths the KGB would go to in their effort to disband our movement. Pitting us refuseniks against one another was a tactic designed to undermine our support system. In my case, the KGB's goal was twofold: to rob me of Svetlana's support by forcing her to flip and, more importantly, to destroy Zach's support system by eroding the foundation of our marriage. (I am happy to report they failed miserably.) I also wanted to show what shaky ground we were all walking on. Most of us managed to stay firmly on our feet. A few may have tripped, but I chose to believe that if they did, it was not due to the meanness of their heart. Weakness, yes. Not meanness.

In mid-February, a strange-looking envelope arrived. I noticed the absence of a return address. *It couldn't be from Zach, could it?* To my delight, it was from him! A bootleg letter! I could not believe my eyes. As I began reading, my joy plummeted with every line. *They are locking him up in the internal prison?* Stung by the news, I kept reading. I didn't realize—just yet—the full extent of the danger the situation presented. It would hit me in a moment, but for now, I was frantically scanning the letter. Smuggled out of the Gulag, it looked like it had been scribbled down in a hurry, causing the narrative to jumble, one theme cascading upon another.

February 4, 1985

Dear Tan'ka,

The Stolypin carriage is trotting along the track; it is getting lighter outside the window, and I am writing you a letter. Today is February 4, and I am being transferred to another labor camp in the Irkutsk region—UK 272/23, Octyabrsky township, Chunsky district.

Now that I am out of there, the Bozoy administration is breathing a sigh of relief. My story is this: my first official complaint, dated September 30 and addressed to Prosecutor Maslov, was thrown out. There, I addressed the beating and the anti-Semitic taunts directed at me. To protest the fact that the paper was simply tossed out, I staged a two-day hunger strike from November 16 to 17. At the beginning of December, in retaliation, the administration went on the offensive. They began to impose on me a job that is considered "shameful"—building a fence in a restricted area. By doing so, they were pitting other inmates against me, thus undermining my security. Here, it is believed that such work in restricted areas is performed only by stool pigeons. I had to refuse. What else could I have done? For refusing this job, I was given two terms in a punishment cell (December 4–7 and December 13–20). To stop their shenanigans and to get a different job, one with a quota— otherwise, if there is no quota, they could simply say that I am not working—I had to declare another hunger strike, this time for eight days (December 17–25). It bore fruit, and the administration retreated: on December 26, they assigned me the job of weaving baskets. For the first month, I was considered an apprentice. By the end of the first month, I was able to make two baskets a day. But the twice-inflated quota for beginners is four baskets. It might as well have been eight baskets, as none of it has any basis in reality. At most, the beginners are able to make two baskets. So did everybody, and so did I. Yet, on January 25, they threw me into a punishment cell for a ten-day term for "failure to produce a quota." On January 31, they informed me of the decree to lock me up in the interior labor camp prison for a six-month term. Immediately, I was transferred from Bozoy to a transitional prison in Irkutsk and then to labor camp #23, a.k.a. Khonyaki, which I will reach by tomorrow. Khonyaki is a Japanese word meaning "Black Hole." The camp was named after Japanese inmates who were kept there during and after World War II.

There were a lot of investigations in Bozoy. They showed me two reports finalizing the investigations, both signed by Vitaly Balandin—the head of management of the labor camp. The reports will be forwarded to you as well. Everything in them is one big *shameless lie. Everything! The conditions in Bozoy were horrific. Imagine this: They provided clean underwear as rarely as twenty days plus (on December 6, 29, and January 18). They fed us worse than in prison. We were starving! Although the bathhouse had double window frames, snow and ice covered their inner side. Also remarkable is the fact that no spoons were available in the punishment cell. Senior Lt. Urmaev, the head of the ward, says that "in accordance with Soviet law, spoons are not allowed in punishment cells." The cold was unbearable. It forced the inmates to cling to radiators like sheep near a shepherd. Dirt, lice—everywhere. The central heating wouldn't function for up to three days, causing your breath to hang in the air. And that's when you are inside! We were freezing to the bone. They claimed the temperature was 62°F to 66°F (as minimally required), but it was nowhere near that!*

The prosecutor's office was useless. Prosecutor Vakhrushkin came once a month, buried his head in the sand, and left. In all probability, our pressure did get to them, plus they thought you knew too much about me, so they decided to hide me away and lock me up in prison. For the last two months, the water supply in Bozoy has been cut off. They drained water out of the radiators and poured it into drinking tanks, and that's what people drank. A total nightmare.

In the transient prison in Irkutsk, I was kept in cell #25. For thirty-five people, there were twenty-five plank cots (with no mattresses provided). If you happened to have a spoon, they would take it away. The thirty-five of us ended up with 7–8 spoons. I'm not sure what the deal is with those spoons. It's mind-boggling! One good thing that happened in Bozoy: they no longer beat the crap out of the newcomers who refuse to collaborate, all thanks to the pain we inflicted on them by making so much noise. One of the collaborators who participated in my beating, someone Zuev, was rewarded—and released ahead of time.

What's known about Khonyaki is that the camp is overcrowded. It houses more than 2,000 inmates. Most inmates are chronic alcoholics. People are starving. Food is disgusting. The quotas for food, even bread, are not being respected. They say that sometimes bread is not delivered for several days. Opposite me on the train sits a man who had spent a month in Khonyaki, then left, and now is being transferred back. He couldn't answer a simple question: Is there a bathhouse there in Khonyaki? Maybe there is, maybe there isn't. He told me, however, that—just as in Bozoy—the newcomers were forced to become collaborators. Those who refused faced the threat of being assigned to unit #11 (designated solely for homosexual inmates).

They asked me how in the world did you know so much about me. Let them guess their brains out. Most likely, I would be locked in a punishment cell right away, but never mind. My weight now is 160 pounds. I feel all right.

You must know I told them I intended to play it cool, not refrain from mandatory work, and that I saw no upside to breaking the camp regime. And I would spare them from my formal complaints once they provide the inmates with minimally acceptable conditions.

Z.[31]

By the time I finished reading the letter, I was physically in pain. It manifested in my temples. I covered them with my hands and felt the relentless beats. *Bang, bang, bang.* Accompanied by this drums-only orchestra, Zach's narrative came into play: *In all probability, our pressure did get to them, plus they thought you knew too much about me, so they decided to hide me away and lock me up in prison.* It was almost like I was hearing him say those words. They rang true, and I agreed with him. But I saw a bigger picture.

I remembered the threat that Kofel's deputy in Bozoy had thrown at me during my visit with him in October: "How about Article 188-3 of the Soviet Criminal Code, which carries an additional three-year

---

31   Tatiana Zunshine's personal archive.

term for regime violation in places of confinement?" I remember shutting him down, unwilling to go down the rabbit hole of his nasty threats. I wasn't going to react to them. "I'm not interested in playing this game," I'd said to him, "so keep your threats to yourself, and don't waste your time on me."

It turned out this was not a game, and the threat of an additional term was no longer just a threat. It was a reality. Let me explain: According to Article 188-3, "malicious disobedience on the part of the inmate is punishable by imprisonment for up to three years, when and if the inmate was sent—within a year—to an internal prison[32] for violations of the regime." That article had the vaguest language possible. What did "within a year" mean? Once a year? Or was it the second time within a year that triggered the charge? It did not say explicitly. And what constituted "malicious disobedience"? The explanation was left out. The truth is, the vague language was hardly accidental. The lawmakers, in essence, gave prison administrations a gift: *Interpret it however you want and use it at your discretion.*

It's that hook again, I thought. *They are trying to hang us on the hook. They are building the case for an additional term, and once done—six months from now—they'll get to decide whether or not to set it in motion. The threat will always be there.*

I was putting those thoughts through the grinder of my mind, realizing how dangerous the situation was. And yet, my brain didn't go frantic looking for solutions, as I knew all too well: there were no solutions. Unlike Svetlana, I was not going to change course. For us, there was no other way to defend ourselves; there was no way to do it safely, either. We had to accept the risk and go on.

Then something else crossed my mind—the way Zach and I exchanged information was now in question. *They thought you knew too much about me,* he wrote, and I did, thanks to the secret code. But

---

32   A prison within a camp.

there, in the internal prison, the letter allowance was limited to one letter every two months. *They will be watching for the leaks to subside*, I thought. *And if they do subside, they'll be able to determine that the leaks had occurred through letters.*

Oh, no!

If Zach's internal incarceration was beyond my reach—by the time I received the letter, it had already taken place—the leak situation was something I could possibly affect. This was vital to Zach's survival. We could not let them find the leak. Whatever it took, we needed them to rule out the letters. How would I do that? *Well*, I thought, *if I can't get information from Zach, I have to get it from somewhere else.* I didn't know exactly how it would play out. I just knew I had to go to Siberia.

First, I'd go to Irkutsk to see people from the regional Gulag and get them to confirm my conclusions. Once confirmed, I, too, would set something in motion! I would ask Pam to telegraph the news all over the world. We would shout it out endlessly, tirelessly, every chance we had, and by doing so, we would try to prevent the second term from happening.

From Irkutsk, I would go to Khonyaki to meet the new administration and get a feel for what they were up to. As importantly, I would cruise around to see if I could get a human being to talk to me and share inside information about the camp. I would talk to anyone who would listen. If I had to, I would stalk a camp laundress or a cook on their way from work. I would do whatever it took to get the flow of information moving.

Before I left for Khonyaki, I dictated Zach's letter to Pam and asked her to get as much mileage out of it as possible.

Arriving in Irkutsk late in the morning, I hurried to the regional Gulag office and requested a meeting with Major Kovalev, the head of the Operative Department. What they called the Operative

Department was, in reality, an arm of the KGB. I thought it would be appropriate to confront those who masterminded the whole internal prison affair, so I insisted on seeing that particular man. He agreed to see me.

I entered the office and saw Kovalev sitting at his desk. He motioned me to the chair, but I chose to remain standing. One other man was in the office as well. He introduced himself as a representative of the Regime Department, Vassily Gusarov.

I went on the offensive right off the bat. "What are the grounds for my husband's incarceration in the internal prison?" I asked Kovalev sternly. "What did he do to deserve it?"

I expected to hear "a lot," followed by a list of "violations," and was prepared to refute every single one of them. Instead, I heard "not much," and that stopped me in my tracks.

"What? Not much?"

"Not much," Kovalev repeated. "He didn't do much to deserve six months. I don't know why they gave him six months; two would have been enough. You understand why it was done, right?"

"Oh, I understand, I understand more than anyone! You are admitting that it's the act of sending my husband to the internal prison that matters, whether it is one month or six months or anything in between. That's what I suspected, and you are not even hiding it! You are blatantly admitting that you are doing this just to lay the grounds for a potential second term!"

What followed was an angry exchange. That is, angry on my part, not theirs. I remember telling them how different they were from what was commonly known as human beings. They said I "misunderstood them." And that they had never met a prisoner's wife like me. I was "different."

They started talking about the fact that I knew a lot about Zach's situation. How come I knew so much? I ignored the question. They had read the letters Zach and I exchanged while he was still in Bozoy.

They threw in a few quotes from my letters and others from Zach's. That was bizarre. *Do they not have better things to do than memorize our letters?* I wondered.

"Instead of writing your husband supportive letters," Gusarov said, "why don't you tell him . . . sort of . . . dear Zach, do everything the prison administration tells you to do, and then things will turn out all right."

I shook my head in disbelief. "The absurdity of this statement," I said to him, "could not be overstated."

Out on the street, I burst into tears. *Those scumbags! They didn't even try to conceal it!*

From Irkutsk, my journey took an unfamiliar turn. No more sixty-mile cab ride, as I had done a few times going to Bozoy. To reach Khonyaki, I had to travel on a northwest-bound train for twenty-three hours.

On the train, accompanied by a monotonous rumble of wheels, I once again found myself in my own world. *I am dragging myself across Mother Russia without any hope of seeing him. My only hope is to get a particle of information about him, a kind of a boost that will give me the strength to go on.*

In my head, the reruns of our story went round and round. The past was flashing in my mind with such clarity and intensity that it could have easily competed with the present. Five years ago, on the train to Riga, accompanied by the same monotonous rumble of wheels, Zach and I felt we were on top of the world. So much promise and so much change were coming our way, exhilarating us as if we were standing on the mountain's peak and observing the vastness before us. That open space was our future. We embraced it. We were ready for it. Were we prepared for a potential free fall? Not quite. Back then, on the train to Riga, the word "KGB" and the dangers of crossing them all seemed academic.

"The stars are our limit, you know why?" Zach had said back then on the train.

I knew where he was going, and it made me laugh. He was leading me on to recite his favorite quote from the German philosopher Immanuel Kant. To paraphrase Kant, the two things that fill the mind with delight are the starry sky above us and the moral law within us.

"So do you?"

"Because of the starry sky above us and the moral law within us," we said laughingly, in unison.

The train ride ended. I arrived in Chunsky, an administrative center situated on the Chuna River. Following the lead of one of my fellow travelers, I went to the bus station and got on the bus. My next stop was the town of Octyabrsky, located on the same river, ten miles southwest of Chunsky.

Despite the short distance, the bus dragged on. I spent the ride glued to the window, observing the moving picture of the landscape. It wasn't too bad to look at. We were passing ridges of hills with smoothed and rounded peaks, all covered in snow. The area was mostly forested, with miles of interchanging pine and larch trees.

Arriving in Octyabrsky, I was pleasantly surprised to see that it was bigger than the minuscule Bozoy. A woman sitting next to me seemed friendly, and I asked her how big the place was. She said the population there was about 8,500. There were a couple of motels, schools, stores, diners, and a medical office.

"Do you happen to know where Khonyaki is?" I asked her.

"Everybody here knows Khonyaki."

She suggested I get off at the bus stop by the river and walk across it. "Khonyaki," she said, "is exactly on the opposite side of the river, but there is no bridge connecting us." She told me the frozen river was safe to walk on. Soon, in April or May, the ferry would resume its operation, shuttling people back and forth. But for now, walking was the only option. "It's not far," she said, "about three hundred yards."

I thanked her and got off at the right stop. The Chuna River was in front of me. I stepped on it, first cautiously, then more confidently, and proceeded to walk. Most of the surface was covered with snow, with occasional snowdrifts formed here and there. At times, patches of ice showed through, naked, or, worse, deceptively covered with a thin layer of snow. I slowed down, just to be careful. The wind was blowing quite hard. I stopped from time to time to turn away from it when the gust was particularly strong. I finally got to the other bank, and there it was: Khonyaki—the infamous Black Hole.

It lived up to its name, that's for sure. Crooked houses half-grown into the earth; dilapidated fences, like village drunks, unable to keep straight; the sound of barking dogs all over the place, resonating in the narrow space of back alleys. Looking at it for a minute or two, observing the place in its entirety, I caught myself shivering, and not from the cold. *It's dreadful*, I thought. *A Black Hole, indeed.*

An older woman dragging a sled with a small water tank passed by. She was dressed in the same manner as most people in places like this, wearing a dark gray quilted jacket with cottonwood filling and a matching pair of felt boots. A warm headscarf wrapped around her head partially covered her face. I asked her where the post office was—just to see if she was willing to talk—but got a short answer: "No post office here. Only on the other bank." She seemed to be suspicious of strangers, so I left her alone.

Suddenly, a passing truck left me in a cloud of exhaust. It was an old, wobbly truck, looking like it could come apart at any moment, but that's not what caught my attention. What caught my eye was the fact that on the side of the truck, in oversized letters, was written the word HUMANS. I found it incredibly odd and didn't quite know what to make of it.

In the headquarters, I requested a meeting with the head of the camp, Colonel Valiulin. Although he agreed to see me, he refused to answer any of my questions and went on the offensive instead.

"Are you here as a reporter, asking us all these questions? Are you interviewing us? Eh?"

"I am the wife of one of the prisoners kept here under your supervision, and that is a plenty good reason for me to come here, ask you questions, and expect answers."

"Your husband is alive; isn't that good enough? What else would you need to know?"

"I'd like to know if *your* loved one were being kept here, would it be good enough to know that they are alive? Or, would you, perhaps, want to know a little more?"

We engaged in a verbal battle, but nothing came of it. He clearly decided (or somebody decided for him) that it was best to keep me in the dark. Feeling at the end of the rope in my frustration, I feared the sparring—if it continued—would push me over the edge. I ended it.

Standing outside of the headquarters, I felt the weight of last week's events crushing me. I was dead tired. Too tired to think straight, I still had to make an effort and decide: *What's next?* My initial plan was to talk to people in town. Before arriving, I did not know how small the town was (I later found out it had a population of 227). I wanted to collect information about the camp to create the illusion that the leak was continuing. But being seen talking to the town's residents would have defeated my purpose. Staying in Khonyaki would not have helped. Staying there was also impossible because the town had no lodging. I had to go back to Octyabrsky.

By the time I crossed the river back to Octyabrsky, it was getting dark. I found a motel near the riverbank and got myself a room. Unlike the room in Bozoy, I didn't have to share it with ten or fifteen other women. *Thank god I can be by myself, close my eyes, and rest. Let's hope tomorrow is a better day.*

The next morning, I went out to see if I could find any locals willing to talk. I stopped at the diner and got some breakfast for one reason, and one reason only—so I could join somebody at their table and strike up a conversation. I saw a group of locals gathered around one table, and I asked if I could join them. They looked at me strangely but didn't say no. We started talking. The food looked inedible, and I didn't touch it, but the conversation was quite fruitful.

I got the scoop on the history of Khonyaki, starting from 1945. That year, 90,000 Japanese prisoners of war were brought to the area. In addition to building labor camps—for themselves and others—they were forced to build a railway. Needless to say, they weren't treated humanely. It's illustrated in a saying circulated in the area: "Underneath every railway tie, there lies a Japanese prisoner of war."

A couple of people from the group had worked at the Khonyaki camp in the past. They crossed the river every day on their way to and from work. "Khonyaki is a tough place to be in," one man said. "It's just across the river, but what a difference." He blamed the natural environment of the area. "There's something rotten in that piece of land," he said. Others agreed. Formerly a wetland, it had been turned into the grounds for a labor camp, but the dampness had never gone away, exacerbating the harshness of the Siberian winter, making the air piercing to the bone. That winter, the temperature had been brutal. For most of February, it stayed at -35°F. It warmed up just a week before I showed up. Another man offered a few details about the camp itself: the uniform the prisoners wore was a joke, not warm enough; the heating system was inadequate, making the inmates suffer from perpetual cold; three terms in a punishment cell could jeopardize one's life.

This was hard to listen to, and my heart was aching, but I had to listen and absorb every word. I thought of the head of the camp, Valiulin, asking me if I was a reporter. At that moment, talking to the locals, I was.

On the train back to Irkutsk, I got more information. One of the passengers turned out to be a former inmate of Khonyaki. I asked him if he knew the rules of confinement in Khonyaki's internal prison. He did. Unlike in the camp, he said, prisoners were kept in cells, with anywhere from six to fifteen men per cell. The food ration was further diminished (as if it wasn't small enough already). The eating utensils—just like in Bozoy—were scarce. Not only was there a shortage of spoons, but there was also a shortage of cups. Meetings with family were prohibited. Correspondence was limited to one letter every two months. One food parcel of limited weight was allowed every six months. The cot situation was similar to that in punishment cells: the cots were bracketed to the walls and lowered only at night, forcing the prisoners to sit on backless benches for the entire day. The fresh air allowance was a half-hour walk in a prison yard. Inside the cell, the air was too warm in the summer, too cold in the winter, and dangerous throughout the year. "Don't ask me where they get cigarettes," the guy said, "but they do. They smoke inside a tiny cell without air circulation, leaving everybody around in a cloud of fumes."

Day after day, month after month. For a period of six months.

That sounded nightmarish.

Sometimes, I wondered if the whole thing wasn't just a nightmare, one I would not be able to wake up from for a long, long time.

CHAPTER 14

WEAPONIZING HUMOR

On my way home, I recorded an account of the whole trip. Having confirmed the KGB's shenanigans around building a case for Zach's second term, I laid it all out in my notes. I asked Pam to shout about it as loudly as she could. I knew she would immediately share this information with all other branches of the Union of Councils for Soviet Jews, as well as with their partners in the United States, Europe, and around the world. I asked them to write letters to Moscow, Irkutsk, the Soviet embassy in Washington, DC, and the camp in Khonyaki. Let those letters show overwhelming support for Zach and outrage at the prospect of an additional term.

I gave Pam the telephone numbers of the Gulag officials in Moscow and Irkutsk and asked her to share them with our supporters. "Let's call those functionaries and express concern over Zach's brutal treatment," I told Pam. "Let's ring those phones off the hook if we can!" I suggested that our supporters call members of the US Congress, asking them to contact the Soviets on Zach's behalf. I suggested that human rights attorneys request a meeting with Zach inside the internal prison—largely a symbolic gesture but one that would shine a spotlight on his case.

"Anything and everything we can do," I said to Pam, "we should do! Take cups and spoons, for example, those infamous cups and spoons the administration refused to provide. Let's make them part of our campaign. Let's send packages of plastic cups and spoons to

Bozoy, Khonyaki, the Gulag office in Irkutsk, the national Gulag office in Moscow, and the Soviet embassy in Washington, DC—another symbolic gesture; this one with a grain of mockery."

Later, I found out that the cups-and-spoons campaign energized our supporters like nothing else. Having received the message, Pam told me, the volunteers took it to heart. They flooded the Soviets with thousands and thousands of those packages, accompanied by notes: *We understand there is a shortage of cups and spoons in the Soviet Union, and we would like to help. Please accept our heartfelt donation.*

Based on Zach's letter, on March 1, 1985, the *Chicago Tribune* published an article titled "Jew's Letter Tells Grim Life in Soviet Gulag," by Howard A. Tyner. Long and scrupulous, the article included every aspect of the letter, from living conditions to, yet again, the lack of spoons. Acknowledging the rarity of such a detailed letter to have reached the outside, Tyner wrote: "A Jewish activist serving three years in a labor camp has smuggled a letter to his wife detailing beatings, intimidation, filth and cold so severe that prisoners huddle around radiators 'like sheep near a shepherd' in the Soviet gulag."[33]

As a part of our campaign, the Union of Councils facilitated sending my letter to Richard Schifter, United States Representative to the United Nations Commission on Human Rights. Richard Schifter was a legend. Having lost his parents in the Holocaust, he fled Nazi-occupied Vienna at the age of fifteen and arrived in the United States. A champion for human rights, he dedicated his whole life to the fight for people's liberty and dignity. Among his immeasurable achievements was his advocacy for political prisoners in the Soviet Union and other Soviet-bloc countries.

---

33   Archives, Center for Jewish History, New York, NY.

February 24, 1985

Mr. Richard Schifter
United States Representative to the United Nations
Commission on Human Rights
c/o the European Office of the United Nations
Geneva, Switzerland

Dear Mr. Schifter:

As far as I know, one of the main objectives of the United Nations Commission on Human Rights is the defense of convicts who have been victimized for political motives. I believe that my husband, Zachar Zunshine, sentenced to a three-year term in a Soviet labor camp, has been the victim of an overall Soviet policy in retaliation against Jews who expressed their desire to leave the USSR.

From the time we first applied and were denied permission to emigrate to Israel, we have been incessantly subjected to many forms of persecution, resulting in the arrest of my husband, Zachar Zunshine, on March 6, 1984. The charges were slandering the Soviet state system. Such a charge serves as an official pretext for instituting legal prosecution. In reality, he was imprisoned for his struggle for the right to emigrate.

The trumped-up and anti-Semitic character of the legal case is illustrated by numerous violations of the law in the course of the prosecution. It is also illustrated by his outright brutal treatment in Riga's prison and the labor camp in the Irkutsk region.

On the first day in the labor camp, he was brutally beaten by criminals instigated by the camp administration. He had to resort to hunger strikes to protest against the beatings, anti-Semitic activities, and the intolerable conditions of forced labor.

Having been transferred to another camp, he was put into the internal camp prison for a six-month term, allegedly for "breaking the camp regime."

He is constantly threatened with the possibility of being sentenced to an additional three-year term under Article

188-3 of the Russian Criminal Code for so-called "violation of camp regime."

The conditions in the labor camp are dreadful. The situation is complicated by blatant violations of sanitary norms. Normal food allocation is not observed. Water is being obtained from the central heating system. The lack of utensils forces five people to use one spoon. Life there is intolerable.

I appeal to the United Nations Commission on Human Rights to make a stand in the defense of my husband, Zachar Zunshine. I appeal to you to take appropriate measures against the terrible conditions he is subjected to and to make every effort possible to obtain his release and our subsequent emigration to Israel.

Signed: Tatiana Zunshine[34]

On March 15, 1985, in Moscow, following the death of Secretary-General Chernenko, a new head of the Soviet state was appointed. His name was Mikhail Gorbachev. Five days later, on March 20, the Third Congressional Fast and Prayer Vigil for Soviet Jewry took place on the floor of the US House of Representatives, with one hundred members of the House fasting and praying for Soviet refuseniks. Needless to say, Congressman John Porter was among them. In his statement, he talked about Zachar Zunshine of Riga, for whom, he said, "I fast today, and whose name I wear proudly upon my chest—a man of courage who is serving a prison term merely for asserting that all people ought to have basic human rights in the Soviet Union or anywhere else."[35]

In addition, the participating members of the House signed an open letter to the newly appointed Soviet leader, Mikhail Gorbachev,

---

34 Archives, Center for Jewish History, New York, NY.

35 *Congressional Record—House* (Washington, DC: US Government Printing Office, 1985), pp. 5695-5696.

urging him to "review your government's policies toward the Jewish community." Zach's name was among the few mentioned in the letter.

Secretary-General Mikhail Gorbachev,
CPSU, the Kremlin, Moscow, RSFSR, U.S.S.R.

Dear Mr. Gorbachev:

We congratulate you on your appointment as Secretary-General of the Communist Party of the U.S.S.R. During recent months, your predecessor, Secretary-General Chernenko, and President Reagan both expressed interest in improving U.S.–U.S.S.R. relations, and we believe the meetings in Geneva are a good step in this direction.

As you assume your new position, we urge you to make another important gesture of your commitment to improving relations. We urge you to review your government's policies toward the Jewish community . . .

During the past year, we in the Congress have raised our voices in support for Anatoly Shcharansky, Ida Nudel, Zachar Zunshine, Yakov Gorodetsky and others who have been denied their fundamental freedoms.

An improvement in this area would make a favorable impression on the opinion of American policymakers concerning your government's sincerity in its expressed desire for improved relations.

Out of a strong desire for a long-lasting peaceful relationship between the U.S. and the U.S.S.R., we hope that you will give careful consideration to this matter.[36]

In mid-April, a rare opportunity arose. Pam told me that a prominent British historian, Martin Gilbert—her personal friend and a

---

36   *Congressional Record—House* (Washington, DC: US Government Printing Office, 1985), p. 5704.

friend of Soviet refuseniks—was on his way to the United States for a meeting with President Reagan and Secretary of State Schultz. She suggested that I write letters to Reagan and Schultz, and she would have Martin hand-deliver them. I jumped on it.

Until then, I had not communicated with Martin Gilbert, but many of my refusenik friends had. They described him as one of the most extraordinary human beings you would ever meet. Born in England to Jewish parents in 1936, he studied history at Magdalen College, Oxford. In 1968, at the age of thirty-two, Martin was appointed by Sir Winston Churchill's family to be his official biographer. He spent the next twenty years in that capacity, completing six volumes of Churchill's biography. By the 1980s, Martin's attention had turned toward the Refusenik movement in the Soviet Union. He was a spokesperson on behalf of Soviet Jewry in large forums, such as the United Nations Commission on Human Rights, small ones, or any venue in between. Martin authored a total of eighty-eight books. For his achievements, in 1990, the British monarchy appointed him Commander of the Order of the British Empire (CBE), followed by knighthood in 1995.

The opportunity to deliver letters to President Reagan and Secretary of State Schultz, utilizing Martin's visit with them, sounded tremendous. I wrote the letters and asked Pam to let Martin know I was ready, awaiting his messenger call. By then, he was already in DC. He called from his hotel room.

"Martin, hi, this is Tatiana," I said, feeling a little starstruck.

Within seconds, I felt like I was talking to an old friend. Our conversation flowed until I started to dictate the letters to him, and then we got disconnected. He dialed back. I proceeded to dictate, only to get disconnected again. And again, and again, and again. Clearly, the KGB was disrupting the dictation. But why in the world would they allow us to reconnect? That wasn't clear. It took forever to get through the letters, but despite many interruptions, we did it.

And Martin was able to hand-deliver the letters to President Reagan and Secretary of State Schultz.

I have never received a response from President Reagan or Secretary Schultz. I have no way of knowing whether or not any action was taken. But if nothing else, this occasion achieved something very important to me. It marked the beginning of my lifelong friendship with Martin Gilbert.

Zach's thirty-fourth birthday was coming up on April 20. I asked Pam to organize our supporters to send him birthday wishes via telegram. But I was thinking, *What else could I do? How else could I lift his spirits?* Then it occurred to me: I needed to be there on his birthday. I would stick around Khonyaki this time so that enough people would see me. From my experience, word spread around those camps like wildfire. If Zach learned I was there, that would be something. For someone kept in captivity, that little gesture could easily make a day, especially a birthday.

This was my second trip to Khonyaki in six weeks. I flew to Irkutsk, got on the train, schlepped for twenty-three hours, and arrived in Chunsky. There, I went searching for flowers. Why flowers? They were going to be my prop. The town of Chunsky was on the bigger side compared to other ones in the area, with a population of around 16,000. I figured that in a town that size, there would be a flower shop. I found it and bought a bouquet of flowers.

I then boarded a bus to Oktyabrsky and exited by the Chuna River. The weather was much nicer than in March when I had been there the first time around. The river ice had already broken up and was well on the way to melting. A single ferry was now operating, and it took me to the other bank.

In Khonyaki, the ground had turned into a combination of puddles, dirt, and piles of blackish remnants of snow. Navigating through that mess, I walked the short distance from the riverbank to the headquarters. There, I requested a meeting with Colonel Valiulin. I stood in the hallway with the bouquet in my hands, sticking out like a sore thumb. Many people saw me as they passed by. They must have wondered what I was doing in the men's prison holding flowers. They must have thought this was odd.

After a substantial wait, Valiulin agreed to see me. I entered the office and saw he was in the company of three other men. They didn't introduce themselves, and that was okay. I was glad he had company; the more the merrier.

"Today is my husband's birthday, and I brought him flowers. I need you to pass them on to him," I said.

They looked at me like I was from another planet.

"What are you doing?" Valiulin uttered after a moment of silence. "Who brings flowers to the penitentiary?"

"I do."

"Flowers are not allowed," he responded, shaking his head in disbelief.

"Why not?" I asked, playing clueless. "Where is it written? And if it is, show it to me. Show me the law that says flowers are not allowed."

"It is not written anywhere. Nobody ever brings flowers to prisons," he said in an icy voice.

"Ah-ha! It's not written anywhere. Other things have been written up, but not flowers. If there is nothing about flowers, then you must take them!"

He was visibly angry.

I didn't know if he knew I was playing him. I didn't think so; he wouldn't have become as angry as he did. As for me, I just wanted to create a scenario where people in the headquarters would hear about my "outrageous" request and talk about it inside the prison. That way, flowers or no flowers, Zach would know I was there.

We went back and forth about the flowers for a little longer. It was quite a spectacle, but at a certain point, I decided I'd had enough. Seeing Valiulin all exasperated, I am sure he had enough as well.

On the way home, I thought about humor as a possible weapon. *We should not dismiss its power, even in unfortunate situations like this. Show them anger, and they'll thrive on it, but humor? They seem to fold in the face of it—something to keep in mind for the future.*

Shortly after I came back from Siberia, a letter from Zach arrived. I was ecstatic! I was also happy to learn that Zach had heard about my presence in Khonyaki on April 20 and had a good laugh about it.

April 28, 1985

Dear Tan'ka,

Although I have been locked up in this Black Hole and have not received any letters for a long time, nevertheless, according to indirect signs—add sensory perception to this—I can perhaps draw a conclusion that cannot but rejoice me: that you, in general, reacted courageously to the lockup, and also to the fact that you have not heard from me for three months.

I recall a character from "The Living and the Dead" by Konstantin Simonov. His name was Serpilin, and he served his time in a camp where correspondence was forbidden altogether. Simonov addressed that phenomenon in this fashion: "Turning the key another half turn, they locked the door that separated him from home even more tightly."

Tan'ka, I could only compare your arrival at Khonyaki on April 20 to the arrival of the battleship "New Jersey" at the Lebanese shore during the crisis.[37] If you say "Battleship New

---

37 US operations during the Lebanese civil war in 1983.

Jersey" in English, that is precisely the nickname I gave you, and that's what I'm gonna call you from now on :).

I reread what I had just written, and I am not that happy with it—the letter is turning into a bore. But I can't spice it up as much as I would have liked to. Talking about the living conditions is strictly prohibited. You can't write about this, you can't write about that, they tell us. What can you write about? Perhaps this: in March, I did not receive a food parcel I was entitled to. Too bad. You know more than anyone how much I adore marmalade.[38] Back in Riga's jail, Investigator Grutup told me: "Zunshine, accept your guilt, and you will receive one year of probation." "What the hell do I need one year of probation for," I thought to myself. "Give me a pound of Latvian marmalade 'Gundega,' and I will accept my guilt and anybody else's." But I didn't say it out loud, the marmalade part, that is, as Grutup has compared me to O. Henry[39] on more than one occasion anyway. Whenever I joked around, he would say, "Santa Maria!" assuming I was making fun of him.

I have been toiling on this letter since early morning, and now it is 4 in the afternoon. Got interrupted by bath time, laundry time, etc. I have not yet opened the textbook on French, nor have I read any Chekhov today.[40] For more than two months, I have studied Chekhov's short stories from 1895 to 1903. I created a method of dissecting a short story by drawing it into circles and squares. I can now draw a 10- to 15-page story into circles and squares using just one piece of paper. Once I did that, the way Chekhov had constructed his stories became clear as a bell. From the short stories, I decided to move on to plays. Chekhov's plays, that is. Right now, I am reading "The Cherry Orchard." With my attitude to literature, I could have taken one book—only if it was

---

38   As prisoners were allowed one food parcel every six months, I sent the parcel with goodies (marmalade included), but the administration must have blocked it.

39   An American writer of short stories (1862–1910) known for his humor, surprise endings, and witty narration.

40   While Zach was still in Bozoy, he asked me to send him a textbook of French, and it was passed on to him; he borrowed a volume of Anton Chekhov from the prison library.

written by a giant like Chekhov—and studied it for the entire six months of my incarceration.

Tan'ka, I want to remind you what I said on March 4 last year when Sasha, you, and I were heading to the Karl Marx monument.[41] I said that one of your biggest objectives is to take care of yourself and stay well. And you should—no matter what— remember this. I hope we get a chance to see each other by the end of the summer (upon my release from the internal prison). Otherwise, do they really intend to allow us to meet less often than once a year?

All things pass, Tan'ka, all things pass (King David had a ring with that inscription). This is as true as "Nothing passes; everything stays." Ten years from now, everything that seemed important today may have a different meaning. Remember that, and do take care of yourself!

Z.[42]

This letter was playful and witty—the opposite of a bore. I re-read it half a dozen times, laughing at the jokes and wondering how he had come up with a method to put a short story into circles and squares. I was intrigued; I am sure Chekhov would have been, too.

Around the same time, the New York-based Committee of Concerned Scientists issued the following press release:

PHYSICISTS AT NATIONAL PARLEY REGISTER DISTRESS
OVER COLLEAGUE MISTREATED IN THE GULAG

NEW YORK, April 29 . . . Deploring the maltreatment of imprisoned Soviet physicist Zachar Zunshine, over 200 participants at the 1985 April meeting of the American Physical

---

41   For our demonstration of protest.

42   Tatiana Zunshine's personal archive.

Society (APS) in Washington, D.C. signed a petition on his behalf. They appealed to the "good offices" of Soviet authorities
"to secure his early release on humanitarian grounds." The
Committee on the International Freedom of Scientists (CIFS),
a committee of the APS, circulated the petition, also on behalf
of the American Association of Physics Teachers . . .

On June 28, 1984, Zachar Zunshine was sentenced to
three years in a labor camp for alleged defamation of the
Soviet state. In fact, he was acting in accordance with his
Government's endorsement of the International Covenant on
Civil and Political Rights and other international agreements
supporting his right to emigrate. The evidence used to convict
him related entirely to his attempts to renounce his Soviet citizenship and to win permission to emigrate.

The conditions of his interment at the Bazoi [Bozoy] labor
camp, where he was held for close to six months, were extremely harsh. Soon after his arrival there, he was beaten by fellow
prisoners. He then became the butt of frequent anti-Semitic
outbursts. When his protest to the local procurator [prosecutor]
did not result in improvement in his situation, he launched a
two-day hunger strike in mid-November. In response, his jailers
assigned him to a work detail in a zone where only informers
worked. Recognizing that his compliance would incite other inmates against him, he refused the assignment. As punishment,
he was twice placed in solitary confinement. Finally, a second
protest hunger strike bore fruit: he was assigned to weaving
mesh baskets.

But this respite was short-lived. On January 25, he was
again remanded to solitary confinement for alleged non-ful-
fillment of his work quota. Six days later, he was informed that
he had been slapped with a six-month term in prison within
another labor camp . . .

Zunshine's plight came to the attention of CIFS chairman Dr. Thomas H. Stix several months ago. His committee
has since considered ways of helping their Soviet colleague. A
member of the committee, Murray Peshkin, telephoned Mrs.
Zunshine in early April to advise her of the group's concern.

She, in turn, urgently pleaded for the support of foreign colleagues in the form of petitions to the Soviet authorities on her husband's behalf.

Dr. Peshkin also sits on the national board of the Committee of Concerned Scientists (CCS). Further information concerning Zunshine and this petition can be obtained from CCS, an independent organization of 4,500 American scientists dedicated to the protection and advancement of the human rights and scientific freedom of colleagues worldwide.[43]

This press release became the basis for a petition sent from CIFS chairman Dr. Thomas H. Stix to the Soviet ambassador to the United States, Anatoly Dobrynin.

THE AMERICAN PHYSICAL SOCIETY
COMMITTEE ON THE INTERNATIONAL FREEDOM
OF SCIENTISTS

May 2, 1985

His Excellency
Anatoly Dobrynin
Ambassador of the USSR
1125 16th St., N.W.
Washington, D.C. 20036

Excellency:

At the Spring Meeting of the American Physical Society, held 24–27 April 1985 in Washington, D.C., members of the Society together with members of the American Association of Physics Teachers expressed their deep concern over the imprisonment of the Soviet physics teacher ZACHAR ZUNSHINE, of Riga.

Enclosed with this letter are copies of a petition signed by 201 physicists and physics teachers who attended this

---

43   Archives, Center for Jewish History, New York, NY.

meeting, appealing to you, on humanitarian grounds, to use your good offices to secure physics teacher Zunshine's early release from internment and to grant to him and his family permission to emigrate, as he requested.

You may be confident that actions favorable to our colleague Zunshine will help significantly to promote cooperation between physicists and physics teachers in our two countries.

Sincerely,

Thomas H. Stix, Chairman[44]

---

44 Tatiana Zunshine's personal archive.

CHAPTER 15

CLOSE ENCOUNTERS WITH THE INHUMAN KIND

On May 4, 1985, at about 10:00 p.m., I was at the train station saying goodbye to friends who had visited me in Riga. Nothing suggested trouble. We stood quietly, talking, waiting for the train to start boarding. Suddenly, a human tornado of plainclothes agents descended on us, whisking me away. It happened too quickly for me to ascertain how many men there were. Nor did I have a chance to see how my friends reacted to this force of nature. I am sure they were left shaken.

I was shaken, too. No matter how many times these things had happened before—too many to count—I still couldn't get used to the scenario that at any given moment, I could be snatched, forcefully and abruptly, and delivered to who knew where, for who knew what, and that none of it—none whatsoever—was in my control.

They took me to the KGB headquarters, where they sat me down in front of the head of the Jewish Department, Lieutenant Colonel Shalaev.

"I hope you like talking," I said to him, "because you will be doing it all by yourself."

"Oh, yes, I've heard," Shalaev said. "That's okay. We need you to listen."

That's when the floodgates opened. He began pouring down on me information concerning my campaign on Zach's behalf, the information that they, the KGB, had accumulated over the last year.

He wanted me to know how much they knew about my activities, and it looked like they knew *everything*.

They had everything I had ever written and signed: my letters and appeals to the Soviet authorities and—most importantly—to their counterparts in the free world; letters to members of the US Congress, to the United Nations, to human rights organizations, to political leaders, including President Reagan and Secretary of State Schultz. My letters to Zach, his letters to me—they had them all. My open-face postcards to the deputies of the Supreme Soviet—they had those as well. My conversations with Pam had been recorded and transcribed. (They mentioned Pam several times, calling her my "collaborator.") They had transcripts of the statements made by members of Congress on the House and Senate floor. They had numerous recordings of radio broadcasts regarding our case, as well as clips of newspaper articles published abroad on our behalf.

The initial shock of having been snatched dissipated, and, surprising myself, I felt calm. In fact, I felt so calm that a daring thought came to my mind: *I would have liked to know which newspapers published those articles.* I almost blurted out, "Can I have the copies for my records?" but realized it might push their buttons a bit too much, so I bit my tongue.

"Your case is all but ready," Shalaev said. "We have collected enough proof for your own charge of disseminating anti-Soviet defamation, at a minimum. There could be a bigger charge. Regardless, this is the last time we will talk to you here."

"Next time, I'll see you some . . . place . . . else," he said slowly, staring at me, making sure I understood what "some . . . place . . . else" meant. I did.

This time, I couldn't stay silent.

"Aah, so you'll be there as well?" I snarled. "In the same capacity as myself, that I am sure of!"

That turned the volume from zero to ten in no time. He was mad.

"Oh, you think it's funny, eh? You think it's funny?" A barrage of threats followed, but within a few minutes, I'd conveniently tuned out. After so many "talks," I had learned how to do just that. I remembered my first encounter with Riga's KGB when, during the "official warning," the officer asked me, "Did you hear what I said? I know you didn't listen, but did you hear?" Since then, not only had I trained myself not to listen, but I had also trained myself not to hear. It's a valuable skill to learn should you find yourself in my position.

I had been in their custody since 10:00 p.m. The talk had ended a while ago, but I wasn't allowed to leave. They kept me in a separate room, with an agent standing guard on the other side of the door. I was wondering what was coming next when, finally, the door opened. "You can go now," the agent said.

It was 2:30 a.m. The streets were completely deserted. Feeling spooked, I walked hurriedly to the nearest phone booth and called for a cab.

The next time I talked to Pam, I told her about my detainment, the "talk," the threats, the promises, their awareness of what was happening, and so on. I asked her to publicize this event as much as possible. "The more we talk about it now," I said to Pam, "the less chance the threats will materialize." I then assured her that this did not change a thing. Things would continue as usual. The only way they could stop us from fighting for Zach was . . . by releasing him.

Pam, in turn, told me that they had made a photograph of Zach into a pin and were handing out those pins everywhere they went. Rest assured, our friend Congressman John Porter was one of the first people to put Zach's pin on his lapel.

On May 7, 1985, wives of House and Senate members announced the formation of the Committee of 21, established under the auspices of the Congressional Human Rights Caucus. The committee paired each member with a political prisoner in the Soviet Union. According to their statement, "each member of the Committee of 21 plans to maintain a continuing correspondence with her adopted prisoner of conscience to express underlying support and to assure them that they are not forgotten."[45] Not surprisingly, John Porter's wife, Kathryn Cameron Porter, chose to adopt Zach and me.

I soon received a letter from her:

May 7, 1985

Dear Tatiana:

I begin this letter as one who knows much about the difficulties of your life and predicament. My husband, Congressman John Porter, talked to you on the phone for over an hour a year ago last March. He described your situation to me and it has motivated him to take a more active role in attempting to help other people in your situation. Your conversation meant much to him and many others who are following your situation here in the United States.

As a wife, my heart goes out to you knowing your husband is in prison and being treated inhumanely. It is such an unfair and unjust punishment to be sent to a prison camp for simply expressing his desire to emigrate. The uncertainty of his health and your future must be agonizing. Please know that my husband and I will do everything we possibly can to help you and Zachar. You are in our prayers daily.

I was concerned to learn that you were recently picked up and interrogated by the KGB. I assure you that we in the West are aware of the precariousness of your situation. These

---

45   Archives, Center for Jewish History, New York, NY.

harassments will not be ignored by your friends and supporters in the United States. We will continue to use all opportunities to call attention to your plight and in particular will raise your case to the Soviet authorities at every possible chance . . .

This will be the first of many letters I will be sending to you. I hope that you will be able to correspond with me on a regular basis and tell me about your struggle for freedom. You have in me a strong supporter and ally.

With warm personal regards,

Sincerely,
Kathryn Cameron Porter[46]

This letter touched my heart immensely. Kathryn remained involved in our case for the rest of Zach's prison term.

Later in May, when the weather turned particularly warm and people traded their spring attire for summer, it meant one thing for me—having KGB agents turn into paparazzi and buzz around me like a swarm of mosquitoes.

What was *that* all about? The answer is simple—clothes. My clothes, to be exact. Apparently, to assist themselves in stalking—to single you out of the crowd, keep you in focus, and do so as effortlessly as possible—the agents needed to be familiar with your wardrobe. No kidding! Every season, as I changed my set of clothes, say, going from fall to winter or from winter to spring, for at least two weeks, the agents put on their paparazzi hats and shot photos of me with vigor. But unlike real paparazzi, the fake ones did their dirty job stealthily, or so they thought.

---

46   Tatiana Zunshine's personal archive.

They carried old-fashioned eighties cameras in a crossbody case, the strap sitting on the left shoulder, while the case resting by the right hip. An opening for the lens was on the side of the case—not the front. The right hand supported the case's bottom, with an opening for the release button. All they needed to do was push the button, and a picture was shot while the camera remained inside the case.

A work of genius, you say? Well, yes, but one thing that "genius" didn't think through was muffling the sound. To catch you, they had to take a lot of shots. And you would hear it, loud and clear: *click, click, click, click, click, click, click, click, click.*

One day at the end of May, I ran into a former co-worker. We were standing on a street corner in central Riga, talking, when, all of a sudden, we both heard: *click, click, click, click, click, click, click, click.*

"What is that?" she asked. "Did you hear it? The clicking?"

"The KGB just took pictures of us," I said. "But no worries, they are exclusively after me."

As the words flew out of my mouth, I realized how out of touch I was with normal people at that point in my life. What was "no worries" to me was an enormous worry to anybody living outside of my reality. I regretted saying it, but it was too late. My friend's face turned white. I tried to assure her that she had nothing to fear—which was true—but she said a hasty goodbye and practically fled the scene.

I shouldn't have said that, I thought, watching her back disappear in the crowd. *I forgot how it feels to live a normal life.*

Later in June, I received a note from Zach. This one revealed a grain of frustration. Our correspondence was sporadic, to say the least. Sometimes, they'd let the letter fly out; other times, they'd block it. There didn't seem to be a rhyme or reason for one action or the other. Some letters with incriminating information were allowed, while others—with not much in them—were not. As a test, I figured, Zach wrote a short note. For the administration, there was nothing to lay their eyes on. But for me, that note contained a gem:

Dear Tan'ka,

Today is June 4, and tomorrow marks exactly four months since I've been here in Khonyaki. Time goes, runs, you can't stop it, and looking back, it seems that a lot happened just yesterday. Summer is here, but on my calendar, it's still spring. May 10, to be exact. Your letters, like the light of a faraway star, come after a great deal of delay, with the last one dating May 10.

What can we do, Tan'ka? I see that they are not in the mood to send my letters out. Someone must have been collecting them, as they are not returning them to me either.

Now a little about myself. If expressed in a few words, it would be something like this: I know where I am, I know who I am and why I am, and, therefore, everything is all right with me.

In Orleans,[47] my very best wishes to all. Tell them I'm touched. I really am. Send Pam my personal regards. Tell her I'm dying to meet her.

Z.[48]

His words, *I know where I am, I know who I am and why I am, and, therefore, everything is all right with me,* struck a chord with me. In time, they became my guiding light. They helped me through severe crises, everyday battles, and moments of feeling sorry for myself (which I was not immune to). *There comes a time in your life,* I thought, *when knowing who you are is all you have. There comes a time when just*

---

47 In the French city of Orleans, under the leadership of Elaine Klein, the Jewish community "adopted" Zach and provided unyielding support throughout his journey.

48 Tatiana Zunshine's personal archive.

knowing who you are makes everything all right. If he can live by that rule, considering where he is, so should I.

That summer, I found myself zigzagging between Riga, Moscow, and Leningrad. My goal was to build as much support for Zach as I could. As importantly, I met dozens of visitors from the United States, Europe, Canada, and elsewhere who came to the Soviet Union as "tourists" but were actually on a mission to get together with the families of refuseniks and prisoners of conscience and collect information on their behalf. Who sent them over? Jewish organizations, like the one Pam belonged to, and others similar to hers.

Coming in, these courageous people would bring all sorts of support, from emotional to financial (that is how I survived the three years of my fight; it would not have happened without the financial support I received—for which I am eternally grateful). We would spend hours talking, hanging out in the tiny kitchens and living rooms of Moscow and Leningrad apartments, creating friendships and lifelong memories. Most of the time, the visitors—for fear of being searched—would absorb the information without writing it down. Past customs, they would spill it all out on paper and send a report to their organizations.

I met so many amazing "tourists" this way, I couldn't possibly mention everyone. I do have to mention two names, however. These were Dr. Konnilyn Feig and Lisa Wilhelm. When we met, Konnilyn was a vice president and history professor at San Francisco State University. A Christian herself, her passion was to tell the world about the Holocaust. She and her best friend, Lisa Wilhelm, shared a passion for travel, books, and life itself. Konnilyn projected strength and an abundance of self-confidence. There was just something powerful about her! Lisa was soft-spoken, the opposite of her friend, but if you hung out with them long enough, you would see what made them the besties they had always been. They both left a tremendous impression on me. They both remained active in our case for the rest of Zach's incarceration.

Around the Fourth of July, I heard that the American consulate in Leningrad was hosting an Independence Day celebration and that some of the refuseniks were invited, me included. Better yet, a delegation of US Congress members was visiting Moscow and Leningrad, and those folks would be at the party on the Fourth, meeting Jewish refuseniks.

I knew I would be going; I just didn't know if getting there would be in my stars.

Nevertheless, I boarded the train to Leningrad and arrived the following day. As always, I went to Yakov Gorodetsky's apartment and settled in the spare room.

"Don't get too cozy," Yakov said, "we are going to see some delegation members in just a few hours." That was good news. If I were to get stopped on the way to the event, at least I would have met some of the delegation ahead of it.

The location of the meeting escapes me—whether it was Yakov's apartment or somebody else's, I don't recall—but the meeting itself stayed firmly planted in my mind. Three out of six members of the delegation showed up: a congressman from Texas, Mr. Steve Bartlett; a congressman from Florida, Mr. Michael Bilirakis; and a congressman from Alabama, Mr. Ben Erdreich, with his wife, Ellen.

After brief introductions, we sat down to talk, and I laid out the entire ordeal for them, starting from the day of Zach's arrest. I emphasized the need for more pressure on the Soviets. "That is the only thing that will save him," I said. "Bring up his name, if you can, in your statements, letters—in all your communications with the Soviets. Let them hear Zach's name over and over and over again. If that doesn't tie their hands, nothing will."

They reassured me they would do their best.

We couldn't keep them there for too long. Hoping to see each other again that same evening at the consulate, we hugged and said, "We are not saying goodbye. See you tonight."

Later that night, Yakov and I headed to the consulate. I was nervous, anticipating some sort of abduction, but nothing happened. We arrived at a centrally located mansion housing the American consulate. People lined up to enter, and I couldn't wait for them to get through the doors. A few minutes later, I was in! Embassies and consulates in foreign countries are legally considered the territories of the country they represent. Having stepped inside, I found myself in the United States.

And what a joy it was to be there! This might have been just another Fourth of July to an average American, but for those of us living behind the Iron Curtain, it was a celebration of spirit and a feast for the eyes.

Where do I start? First of all, everything was decorated with an American flag theme. It was everywhere! The walls, chandeliers, tableware, food—yes, food! Hors d'oeuvres passed around were decorated with a flag theme, as were the cookies and cakes.

A group of American marines were a part of the celebration. The jazz band played the most enticing tunes. And to top it off, the whole party sang "God Bless America" and the "Star Spangled Banner" together.

What a night! I couldn't get enough of it, but I needed to do some business as well. Yakov and I found our friends from the delegation of American lawmakers. They introduced us to the remaining three members: a congressman from Ohio, Mr. Louis Stokes; a congresswoman from Maryland, Ms. Barbara Mikulski; and a congressman from Wisconsin, Mr. Jim Moody. We had a brief but productive discussion.

The party wound down well past midnight. The lawmakers had to return to their hotel. Having accomplished their mission, they left Russia a day or two later.

Excerpts from the statements made by the members of that group upon their return to Washington painted a clear picture of how they had celebrated that Fourth of July and how eye-opening that trip was for all of them. The excerpts below depict Zach's case only; the delegation met with numerous other refuseniks in Moscow and Leningrad and described those meetings in their statements as well.[49]

On the Floor of the US House of Representatives—Barbara Mikulski (D-MD).

July 16, 1985

... I was very pleased to join this bipartisan group to travel to both Moscow and Leningrad in search of agreements in the area of peace, because the issues of peace and human rights are a bipartisan effort. As you may recall, it took us 23 hours to get home from our flights from Leningrad, to Vienna, to Zurich, to Geneva, to Kennedy, back here to Washington. And I can tell you that I did not complain about those 23 hours because I was so glad to be back to the United States after having been in a country where it was the most restrictive environment that I have ever been to . . .

That night [the Fourth of July] I found myself at the U.S. Consulate with a group of marines who give themselves selflessly there, and at midnight, 4 o'clock Baltimore time, they turned the spotlight on the American flag.

We sang "God Bless America" and we sang the "Star Spangled Banner." I thought of that flag flying over Fort McHenry where President Reagan had been only a few days earlier.

---

49   *Congressional Record—House* (Washington, DC: US Government Printing Office, 1985), pp. 19203-19217.

For the rest of my life every Fourth of July that I will now celebrate I will remember that Fourth of July I was with those wonderful gallant marines in Leningrad but I was also with those refuseniks who were willing to give their lives to enjoy freedom.

On the Floor of the US House of Representatives—Ben Erdreich (D-AL).

July 16, 1985

... When my wife and I partook of this journey I really had no idea of what it meant to go into and experience a police state, a state where totalitarian government, it looks like to me, spends about as much of its energy to snoop, and to pry, and to control, and to make conform all the folks in their society as it spends on needed consumer goods, food, clothing, transportation, what have you ...

We went to folks' apartments, had a chance to sit down in the living room and just chat, somewhat like we are chatting this evening about our experiences.

A young couple I remember in Leningrad, Zachar and Tatiana Zunshine. This young lady was with us; her husband was not able to meet with us very simply because he was in prison. They're young; 34 and 32 [29] years old. In 1980 [1981], they asked permission to emigrate. In December 1983, he was held for 15 days, incommunicado, for having asked to leave the country.

After protesting in 1984, writing a letter—and that in the Soviet system can be a protest; if you dare to communicate to the Soviet Government in some way—he was put in prison at the Riga Prison under a sentence for "defaming the Soviet State," a charge that carries up to 3 years in a labor camp, and still, and through this time, no reason has been given for why he cannot leave the country.

On the Floor of the US House of Representatives—Steve Bartlett (R-TX).

July 16, 1985

Mr. Speaker, Tatiana Zunshine came to Leningrad to see us and to be at the American Embassy on American Independence Day on July 4. She came with a story of her husband . . .

What was his crime, what was the crime that he was accused of? The crime was that he asked permission to leave, and then he wrote a letter asking why he was denied permission.

It is important that the West understands that not everyone is arrested. Arrests can come at any time, but most of the refuseniks are simply turned out of society, lose their jobs, are harassed or threatened or followed, but most are not arrested. What is the most difficult is that the arrests are arbitrary.

There was no particular reason to arrest Zachar Zunshine. But the arrests come, and they are unexpected and they are arbitrary and they are always possible. Every refusenik we talked to, we said, "Why are you visiting American Congressmen? Does that not make you subject to arrest?"

They would say, "If the Soviets want to arrest us, they are going to arrest us anyway, regardless of who we talk to and what we say or where we are . . ."

Our trip provided us with a closeup picture of refuseniks who have been denied their rights. I do not think any of us will ever forget them . . .

Refusenik after refusenik told us face to face that their only hope is from the West, that they have no hope from the humanitarianism of the Soviet Government, that their only hope is America, the American people, and the American Government. When we asked them, "What can we do?" refusenik after refusenik said, "Just one thing. Just keep the spotlight on, and remember that America is our only hope.

On the Floor of the US House of Representatives—Michael Bilirakis (R-FL).

July 16, 1985

. . . Our Nation, Mr. Speaker, celebrated its independence several days ago, as we do each year on July 4. This year, however, I, like my colleagues, was not home in America in our Republic to celebrate with the rest of the country. We were in the Soviet Union and while I missed being with my family and friends in the United States on this Independence Day, I cannot imagine a better place to have celebrated this particular Fourth of July than to celebrate American freedom in the Soviet Union.

I say this because now I understand more fully, I thought I understood previously, but I understand more fully what our freedom really means. On this Fourth of July I had the privilege of learning what it is like to be without freedom and I can tell you that is an excellent lesson in appreciating the liberty we have here in America.

Tatiana Zunshine, my colleague from Texas brought up her particular story, I think it is important enough to continue to repeat here. Tatiana and her husband, Zachar, had been waiting for permission to emigrate to Israel since June 1980 [1981] . . . They have actively asserted their right to leave the Soviet Union. Their activism has resulted in charges of hooliganism, which in Soviet parlance means they have refused to accept their Government's denial of their basic human rights. Zachar was a university professor [school teacher] in physics. In March of 1984, as the gentleman from Texas told us, he was arrested and charged with defaming the Soviet state. After demonstrating in Moscow with Tatiana for their right to emigrate to Israel, this is all they did.

When we visited with Tatiana in Leningrad, she told us that her husband was held in a Riga prison and virtually no communication with his wife and friends was allowed. In April [of 1984] he began a hunger strike to protest the refusal of prison authorities to give him paper and pencil so that he could write to Soviet authorities about his case.

Tatiana has been harassed and all her documents, including her passport, were stolen from her in a street attack. Still she and her husband remain committed to their goal of emigrating to Israel.

Shortly after, I went to Moscow for another meeting with a politician. This time, it was a senator from Illinois, Paul Simon. Senator Simon looked as distinguished as it gets. Dressed to a tee, with his signature professorial bow tie, he certainly had a presence. His roaring, deep voice might have been startling for a second, but what shone through was kindness and compassion.

Upon his return to the States, Senator Simon joined Representative John Porter in distributing a booklet of correspondence called "The Zunshine Papers" among their colleagues on Capitol Hill.

UNITED STATE SENATE
WASHINGTON, DC 20510

August 1, 1985

Dear Colleague:

Attached you will find the Zunshine Papers, correspondence from the Soviet dissident and prisoner-of-conscience, Zachar Zunshine, to his wife, Tatiana, and various Soviet officials.

These letters depict the anguish that one man, convicted to prison merely for expressing his desire to emigrate, is currently enduring. Zachar represents the struggle of Soviet Jewry. To want one's freedom is not a crime—it should be a given right.

On Paul's trip to the Soviet Union last month, he had the fortunate opportunity to meet Tatiana Zunshine. John has spoken with Tatiana on the phone. Tatiana's courage and strength of conviction are impressive.

We share with you the Zunshine Papers with the knowledge that Western interest makes a difference.

Our best wishes.

Cordially,

John Porter, U.S. Representative
Paul Simon, U.S. Senator[50]

---

50   Tatiana Zunshine's personal archive.

CHAPTER 16

LOSS

July 4, 1985

Dear Tan'ka,

The sun is beating down mercilessly. The cracked earth is languishing from the heat as if saying, "Let it rain, let it rain!" Not a cloud in the sky. Drought. On a branch of a withered tree, a bird sits, ruffled. No strength to fly. No strength to make a sound. And only the horse stubbornly pulls the wagon uphill. Down here, near the ground, where everything has long dried up, and up there, in the sky, where the hot sun habitually hangs, something ominous is felt everywhere. And in the distant squeaky sound of the wagon's wheels, you hear, "Patience, patience."

Everything ends in this world. It looks like the "drought" for letters has ended. And you received my letter #7a, which I gave up on a long time ago.

Everything is the same in my "boardinghouse": breakfast, lunch, and dinner. In another month, the internal prison will be over. For 4.5 months, I have been reading Chekhov, more Chekhov, and nothing but Chekhov. Chekhov is everywhere. In London, the Royal Theatre is opening the season with the premiere of "The Seagull." The role of Irina Arkadina is performed by a well-known English actress who, twenty years ago, played the role of Nina (played by the actress's daughter this time around).

"First of all, I will have this avenue of pine trees cut down, and then that maple . . . It's so ugly in the evenings . . . Then here I will have bedding plants put in, and here, and there will be a lovely scent . . ." (Natalia Ivanovna, "Three Sisters," act 4).

As for me, I like maple trees. And Canadian "Maple Leafs"[51]—
them I like even more. I was so happy when they won the Cup
last fall. One time—I never told you this—they saved me from
jumping in the river on a cold October day.

This was way back in 1972. The last game in the Summit Series
between the Soviets and Team Canada was coming up. Whoever
won this game would win the series. For some reason, I went (rath-
er foolishly) with my college classmates to a farm before the start
of our senior year. Everybody gathered around the TV, and I, rath-
er cheekily, announced that my team (the Canadians, of course!)
would win. If they lose, I said, I will jump in the river (what was
I thinking?). The game begins. By the middle of the second period,
the score of 5–3 is not in our favor. Phil Esposito is running around
like a madman. A young Bobby Clarke blinds with a full mouth
of teeth (which he later lost one by one on various hockey rinks).
We are losing, and the jump into the cold water seems imminent.
But then we score to tie the game 5–5. And at the very end, Paul
Henderson, this lifesaver, hanging close by the goal, scores to make
it 6–5. We won! I was saved.

Who could possibly not like maple trees? I don't get it.

Summer is here. In the morning, one can hear a rooster crow
in the village or birds chirping unceasingly by the window. After
rain, the air smells of herbs. While escorted to the bathhouse,
you can see the tops of birches and pines from behind the barbed
wire. And above all that green splendor is a high blue bottom-
less sky. And Chekhov would have added something like this:
"Overwhelmed with joy, he knew walking back to the prison was
the last thing he wanted."

Z.[52]

On the surface, what a hodgepodge of a letter he'd written! Sandwiched between the passages that served as an evident study of

---

51   Canadian hockey team, the Toronto Maple Leafs.

52   Tatiana Zunshine's personal archive.

Chekhov, there was a recollection of Zach's student years and his silly bet on the Toronto Maple Leafs (a true story, I should add). But underneath it all was valuable information written in our secret code.

In general, no letter was ever wasted by failing to use the secret code. Take a closer look at this one—seemingly, Zach provided no substantial information. Which meant it was there, behind the text. Notice a contradiction between the first paragraph and the last. In the first paragraph, Zach talks about drought but mentions rain in the last one. The censors didn't catch it, but I sure did. Having written all my letters to him with the secret code, I knew that the choice of words could be limiting. He must have needed the word *rain* in that exact position and decided to go for it.

I remember fishing out two pieces of information. First, our pressure had resulted in daily investigatory commissions at Khonyaki inquiring about Zach. Second, he would be transferred out of Khonyaki on August 7 and undergo a medical examination in Irkutsk, in the hospital within the Gulag, followed by a transfer back to Bozoy.

Having learned that, I decided to go to Irkutsk and stay there while Zach was undergoing his medical evaluation. Since he would be out of the hands of the Khonyaki administration, I wanted to see if I could intercept him for a two-hour meeting (to which we had been entitled for so long).

But the KGB in Riga had different plans for me. We were in the middle of July, about a week after I returned from Leningrad, when I noticed the surveillance had intensified. Was it payback for going to Leningrad and spending time at the consulate with the delegation of American lawmakers? Or were they trying to prevent me from going to Irkutsk? Who knew? The agents were everywhere, suffocating me with their presence, and there was nothing I could do to escape. My attempts to buy plane tickets to Irkutsk failed miserably. The few times I tried to do so, the agents simply stood by the entrance to the ticket office—something I had encountered too many times—sending me a clear signal. I was stuck.

When, just as abruptly, the surveillance ended, I hurried to get out of town before it all resumed.

On August 10, I arrived in Irkutsk. A Gulag official told me Zach was no longer there; he had been transferred back to Bozoy. I had missed him by one day. Well, it was a long shot anyway. Now what? While I was already nearby, I decided to go to Bozoy and try my luck there.

At the headquarters in Bozoy, I learned that the old guard was no longer there. No more Major Kofel—our archnemesis who, in the fall of the year before, had perpetrated a big lie contributing to the tragic death of Zach's mother. Boy, was I happy to see him gone! There was now a whole new management team. The new head of the camp was Mr. Stepanenko. The new head of the Men's Division was Mr. Korenev. Other than that, not much had changed. The place still represented the worst of human inventions.

Mr. Stepanenko denied my request for a meeting with Zach. According to him, Zach was presently being held in a punishment cell.

"Your husband spent fifteen days in a punishment cell in Khonyaki, from July 22 to August 6," he said, "and now he is finishing up another fifteen-day term here in Bozoy. That one started on August 6."

"Wait a minute, what were the grounds for putting him in there?" I asked anxiously.

"Let's see." He skimmed an open folder in front of him and said, "The first one was for refusing to undergo an X-ray. And the second—" he looked down again "—the second is for talking with an inmate during a daily walk."

"And how long was that conversation? Hours? Minutes?"

"A few words, but he was told not to do so."

I had my own few words to say about this, but I knew it was use-less. Instead, I said, "While my husband was here, before Khonyaki, numerous commissions investigated the administration's actions. While he was in Khonyaki, our actions resulted in *daily* investigato-ry commissions. Now that he is back here, I promise you that we will continue to take the same approach to your actions should they not satisfy the laws of the Soviet penal system."

On that note, I left.

But I didn't go too far. I went to the local post office and got a greeting card. I scribbled a few words and went back in the direction of the headquarters. While walking, I spotted a young woman going in the same direction. Hurrying to catch up with her, I asked if she hap-pened to work at the camp. She said yes, but kept walking. Keeping steady with her pace, I introduced myself and then said, "I came here from over 4,000 miles away only to learn that my husband is in the punishment cell and that I can't see him. I have not seen him for al-most a year. I wrote a brief hello for him on this card. Would you take it? Would you pass it on to him? Please?"

She hesitated for a second and then said, "Okay."

"Thank you! Thank you so much!"

All I wanted was to let Zach know I was there in Bozoy. Would she give the card to him or toss it out? That was out of my control. In any event, what did I have to lose?

Before leaving Irkutsk, I called my family in Sverdlovsk. And that's when my world shook again.

My father, who had been fighting a case of leukemia for over a year, was losing his battle. The disease was progressing at a fright-ening speed.

I flew to Sverdlovsk immediately. My mother, my brother, my sis-ter, and I gathered around him in the hospital ward. We were with him, watching with horror how the cancer overpowered his body and how his heart—stronger than anyone expected—pushed back, refusing to give up. And yet, within days, the inevitable happened. The last moments were excruciatingly painful to watch. Sadly, they are, and forever will be, engraved in my memory.

My father was seventy-three years old.

I remember the funeral. A big crowd gathered around, so big it surprised everyone. My father was a gentle soul, soft-spoken, and rather shy. Having spent over thirty years in the same job, he'd earned much love and respect from his colleagues. We didn't know that until witnessing it at the funeral. The outpouring of love from total strangers was heartwarming.

Something heartwarming was exactly what I needed. Left to myself during the funeral preparations, I froze. My heart froze. It was undoubtedly a defense mechanism. When I wasn't feeling numb, I felt desperate, helpless, and angry. Angry at how cruel life was at the moment and how it was not letting up. Selfishly—I admit—I felt that I could not catch a break. I remember talking on the phone with Sasha when I kept repeating an all-too-familiar phrase: "I don't know how to go on." The problem was that in the midst of grieving, I had no choice but to go on. I had to continue my fight, no matter what was happening in my world.

I wrote to Zach, telling him about my father. In about a month, I received a response. Considering the circumstances, *they* must have decided not to interfere in this exchange.

September 22, 1985

Dear Tan'ka,

Life is not easy, and sometimes it's plain dreadful. It is hard, very hard, to lose a loved one. It is painful to see the inevitable unfolding and the efforts—no matter how great they might be—only delaying it just a bit.

Yes, life is not easy, and sometimes it's plain dreadful. But every night, the stars light up the darkening sky. And whether the sky is overcast with clouds, whether it's raining, whether I'm locked in, having not seen the sky for a long time, or looking at it on a clear night, I know that somewhere up there, among the many thousands of stars, there is also my star, my little treasure; just thinking of it touches my soul with ease, and I catch myself saying: "All right."

On August 7, I was transferred out of Khonyaki. On the 8th, I was already in Irkutsk, in the hospital, where, in half a day, I had all the tests done: fluorography, a cardiogram, dental exams, etc. On the 9th, I was already in Bozoy, and on the 21st, as the guard had promised you, she handed me your postcard. But even before that happened, so sure I was that you were in Bozoy that I seemed to have physically felt your presence. I felt it. You were here, nearby.

Then I spent the remaining couple of days in the internal prison, and on the 24th, I was released into the camp. The weather for the past few days has been great. Autumn. It is cold in the morning but warms up in the afternoon. It gets so warm that it feels like the sun is inviting you to sunbathe. In a few days, it will be exactly one year since I was brought to Bozoy. How strange life is, and how unpredictable. A year ago, I was sure they would not give us a meeting, but they did. But this year, it's the other way around.

There is so much more I would have liked to write about, but how can I!? Say hello to your family. And to everyone everywhere here and there, and, of course, in Israel, Chicago, Yale,[53] and Orleans: congratulations on the past New Year, and best wishes to all!

Z.[54]

---

53   Yale University. Having learned of Zach's desire upon release from prison and emigration from the Soviet Union to become a Yale University student, I contacted the school on his behalf.

54   Tatiana Zunshine's personal archive.

If anything could have helped lift me out of that dread, it was Zach's words: *I know that somewhere up there, among the many thousands of stars, there is also my star, my little treasure; just thinking of it touches my soul with ease, and I catch myself saying: "All right."*

I was grateful for his wisdom, wishing for the day when I, too, could say: "All right."

There was more to be grateful for. Zach was out of the Black Hole. He sounded all right. And the young woman in Bozoy? She did give him the card, after all.

My route home included a layover in Moscow. I decided to stay an extra day or two to visit the national Gulag office. I wanted to file an official complaint about the newly discovered gross violation of the law. Let me explain.

According to Stepanenko, Zach spent two fifteen-day terms in punishment cells back-to-back: July 22 through August 6, then August 6 through 21. That was illegal. It was illegal because it was dangerous. The conditions in the punishment cell were such that putting prisoners in there for more than fifteen consecutive days was considered life-threatening. How did they overcome that limitation? By throwing him in there for one fifteen-day term, getting him out, and throwing him back in on the same day, only on a different charge. This was a dangerous practice, and we needed to address it.

After arriving at the Moscow airport, I took a cab to the national Gulag office. There, I requested a meeting with the head of the Compliance Division, Mr. Pobezhimov.

"The head of the division will not see you," his secretary said.

"He cannot see me today? When *can* he see me?" I asked.

"Never."

This had never happened before. This was so outrageous that it threw me off. For the first time, I have to admit, I could not find the words.

I then requested to see the head of the Gulag office of the USSR, Mr. Bogdanov. My visit coincided with the one day per month when the head of the Gulag held an open reception. I was feeling lucky, but in the end, that didn't help me. I was the only one they turned away.

"There are too many people here," his secretary said. "We can't accommodate everyone."

This seems to be a pattern today, I thought, observing a crowd of about twenty families. They were willing to see everyone but me. What does that tell you about our case? My interpretation was this: In their mind, seeing me meant fueling my activities. What they were trying to do instead was stonewall, neutralize, and suppress my efforts. Another reason for not seeing me was to shield themselves from having their names mentioned by Voice of America or some other "unfriendly" radio station or foreign publication.

Whatever their reasoning was, they were dead wrong.

That night in Moscow, I talked to Pam. She already knew about my loss; my friend Sasha must have told her. She sent her deep condolences, personally and on behalf of our supporters. I told her about my trip to Irkutsk, Bozoy, and Moscow, about the wall I had encountered everywhere I went, and how I had been able to achieve little to nothing. I gave her the dates of Zach's incarcerations and explained the danger of double terms. "We need to yell loudly about this," I said. "Zach is no longer in Khonyaki, but we don't want Bozoy to follow suit." I told her about the two Gulag officials in Moscow unwilling to see me and stressed the need to include their names and addresses in all our communications. Pam said she'd gladly do so.

Immediately afterward, the UCSJ issued a call for action: "For the friends and supporters of Zachar and Tatiana Zunshine, please continue sending letters to Zachar; please continue sending letters of complaint to the Gulag administration of the USSR, specifically to the two officials who refused to see Tatiana." The memorandum included their names, addresses, and phone numbers.

On the Floor of the US House of Representatives—John E. Porter (R-IL).

September 26, 1985

Mr. Speaker, as a participant in the 1985 Congressional Call to Conscience Vigil for Soviet Jews I would like to call my colleagues' attention to the nightmare that Tatiana Zunshine has been living.

Mrs. Zunshine's husband, Zachar, has been imprisoned since March 6, 1984, for the simple reason that he desires to emigrate from the Soviet Union. The Zunshines first applied to emigrate in 1981, but were subsequently denied that right. Recently, however, life has become more difficult for Tatiana. She is struggling with Soviet authorities in an attempt to visit her husband in prison.

After learning of her plans to go to Irkutsk for a chance to meet with her husband, who was soon to be transferred from the internal prison, the KGB denied her permission to leave Riga. For 2 weeks she was followed constantly by a team of KGB. When she finally went to Irkutsk prison, she found that her husband was already gone. She then traveled to Bazoi [Bozoy] where Zachar was now being held and requested a meeting with her husband. The officials of the camp denied her request and said that Zachar has been placed in solitary confinement since his arrival, by an order signed by the commandant of Khanyahki [Khonyaki].

In a meeting with Mr. Stepanenko, chief of the Bazoi [Bozoy] Camp, Tatiana learned her husband had been in a solitary confinement punishment cell from July 19 to August 3 [6], allegedly due to his refusal to submit to a medical examination. He was also placed in this cell from August 6 to August 23 [21] for exchanging words with another inmate during exercise. The reason for the first punishment, according to Tatiana, is highly questionable since her husband has sought medical attention repeatedly during his incarceration.

In an unprecedented action by the Soviets, Tatiana was denied access to Government offices in Moscow where she attempted to register her complaints. Mr. Pobezhimov, chief of the board for the Regulation and Fulfillment of Laws of Prisons and Labor Camps refused to see her. Furthermore, Tatiana was the only person not permitted at the monthly reception held by the Gulag office of the U.S.S.R. According to my sources, Tatiana's interpretation of the events is that an official decision has been made by the authorities to neutralize and suppress her activities on behalf of her husband. She has informed the authorities that she will not be silent about continued breaches of Soviet Law and continued denial of her rights as a Soviet citizen . . .

We must not forget the Zunshines and the injustice suffered by other Soviet refuseniks. Their situation emphasizes the need for congressional activity, such as the Congressional Human Rights Caucus and International Parliamentary Group for Human Rights in the Soviet Union, to focus attention on abuses practiced by the Soviet Government . . .

There is no more vital task than to help innocent victims, whose only crime is their desire for human liberty.[55]

---

55 *Congressional Record—House* (Washington, DC: US Government Printing Office, 1985), pp. 25243–25244.

CHAPTER 17

KEEP YOUR CHIN UP

On August 24, after six months of "incarceration within the incarceration," Zach was released from the internal prison back into the camp setting. Shortly afterward, he managed to smuggle two documents out of the camp. The first one was truly explosive. It was an explanatory note he had written to the camp administration.

August 30, 1985
To: The Head of the Labor Camp UK 272/40
From: Zachar Zunshine

Explanatory Note #5

On August 28, 1985, I provided you with a statement (#13) informing you that on August 28, I was deliberately transferred at the lumberyard from one job—working with firewood—to another: shoveling sawdust from under a sawmill. I worked there all day in conditions that monstrously violated minimum safety requirements.

Namely, for the entire shift on August 28, with my height of 6 foot 3, I had to be in a pit under the sawmill (the height of the pit, or, more precisely, its depth, does not exceed five feet). That is, I had to work the entire shift in a position where my torso and legs made an angle of 90 degrees. Whenever I grabbed some sawdust with a shovel, I hit my head or shoulder with an electrical cable that supplied a current of 380 volts to the sawmill. The common practice here is to rake sawdust from under a sawmill set in motion. And—what makes it even more dangerous—there are puddles of water on the ground.

Having worked in these conditions, I wrote you statement #13 requesting that you no longer put me in a job with such gross violations of safety requirements.

However, the next day, August 29, I was once again—clearly, deliberately—assigned to the same job. For the reasons above, I had to reject it. I am getting the feeling that it will soon come to the point when you assign me to a job where I have to wear a cable with a current of 380 volts tied around my neck.

Today is August 30. Having gone to work at the lumberyard, in the presence of the controller on duty, I asked the foreman to provide me with a job—any other job—where the safety requirements were not violated in such an outrageous way. Needless to say, he turned my request down.

From all of the above, it is clear—which I have repeatedly stated before—that I have not refused and do not intend to refuse work that satisfies the minimum safety requirements. But you cannot expect me to work in an environment where I have to tie an electric cable with a current of 380 volts around my neck as the prospect of multiplying the ranks of injured prisoners ("injured" may be an understatement) does not appeal to me—not one bit.

Z.Z.[56]

This was pure madness. Forcing people to work underneath the sawmill while it was set in motion—were they out of their minds? It had become their signature move to assign Zach to a job, whether it was shameful or dangerous, knowing damn well he was going to decline it. They had done it before, and they were doing it again.

Rattled by the news, I dug the second piece of paper from the envelope. It was a list of punitive measures against Zach for the month of September, and it validated my suspicions:

---

56   Tatiana Zunshine's personal archive.

August 30–September 10: eleven days in a punishment cell for refusing to accept a job of cleaning sawdust from underneath the sawmill

September 2: deprived of the right for the next private meeting for refusing to accept a job of cleaning sawdust from underneath the sawmill

September 10–September 20: ten days in a punishment cell for writing a complaint regarding the administration's non-compliance with food rations in punishment cells

I had no time to waste. *I will deal with my anguish later,* I decided, *but for now, I have to act.* I needed to give the latest developments the publicity they deserved. I arranged a phone call with Pam and dictated the explanatory note and the other document. She was as terrified to hear about the sawmill as I was. She promised to share the information with all other branches of UCSJ, with their partners in the UK, Israel, France, and Canada, and our supporters on Capitol Hill.

In response to the latest developments, in anticipation of the upcoming meeting between President Reagan and Secretary-General Mikhail Gorbachev, Representative John Porter wrote a letter to President Reagan, which he presented for the record on the floor of the US House of Representatives.

A LETTER TO THE PRESIDENT

September 30, 1985

Mr. Speaker, as the November summit between President Reagan and Secretary General Gorbachev approaches it is important that the issue of human rights in the Soviet Union is addressed as a high priority concern. We must remember the individuals and their families in the Soviet Union who are the victims of harassment and suffering. Therefore, I submit for the

RECORD a letter that I will be sending to President Reagan on behalf of Zachar and Tatiana Zunshine, who are longing for the day they will be allowed to leave the Soviet Union.

September 27, 1985

Hon. Ronald W. Reagan,
President of the United States,
The White House,
Washington, DC

Dear Mr. President: The American people have long cherished and represented the value of human liberty for all people. Therefore, as you prepare for your upcoming meeting with Secretary General Gorbachev I would like to express my concern that the issue of human rights remains high on the agenda and that the individuals in the Soviet Union who are victims of human rights abuses are addressed specifically.

I would like to bring your attention to the plight of Zachar and Tatiana Zunshine, a family that has become very important to my wife, Kathryn, and I. We have had the opportunity to directly correspond with Tatiana and learn from her firsthand of the suffering that she and her husband have endured. Zachar Zunshine has been imprisoned in the Soviet Union since March 6, 1984. His crime is that he desires to leave the Soviet Union and to live freely in Israel. The Zunshines first applied to emigrate in 1981, but were subsequently denied that right.

Since being imprisoned Zachar has been suffering poor health and has been receiving insufficient medical treatment. While her husband suffers in prison, Tatiana is living a nightmare and will continue to do so until Zachar is released. Recently, life has become especially difficult for Tatiana as she has been struggling with Soviet authorities in an attempt to visit her husband in prison. These Soviet authorities are not only overlooking the Zunshines [Zunshines'] rights as guaranteed by international human rights doctrines, but they are also denying Tatiana her rights as a Soviet citizen.

Mr. President, I know that you share my concern for those whose fundamental freedoms are being overlooked. Your meeting with Mr. Gorbachev is crucial to the freedom of people who are being persecuted in the Soviet Union. It is important that Mr. Gorbachev recognizes that the United States government cares about people like Zachar and Tatiana Zunshine.

America has long symbolized the principle of freedom for the oppressed peoples of the East. The U.S. must reaffirm its commitment to act upon that principle at this critical juncture of the U.S.–Soviet relations and for the Jews of the Soviet Union.

Sincerely,

John E. Porter,
Member of Congress[57]

Another supporter of ours, Dr. Julian Heicklen, a chemistry professor at Pennsylvania State University, had written a letter to Secretary-General Gorbachev. Dated October 7, 1985, his letter was simplistic and plain brilliant. See for yourself.

THE PENNSYLVANIA STATE UNIVERSITY

October 7, 1985

Mr. Mikhail Gorbachev
Secretary General of the Communist Party
The Kremlin
Moscow 103132 USSR

Dear Secretary Gorbachev:

I am writing to you concerning Zachar Zunshine, a Soviet citizen who wishes to emigrate from the Soviet Union. Because

---

57 *Congressional Record—House* (Washington, DC: US Government Printing Office, 1985), pp. 25325–25326.

of this he has had many difficulties with the police, and he is now in prison.

He has continually been mistreated while in prison. His wife, Tatiana, has been denied access to government offices in Moscow to register complaints.

I am appealing to you to listen to Tatiana and to free Zachar. What is the point of all of this harassment? Wouldn't it be an easier solution to let the Zunshines leave the USSR?

Thank you for your consideration.

Sincerely yours,

Julian Heicklen
Professor of Chemistry[58]

This letter makes me smile every time I read it. Seriously, why couldn't the Soviets have just listened to me and freed Zach? What was the point indeed? Wouldn't it have simply been easier to let us leave?

If only they had listened to Professor Heicklen.

Many physicists intervened in Zach's case, including Dr. A. P. French, a British professor of physics at MIT. Dr. French's biography was colorful. In 1944, fresh from Cambridge University at the ripe age of twenty-three, he participated in a nuclear bomb project in Los Alamos, NM, called the Manhattan Project. Later, he dedicated his life to teaching physics. In his letter, dated November 1, 1985, addressed to President Reagan, Dr. French used his current position as President of the American Association of Physics Teachers to urge Reagan to bring up Zach's situation in his upcoming meetings with the head of the Soviet state, Mikhail Gorbachev.

---

58   Tatiana Zunshine's personal archive.

AMERICAN ASSOCIATION OF PHYSICS TEACHERS

November 1, 1985

President Ronald Reagan
The White House
Washington, DC 20500

Dear Mr. President:

I write to you in my capacity as the current President of the American Association of Physics Teachers, to urge you to do anything you can on behalf of Mr. Zachar Zunshine, a physics teacher currently being held in confinement in the USSR.

In April a letter about Mr. Zunshine, written at considerable personal risk by his wife Tatiana, was delivered to you personally by Dr. Martin Gilbert (of Oxford University) who for many years has been deeply and actively concerned with the oppression of Jewish people worldwide. Let me, however, summarize again here the facts of Mr. Zunshine's case: Zachar Zunshine is from Riga, received a B.A. [equivalent to an MA] in physics from the University of Gorky in Sverdlovsk, and then taught high-school [night school] physics until 1980 [1983], when he declared his desire to emigrate to Israel . . . His pursuit of the right to emigrate led, on June 28, 1984, to a three-year sentence in the Bazoi [Bozoy] labor camp. While in this camp he was beaten by fellow-prisoners, was twice [many times] placed in solitary confinement, and was then sentenced to six months in the Siberia Internal Labor Camp Prison under inhuman conditions.

The situation of Mr. Zunshine is of particular concern to the American Association of Physics Teachers because, although there have been many authenticated cases of oppression of Jewish research physicists in the USSR, this is the first clear-cut example we know of concerning a school teacher in our profession.

I hope that you might find it possible to bring up this matter in your forthcoming meetings with Mr. Gorbachev, and to take any other steps that might help Zachar Zunshine and his wife to fulfill their desire to emigrate. This request comes to you with the unanimous support of the Executive Board of the American Association of Physics Teachers.

Respectfully yours,

A. P. French
President, AAPT
Professor of Physics, MIT

On October 20, another piece of bootleg mail arrived. Seeing an obscure envelope with no return address made me jump. Another one of those! Zach seemed to have established his own channels of communication. This was great! But wait, having fished out a tiny piece of paper covered with hurried handwriting, I hesitated. No, that didn't spell good news, did it? It didn't.

October 8, 1985

Tan'ka, I have contracted hepatitis B. Tomorrow, I'll be transferred to the hospital in the town of Angarsk. Keep your chin up. Everything will be all right.

Z.

This shook me badly.

Keep your chin up, he'd written. Keep my chin up? We hadn't even finished the battle over the sawmills, and now this? Hepatitis, of all things! This had gone too far.

I am scared; I really am. I am frustrated beyond belief. I don't know how to stop that grizzly bear of a Gulag from crushing Zach—physically, not in any other way, but crushing nonetheless. We don't seem to be able to stop it. What are we doing wrong?

For the first time, I felt a cloud of doubt descending on me.

I was in that dark place for hours, feeling hopeless and wanting to cry. But tears had abandoned me. *If tears would no longer come to my rescue*, I thought, *who would?* The answer was obvious—my friend Sasha, my rock and my right-hand man.

I went out to the phone booth to call him.

"Tan'ka, what happened? You sound awful," Sasha said when he answered the phone.

"Zach's contracted a case of hepatitis, and I've contracted a case of self-doubt," I said gloomily.

"I'll be there."

We talked for hours. "Don't expect to stop 'the machine,' as you call it; it's impossible," Sasha said. "Go for little wins. One little win at a time. And count your blessings with every single one of them."

That's what I needed to hear, and it did make things a bit better. He was right—little wins were all I could count on.

Together, we called an infectious disease doctor.

"With proper treatment," she said, "it's curable."

"With proper treatment, you say, and that's the key. Can we rely on the Gulag system to provide proper treatment? And what happens if they don't provide it?" I asked.

"Then it could cause a chronic infection and serious liver damage."

"Damn!"

From her, I learned that hepatitis B commonly occurs from sharing hypodermic needles between individuals. But how was that possible? Where and when could it have happened? I went through every piece of correspondence I had in search of clues, and then I found it. There it was. Zach's letter dated September 22: *On August 7, I was transferred out of Khonyaki. On the 8th, I was already in Irkutsk, in the hospital, where, in half a day, I had all the tests done.* The tests! The blood test, to be exact. Whoever administered it must have used an unsterilized needle.

One question remained: What was the incubation period for that particular virus? The test had taken place in August. We were now in October. Was it plausible? My consultant doctor confirmed: yes, highly plausible, and most probable—the incubation period for that virus was anywhere from 60 to 150 days.

Case closed. *They* had infected Zach with hepatitis. *Oh, my god! What was that? A case of gross negligence? Or criminal intent?* My go-to thought was that they'd done it on purpose, but I quickly stopped myself from going there. I had no proof, nor did I have proof to the contrary. *We'll get to the bottom of it, but I can't think about it right now*, I thought while throwing things into my suitcase. I had to go. I needed to go to the hospital in Angarsk to meet the doctors and get a feel for what they were like. We were in their hands, and I needed to know how competent—if at all—those doctors were.

Arriving in Moscow in the morning, I had the whole day to kill before my red-eye flight to Irkutsk. I used it to collect everything I needed for my visit. At the central market, I bought lots of fresh fruits and vegetables. My next stop was a pharmacy for a supply of vitamins. Lastly, I went to the largest delicatessen in the USSR—Eliseyevsky grocery store—to get a can of caviar. Why caviar? The most beloved food for any Russian, it was more than just a delicacy. It was highly nutritious and packed with omega-3 fatty acids, B_{12} vitamins, and other vitamins and minerals. In addition, before leaving Riga, I had packed a few items of clothing—new warm Canadian underwear, warm undershirts, and socks. Between that and the food, I had too much to carry. I hoped to come home empty-handed (literally), but I certainly wasn't counting on it.

The flight was uneventful. The night dragged on, and I was unable to close my eyes. I was worried about Zach. How was he? How was his treatment going? Was it adequate? Were his doctors competent?

I would be dealing with a whole new camp, new camp commanders, and, most importantly, with a group of camp doctors. What would that be like?

Arriving midmorning in Irkutsk, I then took a cab to Angarsk, located thirty-seven miles northwest. It was an administrative city with a population of 265,000. Before I knew it, I was there. The cab stopped at the labor camp headquarters. (That particular camp housed a built-in infectious disease hospital.) The driver helped me get my luggage out and then took off. I stood there for a few minutes, mentally preparing myself for a battle. Nothing happens in places like that without a battle.

I took a deep breath and opened the door.

In a rather large office, three men stared at me as I came through the doorway, suitcases and numerous food packages in tow. It must have been quite a scene—me holding the door open with my rear end while pushing my luggage piece by piece over the threshold. I noticed the men smiling, but it must have been below their ranks to help me.

Once I'd settled in the room, I introduced myself; I didn't have to—they knew who I was.

And who were those three? The chief medical officer (and Zach's doctor), the head of the camp, and the head of the Regime Department of the regional Gulag, Fedor Katiuchin.

My grand entrance into the room must have struck a lighter note as the men appeared to act friendly, especially the doctor. Something about this doctor told me I could talk to him.

I asked him about Zach. How was he? The doctor proceeded to tell me that Zach was responding to treatment well. His blood markers had improved. He would spend up to forty days in the hospital, followed by discharge back into the camp, where he would receive a special diet and lighter labor assignments for one year.

The conversation moved on to what else could be done to help the situation. "I brought all sorts of fruits, vegetables, and vitamins," I said, "and I need you to pass them on to my husband."

"We can't do that," Major Katiuchin interjected. "Your husband's allowance for a food package has been taken away. The next one is not scheduled until—"

I stopped him right there. "His hepatitis B was not scheduled either."

"No, it was by no means scheduled," the doctor said agreeably.

"And yet, he got it, and we are dealing with it, aren't we, so the least you can do is accept an unscheduled package," I said in one breath.

Katiuchin backed down rather quickly. "Let's see what you've got."

Elated but cautious about celebrating too soon, I began putting the contents of each package on the head of the camp's desk, turning it into a supermarket counter.

They looked at me in disbelief. "How much did you bring?"

"As much as I could carry."

"And what's that?" Katiuchin asked, pointing at the can of caviar.

"That's a can of food. Canned food is allowed. The rules specifically say so."

"Yes, but that's caviar. It's not just a can—it's caviar. You don't get to eat caviar in a penitentiary."

What followed was a courtroom drama. Once again, I put on a lawyer's hat and argued that the can was a can, no matter what was in it, and if cans were allowed, then this particular can should be allowed as well. Unless it was explicitly disqualified, in which case they had to prove it. "Show it to me," I said.

"I am a colonel," the head of the camp said, breaking his silence. He had said nothing until then but must have felt the need to contribute to the caviar dispute. "I am a colonel," he repeated, "but I don't get to eat caviar. And you want us to pass it on to an inmate?"

"I don't get to eat it, either. And yes, I want you to pass it on to my husband, as it is highly nutritious and may help his recovery. Plus, for the millionth time, canned food is allowed!"

We went back and forth until, one hour into it, they asked me to step outside the room so that they could discuss the situation. I did so gladly, as I was exhausted from having to spend all my energy battling over a can of caviar.

It took them a while, but they did ask me back into the room.

"We'll take it," the colonel said.

"Aah, thank you!" I couldn't contain my joy. This can of caviar had clearly become more than just a can. It represented a "little win," the kind Sasha had talked about.

They did accept everything—all the food, the Canadian underwear, and socks—leaving me empty-handed. I was happy. Flying out of the camp, I couldn't help but notice the dreadful scenery surrounding it, but I didn't care. This was a win, and I was celebrating it in my heart.

Years later, that same can of caviar gave me severe trepidation. All of a sudden, it occurred to me that salty caviar might not have been the best food for a damaged liver. Sure enough, that turned out to be true. Nothing bad happened to Zach as a result, but to this day, the thought of me inadvertently passing on to him a potentially harmful product sits heavy on my heart.

It wasn't a win after all.

CHAPTER 18

THE END OF AN ERA

In early November 1985, out of nowhere, my best friend Sasha Balter received permission to leave the Soviet Union. If you are speechless, so was I.

The emotions every one of us refuseniks experienced when close friends received permission to leave were truly indescribable. It was jubilation for your friends and a pity party for the rest of us. "What about me?" you'd sulk in solitude, feeling left out. It was only human to feel that way. Happiness and sorrow were both there, colliding in one big clash of emotions. That is how I felt when Sasha told me he and his family were leaving.

"You WHAT?"

"We got our permission to leave," Sasha said. "It doesn't seem real, but it is."

"I'm so happy for you! I can't believe it! This is incredible!" Did the pity party start at that moment? It probably did. Sasha might have sensed it.

"Don't worry, Tan'ka, I will help you as much, or more, only on the other side."

"Oh, no, no, I am not worried at all! I am so happy for you I wanna cry!"

Sasha was my rock. He was my travel companion, sounding board, editor (sometimes, writer), shoulder to cry on, and comic relief —all in one. What he and Polina provided for me was invaluable.

Not having my own family in Riga, they were my second best. I spent endless nights in their crowded apartment, the one they shared with Polina's mother—me, on a pull-out bed in the living room, feeling every spring of the mattress, but, more importantly, feeling like a part of the family. Over the years, my relationship with Sasha grew beyond friendship. I treated him like he was my younger brother. He, on the other hand, treated me like I was his younger sister. One incident in particular illustrates this dynamic.

I got mad at him for something. It may have been the only time I have ever been mad at him in all the years I've known him. What was it about? I don't remember. But I do remember this: the minute I saw him at my door, I started yelling.

He paid no attention to me and went straight to the kitchen. There, he opened the refrigerator. I followed him to the kitchen, still yelling. He shut the door of the fridge and headed for the exit. Before I knew it, he was down a few flights of stairs.

"Where are you going?" I shouted down the stairs.

He looked up and yelled back, "Your fridge is empty! I am getting you some groceries. Eat something! It may sweeten you up a bit." Then he disappeared.

I was speechless. How clever he was. And how sweet! I couldn't help but burst out laughing. Too bad he wasn't there to share it with me.

Sasha's impending departure opened up an opportunity for the KGB to persecute me for "social parasitism." Let me explain.

In the Soviet Union, every adult was obligated to work, except for retirees of official age, mothers of young children, students, and people with disabilities. Those who refused to work risked criminal charges for social parasitism (punishable by up to five years of internal exile). Jewish refuseniks frequently faced such charges. To avoid trials for parasitism, many took unskilled jobs, like street sweepers, boiler room attendants, and elevator operators. One of the most outrageous trials on the charges of social parasitism was conducted against the poet Joseph Brodsky. In 1964, despite the number of odd jobs he had held, Joseph Brodsky was wrongfully convicted and sentenced to eighteen months of internal exile. He served his sentence in the village of Norenskaya, in the far north of Russia. After Brodsky's release and subsequent emigration to the United States, he won the 1987 Nobel Prize in Literature and became the poet laureate of the United States.

Many dissidents and refuseniks, myself included, faced the challenges of being threatened with charges of social parasitism. Since the day of Zach's arrest, I had quit my job and engaged in an around-the-clock campaign for his release. Due to the nature of my campaign, I couldn't have been constrained by a job, even an unskilled one. I needed to be able to move freely at a moment's notice.

To the KGB, pinning me down to a job and, by doing so, forcing me to stay in Riga was too appealing to pass up. In the fall of 1984, I received an official warning that should I not find a job within a month, I would be charged with social parasitism. This turned out to be an easy fix. I began "working" as a housekeeper for Sasha and Polina.

The reason the KGB allowed Sasha and his family to emigrate may have been to undercut my support system, terminate my "employment," and expose my vulnerability.

Meanwhile, Sasha's family was getting ready to leave. The days and weeks before their departure turned into a prolonged farewell party. Their apartment became a virtual revolving door, with friends coming over to say goodbye and wish them the best of luck. These spontaneous get-togethers were colorful. Though desperately needing to pack, the hosts would gladly abandon the effort and greet whoever happened to be at the door. Food would magically appear on the table, and so would vodka. And in the best Russian tradition, the toasts would start and seemingly never end.

One of the frequent guests at Sasha and Polina's was a close friend of theirs, a refusenik named Sergey Gaibovich. I hadn't known Sergey before, nor did I know that Sasha was talking to him about taking over his role of assisting me. We got to know each other, and I learned that, just like Sasha, Sergey was a computer programmer. He was married to Bella, whom I also met, and they had a young daughter. When Sasha said, "Gaibovich will take my place helping you," I was grateful. Would I get a younger brother? In my mind, probably not. But I might get a friend!

As it turned out, the friendship never blossomed, but one thing served Gaibovich and me well. Taking a gamble, he offered me another fake position.

"You could be our daughter's nanny!" he suggested.

Brilliant idea! No doubt the KGB had already blacklisted my name at the agency registering housekeepers. Registering as a nanny required approval from an entirely different agency.

"That would do it. Thank you! Let's beat them to it."

We proceeded quickly, and in no time, I became a nanny. It didn't last long—within three months of my starting, Sergey and Bella received permission to leave the country. No kidding! Before that, the KGB attempted to pressure Sergey into abandoning me. He stood firm and refused to budge—for which I give him a lot of credit—and in the end, it paid off.

Before leaving, Sergey introduced me to another friend of Sasha's, Alik Kupershmidt, a.k.a. "Cooper." He, too, was a refusenik. And just like Sasha and Sergey, Cooper was a computer programmer. He was a few years younger than me, married to his wife, Fanya, and had a young daughter. He was smart, personable, funny, and warm; they both were. Working as a nanny for their child was no longer an option, as that door had been closed. So, what did we come up with? I became their English tutor—a fake one, of course.

For the next six months, we hung out together. I spent numerous nights at their apartment, on the couch in their living room, just as I had at Sasha and Polina's. It gave me a feeling of belonging and meant the world to me. Until one day, Cooper said, "You won't believe what has just happened. We've gotten our permission to leave."

"You WHAT?"

He wasn't kidding. Thirty days later, after Cooper and Fanya departed, I jokingly said to my friends, "If every refusenik signs up to be my employer, one by one, we could potentially solve the emigration problem in the Soviet Union."

But I am jumping way ahead of myself.

As November 1985 drew to a close, we were saying our goodbyes to Sasha and Polina. The day before their departure, a group of us went to Moscow to see them off. The morning we arrived, reality sunk in. They were leaving, for real. On the platform, next to the train, emotions overcame me. My eyes filled with tears, and I didn't try to hide them.

"No worries, Tan'ka," Sasha said, "you are in good hands."

I nodded. "I know. It's not about that. Thank you for *everything*. And best of luck!"

The train started moving slowly and then picked up speed.

It felt like the end of an era, and it was.

I decided to stay in Moscow a little longer to take care of a few things. By then, I still hadn't received a clear answer on how Zach had contracted hepatitis B. I needed to get to the bottom of it. I knew they

wouldn't admit to it being premeditated, but I still needed to hear
their explanation of how the virus had been contracted. Who exactly was at fault?

Going in, I had two official papers in my hands.

The first one, from the head of the Gulag Compliance Department
of the Irkutsk region, A. A. Bolshakov, was dated August 15, 1985,
and stated: "Zunshine was assigned to central hospital N1 in the city
of Irkutsk [the hospital of the Ministry of Internal Affairs], where
his medical examination was carried out in the course of three days
from 6 to 8 of August, 1985."[59]

The second letter, dated November 21, 1985, was from the
head of the Gulag Medical Department of the Irkutsk region, R. G.
Medvedev, and read: "Your husband, Zachar Zunshine, from October
10 through November 13 was treated at the Institution hospital
UK-272/2 in connection with his illness, final diagnosis—viral hepatitis, type B."[60]

Based on these two letters, Zach's contracting the virus coincid-
ed with his undergoing a medical examination. With that in mind,
I opened the door of the Medical Department of the Ministry of
Interior.

"I am here to see the head of the Gulag Medical Department,
Romanov."

His secretary told me to wait, and it took a while. I watched
people go in and out of his office. Finally, she opened the door and
motioned me in.

A man sitting at the desk introduced himself as a psychiatrist. I
was in too much of a shock to be able to catch his name. *Psychiatrist?*
What was he doing there?

---

59   Tatiana Zunshine's personal archive.

60   Tatiana Zunshine's personal archive.

"This is outrageous," I said. "I have no intention of talking to you, but I am not leaving either. I will sit here and wait until you bring Romanov in."

He asked me how I was doing, but I employed a familiar tactic—not talking. He tried a few more rounds but got nowhere. Then he got up and left the room, but not for long. Coming back, he announced, "He will be in shortly."

I couldn't believe he had folded so quickly.

Romanov stepped in, but the psychiatrist did not leave. He moved to a chair by the opposite wall and sat there, staring at me.

I presented to Romanov the two documents, coupled with my conclusion: "Everything points to my husband's stay at the hospital. That is where he was infected. The question is, how did it happen? And most importantly, was it deliberate or accidental?"

He admitted that it had happened in the hospital and that medical personnel were at fault. Naturally, he denied it being deliberate.

"Okay," I said, "suppose it was accidental. But still, those whose task is to cure the ill have caused the illness of an otherwise healthy person. Somebody should pay a price for it, don't you think?"

"That's been done," the psychiatrist interjected. "We have dismissed Medvedev from his position."

"What? Medvedev? You fired the head of the Gulag Medical Department of the Irkutsk region. Is that what you are saying?" This was the author of one of the two letters I'd brought in with me, and the last thing I expected to hear was that he had lost his job in connection with Zach's case.

"Yes," the so-called psychiatrist said, further revealing his awareness of our situation and thus confirming who he really was. He was as much of a psychiatrist as I was.

Bringing attention to Zach's case was vital for ensuring his post-treatment regimen. At my request, Pam's organization contacted physicians in the United States and elsewhere, asking them to write to Soviet officials on Zach's behalf and to stress the importance of a proper post-treatment regimen. One of the physicians who responded was Dr. Herbert L. Abrams, a radiologist at Stanford and Harvard universities and a first-generation Russian American. He was a founder of International Physicians for the Prevention of Nuclear War—the organization that had won the Nobel Peace Prize for its work in publicizing the health consequences of atomic warfare.

STANFORD UNIVERSITY MEDICAL CENTER

December 30, 1985

Ambassador Anatoly Dobrynin
1125 16th Street, N.W.
Washington, D.C. 20036

Dear Ambassador Dobrynin:

I have learned of a distressing situation pertaining to Mr. Zachar Zunshine, a 34 year old prisoner who has received a three year sentence in the Irkutsk region of the U.S.S.R. As a physician, I take a particular interest in this individual because of the nature of the health problem involved.

My understanding is that following a medical check-up on August 16, 1985, Mr. Zunshine contracted infectious hepatitis B. As I know you are aware, this is a most serious condition requiring strict diet, conservation of energy, and separation from any hard labor that may impede the recovery process. I am particularly concerned that failure to provide the appropriate conditions for recovery from hepatitis B could result in irreversible liver damage and ultimately in liver failure and death as a consequence.

I write not as the National Co-Chairman of Physicians for Social Responsibility, or as the founding Vice-President of International Physicians for the Prevention of Nuclear War, but rather as an individual doctor in an effort to bring a specific medical problem to your attention and to make certain that the opportunity for the kind of medical care that will forestall extensive hepatic fibrosis may be rendered to Mr. Zunshine.

I thank you for your consideration. I would appreciate hearing from you that this matter will be pursued.

Sincerely,

Herbert L. Adams, M.D.
Professor of Radiology and Member-in-Residence,
Stanford University
Center for International Security and Arms Control[61]

Toward the end of 1985, I received a letter from Zach. In this letter—as in many others before—he transported me to his world.

December 1985

Dear Tan'ka,

Sunday morning. Last day of Hanukkah. Somewhere out there, far away, somewhere in a different life, there is a holiday; candles are burning. But here, the stove is buzzing; the radio is on; one man is semi-lying, the other is sitting, a third one is rising, the fourth is climbing up on a stool to take down his valenki[62] from the top of the furnace. On their faces is a tired, frozen countenance, typical for men awaiting something to happen. (In my aisle, between the lines of cots, a human bottleneck is always the case, all due to the furnace being next to my cot.) Everyone is subconsciously checking out the clock. Any minute now, a roll call will be declared. By the furnace, it's warm and cozy. Everyone in this corner feels too lazy to talk. Silence. Nobody wants to go out and line up, but the radio announcement is about to come on. It's time to put on coats and go out.

---

61 Tatiana Zunshine's personal archive.

62 Felt boots.

Turns out, it's really nice outside. The frost has abated. The snow is as white as pure milk. If they don't come up with something else for us to do in half an hour or so, there will be time to finish this letter. Afterward, there is a lecture to attend. The administration here is crazy about lectures. A rare day passes without them. According to them, everyone is supposed to improve their level of education—those who are lecturing and those who are (not) listening. The other day, the lecture was on the harmful effects of overeating. The grande dame who was delivering the lecture cast defiant glances through the lens of her glasses. Maybe it was just a perception caused by the lecture's subject—overeating.

On October 10, I was taken to the hospital. Upon admission, my blood markers were three times worse than normal. By November 1, all tests came back normal, and two weeks later, on November 14, I was taken to a transitional prison where I spent a week awaiting etap.

On October 21, I had a hunch that you had flown into Angarsk, and on the morning of the 25th, I told the inmates in my hospital ward that I could literally smell it with my nose that my wife was here. And indeed, I got the package from you later that afternoon. It just happens that every time you, my little treasure, stick out on the other side of the fence, I know it; I know it for certain.

Since November 21, I have been back here in Bozoy, and since the 23rd, I have been assigned to work in a weaving shop where mesh sacks are being produced (light or, as they say here, easy work). Since December 1, I have been receiving a special diet, which is—surprisingly—quite decent.

I—of course!—am very happy for Sasha. You are right to say that life without him here in Russia will be much harder. What can you do, baby? Give him my most heartfelt greetings and best wishes. I really am very happy for him; he is a man of rare qualities.

He is also fortunate to be leaving by train rather than by plane. That way, you truly feel it. You can experience the whole process of the physical departure, looking out the window, seeing how this land remains behind you, how the distance to what you have been striving for so many years is decreasing with every passing hour, every passing minute.

My best wishes to everyone, and happy Hanukkah!

Z.

PS. They stopped putting me into punishment cells for the time being, thanks to my hepatitis. It's been three months since the last one. I even put some weight back on; some may even say, "got fat," but they, of course, are joking.[63]

Reading the lines, *It just happens that every time you, my little treasure, stick out on the other side of the fence, I know it; I know it for certain,* made me smile. But what made me throw my hat up in the air, so to speak, was this: learning that they *had* assigned Zach to light labor, that they *had* given him a special diet, and that they hadn't thrown him in a punishment cell for the last three months.

Finally! Had the tide started to turn?

---

63 Tatiana Zunshine's personal archive.

PART 3

1986

CHAPTER 19

WHEN IT RAINS, IT POURS

In early January, I found a small envelope in my mailbox. Overstuffed with papers, it was bursting at the seams. As I ripped it open, an uneasy feeling started to brew in me, though I didn't know where it came from. My intuition didn't fail me; the papers inside contained a trove of damning information about the camp administration's rotten practices. Among them was a letter from Zach.

January 1, 1986

Dear Tan'ka,

About the conditions that surround me: The top issue is tuberculosis! On the adjacent cot—as close to me as it gets—a guy is sleeping, age twenty, with a disability in the second degree. He has just come back from the hospital where, for the last five months, they treated him for TB. Coughing, especially at night, he wheezes so much that it seems like he is about to keel over. One of his lungs is completely shot, and, as he told me, he is about to undergo surgery to remove it. At my workplace, in the weaving workshop, next to me, there sits another guy—this one is even younger—who had a bout of tuberculosis. Despite having had it, he smokes (!) makhorka.[64] All in all, there are about thirty-five men in the shop, and everyone smokes but me. In addition, there are two iron furnaces there. All that combined creates an

---

64 A low-grade tobacco.

environment where blowing your nose makes the handkerchief turn black. It wouldn't hurt to put a gas mask on, you know. At the moment, their disease is dormant, yet triggered by a cold or something, it can once again become acute. As for me, having had a bout of hepatitis, I am in a weakened state of health, and you, Tan'ka, understand what that means. Anything could happen. Needless to say, adding tuberculosis to my health problems is the last thing I need.

It is clear as a bell that TB inmates should be kept in a separate unit, or at least in a separate section, but that's "Bozoy-ville" for you.

In the barracks, there is no ventilation pane. It's too dark to read or write; your eyes hurt from the strain. About all these issues—TB, ventilation, light—I turned to the head of the camp, but he took no measures whatsoever. They maintain that everything is just fine around here and couldn't be better. I decided not to waste my time on that guy and will, in a few days, send an official complaint to the prosecutor's office and the Gulag office of the USSR.

Now about the situation in the unit, which has grown a great deal worse since the same time a year ago. Last year, at least, I hadn't witnessed any brawls here in the unit; not the same this time around. The last one happened on December 25, 1985, right in the section where I sleep. One of those in a leading position (a.k.a. "firmly established on the way to self-correction") started a brawl. He grabbed a stool and tried to hit another inmate with it, then jumped up on the top bunk of the bed and struck him in the face. Two or three inmates hold a leading position and are running this unit. They have such a grip around here that they—as a warning to others—can fix things up so that any unlucky one—who is not a bigger transgressor of the regime than anybody else—can find himself perpetually thrown into a punishment cell. They say it openly: anyone who dares to object to them is doomed. To no one's surprise, some inmates, having been driven to despair, charge at these bullies, sometimes with a metal rod, other times with a brick. Those attacks, just like the fights, are being hushed up. On December 27, a unit meeting took place, but everybody was tight-lipped about the accidents (the poor guy who hasn't seen the light of the day, spending term after term in a punishment cell, was not given a chance to speak). All of this will undoubtedly end with a tragedy on their hands.

These punks in leadership positions entertained the idea of forcing me to clean the floors (although this is usually done by inmates at the very bottom of the food chain). Soon, perhaps, they will want me to shine their boots?! The administration lets those punks get away with murder, which suits both sides just fine. The latest on the administration: they claimed that the Operation Department has collected "evidence" that I allegedly attacked the senior duty man (or some other similar nonsense). They sometimes request explanatory notes from me several times a day. What are the pretexts? Those are too ridiculous to mention.

It got to the point that some of them began paying lip service to the subject of Jews, and that's just plain annoying.

Now about my job: I weave large mesh potato sacks, which is considered light labor. To weave one sack, one has to make more than 1,000 rather sharp movements with one's right hand; to weave two sacks—more than 2,000; to weave three sacks— more than 3,000, and that's my limit. And all this time, since I started the job on November 23, I have had pain on the right side of my abdomen. At first, I thought that this was muscle pain, but forty days later, it is still here. I talked to the doctor, and he admitted that making that many sharp movements a day without breaks could irritate your liver.

You know, Tan'ka, I'm not sure why, but I have a hunch you will receive this letter. My personal and fondest regards to everyone we know around the world.

Z.[65]

Shaken, I turned to the other papers.

---

65   Tatiana Zunshine's personal archive.

To: The Deputies of the Supreme Soviet of the USSR

January 1, 1986

It will be a miracle if I don't catch TB while I'm recovering from hepatitis.

Those who have had a bout of TB must be isolated in separate living quarters. However, in labor camp #40, this is not the case. Right beside me sleeps a TB inmate, age twenty, with a disability in the second degree. During his coughing bouts, he wheezes so intensely that it looks like he is about to keel over.

At my workplace, the situation is equally dangerous. The weaving shop is located in an unsafe building. Supporting beams look like they could collapse at any moment (that did happen to me in the laundry room; fortunately, I escaped with just a few scratches). Soot, smoke, dirt—everywhere, including the windows and windowsills. No ability to wash hands as there is no running water on the premises and neither are washbasins or water pumps. There is mold in the corners and on the ceiling. As weaving mesh sacks is considered an "easy" job, many TB inmates are being assigned to it.

I consider it a crime. What is your opinion, Comrade Deputy of the Supreme Soviet?

Zachar Zunshine[66]

I was dumbfounded. These letters had come through official channels. Why? Why give me so much ammunition? Or had they simply fallen through the cracks?

I turned to the last one.

January 12, 1986

To: The Ministry of Internal Affairs of the USSR
From: Zachar Zunshine, labor camp #40 of the Irkutsk region

---

66 Archives, Center for Jewish History, New York, NY.

Insulting one's ethnic dignity (by using racial and ethnic slurs) constitutes a violation of Article 36 of the Constitution of the USSR.[67] Anti-Semitic attacks waged against me with the apparent goal of humiliating me contain all attributes of the violation mentioned above.

Turning the inmates against me, forcing them to write a never-ending array of denunciations containing absurd accusations against me (ex: "Zunshine wouldn't let us wash the floor," or "Zunshine disturbed inmates' sleep"), initiating transparent attempts to throw me off, engaging in endless anti-Semitic stunts—all of these actions have been carried out with the approval of the administration of the labor camp #40.

The main character in this charade is inmate Biryukov (one of those "firmly established on the way to self-correction"), who, with the administration's blessings, is serving the remaining part of his sentence under fewer restrictions.

I consider the administration's unwillingness to put an end to these antics an attempt to push me over the edge, to create a scenario where I have no choice but to grab a poker or something (incidentally, I sleep by the furnace) and smash the heads of these "firmly established on the way to self-correction" cynics.

On January 10, 1986, they asked me to submit yet another explanatory note addressing the fact that I had called one of these wise guys an "imbecile."

On January 8, 1986, sometime after 9 p.m., two senior on-duty inmates approached me while I was sitting on my cot. These were inmate Levashov and inmate Biryukov. I suggested for them to get lost, but they started talking anyway. Accompanied by Levashov's giggling, inmate Biryukov began reading aloud an extract from a newspaper article, replacing the words "Jewish Defense League" with "Defense league of kikes,"

---

67   Constitution of the USSR, adopted on October 7, 1977, Article 36: "Any direct or indirect limitation of the rights of citizens or establishment of direct or indirect privileges on grounds of race or nationality, and any advocacy of national exclusiveness, hostility, or contempt, are punishable by law."

and at that moment, gathering all my strength not to reach for a poker, I instead called him an imbecile.

The facts mentioned above sufficiently constitute a violation of Article 36 of the Soviet Constitution and warrant proceedings to punish those who infringed on my ethnic dignity.

It is crystal clear to me that, if needed, the administration will present 20–30–40 inmates who will undoubtedly testify to the contrary (as soon as inmates cross the threshold of the camp, they, with rare exceptions, establish themselves "on the way to self-correction" and become collaborators; what must have been the scale of their duress to justify turning themselves into tamed idiots, willing to testify to whatever the administration tells them to; those, on the other hand, who dare to assert their human dignity are dealt with accordingly).

Nevertheless, I request that you consider initiating the proceedings in connection with the facts (mentioned above) of insulting my ethnic dignity.[68]

By the time I finished reading, so much anger and so much fight brewed in me that I could hardly contain it. Fuming, I reached for *my* mental poker—my typewriter—and started typing. I wrote one letter after another: to the Communist Party of the USSR, to the Ministry of the Interior, to the national Gulag, to the prosecutor general of the USSR, to the deputies of the Supreme Soviet of the USSR, to the World Health Organization, to Amnesty International, to the United Nations Committee for Human Rights—you name it, I wrote to them all.

Regarding tuberculosis, I promised to battle the camp administration until I myself turned blue. I cited medical sources, urging the separation and isolation of latent TB carriers from the rest of the camp's population. I attached Zach's letter and stated that "the

---

68 Tatiana Zunshine's personal archive.

documents enclosed provide evidence that in labor camp #40 where my husband, Zachar Zunshine, is being confined, preemptive sanitary measures are being utterly disregarded, not only concerning TB but also concerning basic sanitary norms; all of that serves as a factor conducive to proliferation of the TB agent and provides a prerequisite for group mortality."[69]

I demanded the convening of commissions to investigate the activities of the camp administration. I demanded the isolation of TB inmates without further delay. I urged the Gulag higher-ups to conduct epidemiological and medical observations of people who were in contact with TB inmates, in particular of my husband. I also urged them to punish the administration for blatant disregard of the laws of public health.

On the subject of anti-Semitism, I demanded that the administration cease anti-Semitic attacks against my husband once and for all. I sent open postcards to 200 deputies of the Supreme Soviet, asking them to take urgent measures to protect the honor and ethnic dignity of my husband, to stop the campaign of unabated persecution and anti-Semitism, and to bring to justice those who were responsible for it.

I worked around the clock, hardly noticing the days passing by. One thing I did notice, however, was the intense surveillance. On average, three cars filled with agents accompanied me on every trip outside the house. I planned to finish my letter-writing campaign and leave for Siberia, but I wondered if the surveillance would stand in the way.

It wasn't the KGB who interfered with my plans. It was my friend Yakov Gorodetsky.

"I have news for you," he said to me on the phone. "We have gotten permission to leave the country."

"Are you serious?"

---

69   Archives, Center for Jewish History, New York, NY.

"I wouldn't joke about stuff like that."

"Well . . . then . . . huge congrats!"

I wasn't faking it. I was truly happy for Yakov. Ever since my friend Sasha Balter's departure, I realized I was making it too much about myself. Back then, I was worried. *How would I be without my best friend and confidant? Could I survive in that kind of vacuum?* The truth is, it wasn't about me. It was Sasha's moment, and I needed to be able to enjoy it with him. Lesson learned.

"I was planning on going to Irkutsk," I told Yakov. "But I will swing by Leningrad, say goodbye, and be on my way."

Having the tail of KGB agents follow me to the train station, I was not at all sure they would let me board, but they did. You just never knew with them! You thought you had learned their moves, then they threw you off by letting you get away. Go figure.

Yakov and Lina were departing within a few weeks, but I knew this would be the last time I would see them in this part of the world. The last time staying in this apartment, in that den, on that couch. The last time for all of that. But this wasn't the end of Yakov's fight, not by any means. While he and Lina chose to emigrate to Israel, he was already planning on going to the United States and engaging in a speaking tour in support of those left behind.

Saying goodbye was emotional, no matter how well I prepared for it. I was grateful for everything Yakov had done for Zach and me, and I tried to tell him that, but he shied away from it.

"I know, I know, you don't have to tell me," he said.

"Hug Sasha for me, please," I asked, "and Pam, and Marillyn, and Martin, and everybody you meet in the States."

"Will do."

The three of us hugged, and I hurried out of their apartment, trying to keep myself from openly breaking down.

Before leaving the city for the airport en route to Irkutsk, I went to the market and bought ten pounds of fresh produce. No scheduled parcel was allowed for Zach, but that wasn't the point. The point was to bring the parcel to the camp and push the administration to accept it. I did that on every trip I took. Some of my previous attempts had worked; most had not. But I was going to try.

The cab brought me to Bozoy around 11:00 a.m., and I went straight to the headquarters. I asked to see the head of the camp, Mr. Stepanenko, but what I heard shocked me: Stepanenko was no longer the head of the camp. At that moment, he was transitioning his position to a new head, Mr. Mouzh. Did we have anything to do with it? I later found out that we sure did.

Needless to say, Stepanenko didn't want to see me. Instead, they directed me to the office of the head of the Political Department, Mr. Ploscharin. He was there in the company of two men: the officer serving in the Operative Department,[70] Mr. Uvarov, and the camp's new doctor, whose name I didn't catch.

I marched straight to Ploscharin's desk and put the copies of Zach's letters in front of him. He examined them while I stood silently, waiting for him to finish. Then I started talking. I told them that I was there to address all of those violations. I brought up the situation with TB, poor sanitary conditions, anti-Semitic touts, and other stunning revelations I had learned from Zach's letters.

From my very first exchange, I sensed that something was different. I felt no resistance. It seemed like the administration was testing a new tactic—appeasement. For every issue I raised, they gave me a cookie-cutter response: "The matter is currently under investigation. Once completed, we will let you know."

"This is an outrage, and it must stop," I summarized my demands.

---

70   An arm of the KGB.

"The matter is currently under investigation—" one of them began.

"And you will let me know," I said sarcastically, finishing his sentence for him. "This is not going to work, you know. You will not hide behind some bogus response while continuing to do whatever you are doing. I can see through that nonsense, and you are not gonna get away with it."

But I must have been right about the appeasement, as this blunt statement of mine did not change the course of the conversation. Still no resistance.

Then I asked to pass on a food parcel to Zach, and they said, "Okay."

"Okay?" Their answer threw me off a bit, and I wanted to make sure I'd heard it right.

"Yes, okay. We will give the parcel to inmate Zunshine at 7:00 p.m., once he is off work," one of them said. "Meanwhile, you are free to leave."

Hmm. Suspicious of their newfound subservience, I didn't quite know how to react. I looked at my watch; it was showing twelve noon.

"I will wait till 7:00 p.m.," I said. "Once you give him the parcel, I'll leave."

They asked me to step outside the room, and I did. When they called me back, Uvarov said, "We will give your husband the parcel right now and provide you with a receipt. Is that okay?"

"Of course it is!"

And that's what happened. They brought a receipt with Zach's signature on it. But more, in a true spirit of appeasement, they offered me a car with a driver to take me back to Irkutsk. *They just can't get me out of here soon enough*, I thought, taking them up on their offer.

On the ride back, I had a little win to celebrate and questions to answer. Mainly, what was all *that* about? If this was just a phase—which

I thought it was—how long would it last? I didn't think it would last
till the next visit, and it turned out that I was right.

In Irkutsk, I learned that more heads had been put on the chop-
ping block over Zach's hepatitis. I believe it wasn't because of the
infection itself but because of their admission to it in a formal letter
to me. Who admitted it? The head of the Gulag Medical Department
of the Irkutsk region, Mr. Medvedev, whose signature was on the
letter. I found out that in addition to Stepanenko and Medvedev,
the head of the Compliance Department, Mr. Bolshakov, had been
dismissed as well.

I didn't feel sorry for them. Not that I thought their replace-
ments would be any better.

On my way back from Irkutsk, I stopped to see my family in Sverdlovsk.
My sister, Lora, was in town with her two-year-old twin boys, Robert
and David.

Twins ourselves, Lora and I were inseparable. We lived in two different republics on the Baltic Sea, me in Latvia, her in Estonia. Yet
in spirit, like a pair of Siamese twins conjoined at the heart, we were
together every step of the way.

Growing up, our parents didn't separate us enough. We attended
the same school, had the same friends, read the same books, and wore
the same dresses and coats. One thing wasn't the same, however: she
was outgoing, and I was shy. In old family photos, Lora's smiling eyes
stand out, round as a pair of buttons. Mine are almond-shaped and
often sad. Looking at those photos makes me wonder. *Why was I sad?*
I don't know! I don't remember. One thing I do remember: as a child,
I wanted my sister all to myself. Having to share her with friends,
I often felt bitten by a green-eyed monster, jealousy. Unequipped to
handle it, I shoved it deep inside. I wasn't going to admit to it, nor was
I going to admit that I wanted to be more like her.

Needless to say, I adored my sister. My very first test of character happened at the age of nineteen when she got married and moved out of the house. And how I felt that void! I was lost. It was as if somebody had split me in half and taken one of the halves away. I realized then that I had no choice but to grow that other half. As difficult as it was, growing the other half was one of the most rewarding things I've ever done for myself.

As for my shyness, that went away; I washed it off with the tears I shed the night of Zach's arrest.

My brother, Gena, met me at the airport. I was giddy, anticipating spending time with Mom, Lora and the boys, Gena and his family—his wife, Tanya, and his daughter, Natasha. I thought I could use a break for a few days before going back to Riga.

Driving out from the airport, we noticed several cars following us, which I found utterly annoying. This wasn't the first time they had followed me in Sverdlovsk. The worst part was that, even after I'd left, they'd continued following my brother for days. I felt responsible for that, and it made me want to stay away from Sverdlovsk.

"You are not going anywhere," Gena said, "but I do need to tell you about something."

A few months back, he told me, he had flown to the Siberian town of Krasnoyarsk on a business trip. Having visited it numerous times and having stayed in the same hotel, he had developed friendly relationships with the women at the reception counter. And it paid off. He was in his room when he got a phone call from downstairs. "Get down here *now*," a receptionist said convincingly. When he got downstairs, she took him aside. "Soon after you checked in, two men came by," she said. "They went to the manager's office and spent a good chunk of time there, talking. Once the meeting ended, the manager told us to vacate the room next to yours and check the two men into it. I thought you should know."

Within minutes, Gena was in a car, having a local co-worker drive him to the train station. To fall off the KGB radar, the best way to go was by train (as opposed to a plane). To eliminate any chance of exposure, he bought four tickets—for the whole compartment—and locked himself in. The journey took thirty-six hours, but he arrived home safely.

Listening to this, I had chills going up and down my spine. I was terrified. That situation wouldn't have happened had he not been related to me. I had brought it upon him. Me.

"I am so sorry you had to go through this!"

"No worries," Gena said. "Nothing happened in the end."

So what was it? A setup for a potential provocation? A scenario for planting drugs? No one would ever know. Luckily, Gena dodged the bullet. As for me, I started having recurring nightmares about the KGB throwing my brother in jail as a way of getting back at me.

CHAPTER 20

MY FAIR LADIES

On the way home, I stopped in Moscow and, as always, went to my friend Dina Zisserman's apartment. When we first met in the fall of 1985, Dina gave me the key to her apartment and extended an invitation to stay with her whenever I needed it.

Who was Dina?

A journalist in her pre-refusenik life, she was a rare gem. Tiny in size, she was an intellectual giant, but that's not what defined her. What defined her was the amount of warmth and kindness she exuded. We all felt it. Who were "we"? The cast of characters hanging around her apartment, me included.

Dina was the wife of a political prisoner, just like I was. Her husband, Vladimir Brodsky—a forty-one-year-old physician—was arrested in July 1985 on trumped-up charges of "assaulting a police officer." He was convicted and sentenced to three years in the Gulag.

When Vladimir's trial began, Dina was eight months pregnant with their first child. By the time their daughter, Rachel, was born, he had already been convicted and was in the process of being escorted to the labor camp in the Gulag. I always wondered how Dina managed to fight for her husband while having an infant on her hands. I couldn't imagine being in her shoes. But she did what she had to do simply because she had no choice. Friends chipped in as much as they could. When I was in town, I often stayed with the baby when Dina needed to be out and about. Coming back, she'd trade places with me.

The real reason for Brodsky's arrest and conviction was his membership in an independent group called the Moscow Group for the Establishment of Trust Between the USSR and the USA (a.k.a. Trust Group). Founded in June 1982 by a twenty-five-year-old Russian artist, Sergei Batovrin, the group's goal was to "harness the enormous creative potency of the broad public in search of disarmament and peace."[71] From the moment of the group's formation, the Soviets, in a display of their true colors, tried to suffocate it to the best of their abilities. The crackdown was vast. Sergei Batovrin found himself committed to a psychiatric hospital. Another member, Oleg Radzinsky, was arrested and sentenced to six years in the Gulag on charges of "anti-Soviet agitation and propaganda." Lastly, Vladimir Brodsky got his three-year conviction. These were just the highlights. The KGB assailed the group with house arrests and fifteen-day jail sentences. But the lowest of all was their puncturing one member's automobile tires in an apparent attempt to involve her in an auto accident.

And that brings me to my other best friend and soulmate, Olga Medvedkov.

Olga and her husband, Yuri, joined the Trust Group in July 1982. In their pre-refusenik life, both had successful academic careers in geography. Once they joined the group, they became its heart and soul. It was Olga's tires the KGB punctured, causing her to nearly lose control of her car. But it didn't end there. In 1983, they slapped her with the trumped-up charges of "assaulting a police officer," punishable by up to three years in the Gulag. After an enormous outcry from the international community, in March 1984, Olga—mother of an eight-year-old son, Misha, pregnant with a second child—received a suspended sentence of two and a half years.

---

71   "U.S. Group Assails Soviet Repression," *The New York Times*, September 5, 1982.

A true force of nature, Olga had a magnetic personality. Besides being wickedly smart, she was fearless, assertive, and hilariously funny. Combine that with her generosity of heart, and you had a shining star, somebody you couldn't help but admire.

It just so happened that Olga and Dina were best friends. How did I get so lucky to have met these fabulous women and be able to call them *my* best friends?

On February 16, 1986, in Moscow, Dina and I headed toward our friends' house on Vernardsky Avenue. It was about 4:00 p.m. Approaching the entrance of the building, we saw three men hanging by the door, talking. *It's them, no doubt,* crossed my mind, and sure enough, the men turned toward us and then pounced.

One man held Dina, and another held me, keeping us apart while we tried to wriggle our way out. The third displayed a badge and introduced himself.

"First Lieutenant of the Latvian KGB, Narnitsky."

He then joined the guy holding me, and the two of them dragged me a few yards to the sidewalk, where a car waited at the curb. They pushed me into the car and got in, each on either side of me. The last one let go of Dina and briskly walked toward the car. What did she do? Anybody else would have backed off, but not Dina. She ran up to the car and started banging on the windows, yelling, "Let her go!"

The car took off.

Narnitsky was a familiar face. In May 1984, he escorted me on the train from Leningrad to Riga. Little did I know back then that I would be stumbling over that guy time after time after time.

Observing the road, I figured they were taking me to the airport. *That's a change,* I thought. I was accustomed to them putting me on trains. I wondered if there was any significance to it. *Somebody put a rush on it. Who would that be, and why?*

We drove for forty-five minutes and arrived at Sheremetyevo Airport at about 5:00 p.m. We all got out of the car. The two men shook hands with Narnitsky and parted ways with us. He took me to the airport's police station and directed me into an empty office. I went in, and the door closed behind me.

Left alone, I tried not to let thoughts of uncertainty overcome me. My mind wandered off to a happier place. Having just visited my hometown of Sverdlovsk, the images of my childhood were freshly painted in my mind.

The L-shaped building I grew up in was built in the mid-1950s. Most of its residents had moved in back then and seemingly never left.

On both sides of each of the five building entrances were comfortable benches. These belonged to older women, widows mostly, who sat there day after day, night after night, keeping each other company, gossiping, observing. They were the gatekeepers. With headscarves covering their hair and layers of cardigans allowing for a change of weather, those ladies were a tough crowd. To pass by them in peace, you had to show respect, or your mother would hear about it. Growing up, we were intimidated by those silver-haired dandelions, but now, just thinking about them makes me smile.

In a large circle in front of the building was a park full of decades-old apple trees, acacia bushes, benches, and picnic tables. In the center of it all was a playground. In late spring and early summer, the smell of apple blossoms penetrated the apartments through open windows and balcony doors. Aah, I loved it. I loved the trees and the acacia bushes—those had a balsamic smell to them—and I loved the park. There were other occupants of the park besides the kids. Older men in flat caps took over the benches and picnic tables. What were they doing there? Playing chess, or dominoes, or simply talking. A picture solidly imprinted on my mind is of a group of men sitting on a bench, and all of a sudden, in the middle of their conversation, you see one man's head droop down to his chest or shoulder, his eyes closed, his mouth open just slightly, as he falls asleep. Oh, those wonderful memories! For us—the neighborhood kids—the park was our kingdom. We spent most of our summer days playing in its alleys. Around ten or eleven at night, the mothers' voices would ring from the balconies and interrupt the magic: "Time to come home!" On the third call, you reluctantly went inside.

Narnitsky opened the door and interrupted my magic. Standing in the doorway, he motioned me out: "Let's go."

He took me straight to the gate. The plane wasn't boarding yet, but he showed his badge and the tickets, and the gate agents let us on board.

More waiting. Then people started showing up in a steady flow.

An hour and a half later, we landed at the Riga airport. By then, the clock read eleven. I was tired and wanted the ordeal to end, but apparently, Narnitsky wasn't done with me. We were walking along the airport ramps when I decided to break the silence (which had begun as soon as they'd abducted me) and asked where we were going. He just said, "Follow me," and kept walking.

We entered a police station at Riga's airport. Narnitsky flashed his badge, and a policeman on duty took us to a nearby office. He was clearly aware of what was happening—I wished I had the slightest notion.

A man sitting at the desk raised his head. It was none other than Lieutenant Colonel Shalaev. That same Shalaev, the head of the KGB Jewish Department, who had promised me in June 1985 that the next time he and I saw each other would be "some . . . place . . . else." It was a rather transparent threat, but I remembered trying to defuse it by saying, "So you'll be there, too?" I also remembered him being utterly annoyed by that.

"Take a seat," Shalaev said.

I sat down in front of the desk. The apparent urgency in bringing me back on a plane was wearing me down. I was tired of waiting and needed them to show their cards.

"This is to inform you," he said sternly, "that you are not to leave the boundaries of Riga until March 5. Any attempts to do so will be fruitless; complaining won't bear any fruit either."

This was it? That's what I was there for? I felt a sense of relief. But then, what was with all the rush? This could easily have waited till the next day. I thought of bringing it up but decided not to mess with him this time around.

Shalaev wasn't lying about me not being able to leave Riga. From the night at the airport onward, the surveillance took a very aggressive turn. It was arrogantly open and purposely in my face. Three cars stood by the entrance to my apartment building. Between them, about ten agents kept a watchful eye on the door. When I showed up, some agents would get out and follow me on foot while keeping me at arm's length. Others stayed inside the car, moving slowly, block by block. If I happened to take a cab or hop onto public transportation, the team would quickly consolidate and follow me to my destination.

About two weeks into my confinement, I received a letter from Zach. Not only was it my consolation prize, but it was also a pure treat. Like many letters before, it had a generous serving of humor with a side of sarcasm.

February 19, 1986

Dear Tan'ka,

It's past 10 a.m., but I just now sat down to write you a letter (which I had intended to do since early morning). One thing or another stood in the way.

On Sundays, reveille is a half hour later than usual—at 6:30 a.m.—designed to let the youth around here sleep a little longer (an overwhelming majority of the inmate population is about twenty years old). Right after reveille comes sweeping of public grounds, or, as I call it, "snow retention." Boy, do they love snow retention over here! They love it so much that if it did not happen every day, several times a day, and if the whole unit of 100 men did not partake in it, then—riot or no riot—something horrid would be bound to happen, and just thinking about it gives me severe trepidation.

Today, after breakfast, there was a snow retention stint, and then another one after the morning roll call. The trouble is that atmospheric precipitation around here is extremely low—this isn't Riga, after all!

A thrilling thing is this snow retention. Imagine this: Black sky. Light coming down onto the observation decks. A dazzling white snow-packed ground. Add the stars scattered here and there across the black sky on a clear night and also the moon. There is nothing to scrape, as there is no fresh powder—none whatsoever! But this ritual dance of snow retention is still being performed. There is so much mystery in it, so much expressiveness in its meager colors, gestures, and movements, that, honest to god, every time I observe it, I discover something new—a feature or a look— that excites the hell out of me. A solemn moment is about to start; everyone lines up, everyone is set and ready, even stars and the moon flex their muscles, imaginative fanfares are about to erupt, one more particle of time, and a sacred ritual begins!

On January 10, they sent you a wire for 414 rubbles. You must have already received it. This is a reimbursement for my personal belongings, which, to put it mildly, have vanished into thin air. In March of last year, I filed a lawsuit against this "lovely" institution. The case dragged on, and, at first, my lawsuit got thrown out. But eventually—I still can't grasp how it all happened and why—on August 6 last year, the People's Court ruled in my favor. So, having received the money, remember your unfortunate one, who looks after you daily and nightly from the distance of this godforsaken land.

I am still working in a weaving shop, making mesh sacks. By the way, they offered me a different job. Let me explain to you so you understand: Imagine a gate, the one inmates go through on the way in and out. A guy opening and closing the gate, sort of a watchman, is called an "orderly." Surely, in this country, every kind of job is held in high esteem. It rings especially true in places of incarceration, as reeducation and redemption of those who have gone astray can only be achieved by socially beneficial labor. And it is hard to imagine more socially beneficial labor than opening and closing the gate.

As you have already guessed, Tan'ka, I refused to take it. That surprised the hell out of the head of the unit, who did not doubt that I would accept it. What can you do? It was not in my stars.

To everyone, everywhere, my personal regards and best wishes.

Z.[72]

I couldn't believe it! He had won a lawsuit against the camp administration. How was it possible? We lived in the land of lawlessness. He, as a convict, had been stripped of the remainder of his rights, and yet, he had sued his captors in the court of law—Soviet law, to be exact—over the loss of his belongings and won? How remarkable! Let

---

72 Tatiana Zunshine's personal archive.

me tell you what the sum of 414 rubles back then translated to. For a college-educated person, it was more than three months' salary.

In secret code, Zach told me that he was planning on declaring a one-day hunger strike on March 6—the second anniversary of his arrest.

The March 6 anniversary was around the corner. Not only had I decided to join Zach in his hunger strike, but I chose to do it with a bang. I asked Pam to organize a sympathetic hunger strike among our friends and supporters. Soon, the Union of Councils' branches shared the following press release.

ZUNSHINE: SYMPATHETIC HUNGER STRIKE

Tatiana Zunshine has asked that in sympathy with her husband, who is planning to begin a hunger strike on the second anniversary of his arrest on March 6, friends and supporters join in the hunger strike for that one day.

On March 6, Chicago Action is planning a one-day symposium, teach-in, and fast. The program, as planned, will include Rabbis' participation, Psalm reading, postcards, slides, statements by ex-refuseniks, and they will also attempt to phone the labor camp in Irkutsk, where Zunshine is now being held.

Everyone who is interested in undertaking a similar program should contact Marillyn Tallman, Chicago Action, who will assist with planning ideas and suggestions.[73]

This was turning into a major event, the scope of which I myself had not envisioned. In the aftermath of March 6, Chicago Action for Soviet Jewry issued a press release describing what the event had entailed.

73   Archives, Center for Jewish History, New York, NY.

FOR IMMEDIATE RELEASE

SOVIET JEWRY ACTIVISTS HOLD HUNGER STRIKE
IN SYMPATHY WITH WIFE OF PRISONER-OF-
CONSCIENCE IN USSR

On Thursday, March 6, 1986 members of Chicago Action for
Soviet Jewry, including rabbis, educators, and attorneys,
gathered at the office of Chicago Action for Soviet Jewry, 1724
First Street, Highland Park to hunger strike in sympathy with
Tatiana Zunshine of Riga whose husband, Zachar Zunshine, is
a prisoner of conscience in Irkutsk, Siberia.

The hunger strikers placed a call to the mayor of Riga, Mr.
Rubiks, to inform him of Western awareness of the abuse of
Soviet law in the Zunshine case, and of the many people who
are concerned for the KGB isolation of Mrs. Zunshine in Riga.
Telephone calls to the prison camp in Irkutsk and the office
of the General Procurator [Prosecutor] in Moscow notified the
Soviets of the deep interest of Americans vis-à-vis this case.

David Cohen, Press Officer for Congressman John Porter, reported that Katherine [sic] Porter, a member of the "Committee
of 21," an organization of Congressional wives working on behalf of Soviet Jewish prisoners, delivered to the Soviet Embassy
a written appeal to Soviet leader, Gorbachev. Mrs. Porter wrote,
"Mr. Gorbachev, I am appealing to you as a concerned woman, a
wife, a mother and a citizen of the United States. Please use your
influence to intervene in this case to assure that the Zunshines
are accorded their basic human rights. As our two countries
move toward improved relations it is vital that the Soviet Union
take steps to legitimize its commitment to peace through humanitarian gestures. I appeal to you to release Zachar Zunshine
from his imprisonment, to end the harassment and repression
of Tatiana Zunshine, and allow them to emigrate to Israel. By
these actions, you will be demonstrating your country's true
commitment to human rights."

Chicago Action for Soviet Jewry, the Highland Park based human right's [sic] agency, announced the participation of Rabbi Mordecai Simon, Executive Director, Chicago Board of Rabbis, Rabbi Samuel Fraint, North Suburban Synagogue Beth El, Highland Park, Rabbi Stuart Weiss, B'nai Shalom Traditional, Buffalo Grove. Rabbi Fraint read appropriate Psalms in Hebrew and English.

Pamela Cohen and Marillyn Tallman, Co-chairmen, Chicago Action for Soviet Jewry, said "this is a very significant day—an expression of the solidarity for Tatiana Zunshine and her husband, Zachar, in their struggle."[74]

I was floored. This grew beyond my wild imagination. But there was still more to it.

ACTION FOR REFUSENIK WOMEN AND CHILDREN
c/o Devra Noily
1827 33rd Avenue
San Francisco, CA 94122

February 28, 1986

FOR IMMEDIATE RELEASE

ACTION PLANNED AT SOVIET CONSULATE

A rally and vigil will be held beginning at 5:00 pm on March 5 at the Soviet Consulate (2790 Green Street in San Francisco) to protest the worsening conditions of Soviet prisoner of conscience Zachar Zunshine and his wife Tatiana Zunshine.

March 6 marks the second anniversary of Zachar Zunshine's arrest, and the completion of two-thirds of his three year term in a Siberian labor camp on charges of "anti-Soviet slander."

---

74   Archives, Center for Jewish History, New York, NY.

Tatiana Zunshine has declared a hunger strike on March 6 to protest these latest assaults on the rights of her husband and herself.

Hunger strikes will be held in solidarity with her on March 6 in San Francisco, Chicago, London, Jerusalem and Tel Aviv.

The 5:00 pm rally will be followed by an all-night vigil and hunger strike outside the Soviet Consulate, ending at 12:00 noon on March 6.

Rally participants will include San Francisco Supervisor Carol Ruth Silver, Holocaust scholar and human rights activist Dr. Konnilyn Feig, and Morey Shapira, executive director of the Union of Councils for Soviet Jews, among others.[75]

Reading these documents from Chicago to San Francisco, I felt my heart swell with boundless gratitude for those who had dedicated their lives to help rescue us—Soviet Jews—from the claws of the Soviet regime, who sacrificed their own days (and nights!) to fight alongside us, and did it with such selflessness and generosity of heart. I knew I would forever be indebted to them.

I learned that, in addition to me, the vigil was staged in support of two other women. These were Tanya Bogomolny, a long-term refusenik and a cancer patient fighting for her life in Russia, and Yelena Bonner, a human rights activist and wife of a prominent nuclear physicist, dissident, and Nobel Prize winner, Andrei Sakharov. None of us could be there in person, but undoubtedly, we were there in spirit. And what an honor it was to be in the company of such remarkable women!

Years later, I came across a speech delivered by my friend Dr. Konnilyn Feig at the San Francisco vigil (she and I had met in Moscow when she and her partner, Lisa Wilhelm, came to visit, posing as tourists). That speech broke my heart in the best possible way.

---

75   Tatiana Zunshine's personal archive.

VIGIL
MARCH 5-6 1986
SOVIET CONSULATE, SAN FRANCISCO

In recent weeks, the release of Anatoly Sharansky[76] has brought recollections of his wife Avital's relentless campaign in defense of her husband and his right to be freed. For the last two years, Tatiana Zunshine has carried out a campaign calling for her husband Zachar's release, and for his humane treatment while he remains imprisoned in Siberia: a campaign with the intensity, determination and sacrifice of Avital Sharansky's, but pursued inside the Soviet Union, where she is followed not by journalists but by KGB agents, where reports of her activities appear not in the *New York Times* but in the overflowing files of the state security police.

Tatiana finds her predicament to be not only unbearably unjust, but also deeply ironic. Neither she nor Zachar has done anything illegal; on the contrary, certain Soviet officials—in arresting Zachar, in the conduct of his trial, in abuses of his rights and assaults on his health in the labor camp—have repeatedly violated provisions of the Soviet Constitution and Soviet laws. To each such violation Tatiana has responded with persistent appeals to the Soviet authorities, calling for investigations into the crimes committed against her husband.

The most recent information from the USSR is that both Tatiana and Zachar have come under new threats. Rumors are being circulated in the prison by camp collaborators claiming that Zachar assaulted a camp official. This is a prelude to possible new charges against him which would lead to a trial in the camp and an extension of his sentence. On February 16, Tatiana was picked up in Moscow, forced into a car and taken back to her home in Riga under KGB guard. She's being kept

---

76   The February 11, 1986, release and subsequent exchange of Anatoly ("Natan") Sharansky—a Prisoner of Zion who served nine years out of his thirteen-year sentence for so-called espionage—was the most celebrated event among the international community of human rights activists. During the years of her husband's imprisonment, Avital Sharansky—a citizen of Israel—relentlessly campaigned on her husband's behalf.

in Riga, and all attempts to reach her by phone from the west have been futile.

The more public attention outside the USSR is focused on the Zunshines—on Zachar's treatment in the camp and Tatiana's struggle to defend him—the greater are the chances that Zachar will be released, in reasonable health, at the end of his term in March 1987. Without such attention, the authorities are far more likely to extend Zachar's sentence and to arrest Tatiana as well.

March 6 marks the second anniversary of Zachar's arrest, and the completion of two-thirds of his prison term. On that day, Tatiana will hold a hunger strike in Riga to protest these latest abuses.

At Tatiana's request, on the same day, she will be joined in her action by supporters in San Francisco, Chicago, London, Jerusalem and Tel Aviv. A rally will be held at 5:00 pm—followed by an all-night vigil and hunger strike—at the Soviet Consulate in order to demonstrate international awareness of and support for her struggle. Our hope is that the vigil will encourage Soviet authorities to allow Tatiana, or others genuinely concerned with Zachar's well-being, to see him and to ensure that his treatment is legal and humane until his release on March 6, 1987.[77]

I was flattered to be portrayed that way and felt an overwhelming appreciation for what transpired in front of that consulate. I later learned something else had happened that night: two local actors— Stephanie Hunt and Bill Peters—presented a dramatic reading based on letters Zach and I had written to each other.

---

77   Tatiana Zunshine's personal archive.

On March 1, 1986, I received a notice that Zach and I had been grant-ed permission for a two-hour supervised meeting scheduled for March 11. I reread it a few times just to make sure. Then I started screaming.

"I can't believe it! Is this for real?!"

Having not seen Zach since September 1984—for seventeen months—I would have seized any opportunity to meet. Yes, this would be a short meeting in a room separated by a glass partition, but I was still grateful. Partition or no partition, I was going to see Zach!

Knowing that the surveillance would last till March 5, I planned to leave that day. I would spend a few days in Moscow and then head to Bozoy.

On the morning of March 5, at about 7:00 a.m., I left the house to start for the airport, only to see the same cars parked by the en-trance of my building. I got in a cab. We drove off, but the KGB cars were on our tail. *It was supposed to be all done with, wasn't it? Did they not get the memo?*

The cab driver let me out by the airport terminal, and I went in-side. And who do you think I ran into first thing? None other than my stalker-in-chief, KGB Lieutenant Colonel Shalaev.

"Not again!" I almost screamed. "Another lecture? I don't have time for this! I have a plane to catch."

"Nobody is catching any planes," he said. "We've got to talk."

"No, we don't!"

He took me to the airport police station—a place I'd become quite accustomed to—where he declared, "We are extending your confinement in Riga till March 10."

I couldn't believe my ears.

"You kept me from leaving," I growled. "You told me it would last till the 5th. Today is the 5th, isn't it?"

"The plan changed," he replied rather calmly.

"I don't know about *your* plan. *My* plan is to go to Irkutsk. I have a letter authorizing my meeting with my husband on the 11th. I have to be there, have to. You understand?"

"Leaving on the 10th would allow you to get there on the 11th," he said, but I jumped on him.

"How do I know you won't pull the same stunt?"

It was pointless, and I was too upset to continue. I went outside and saw the KGB cars waiting for my next move. I took a cab. I just wanted to go home and have a good cry.

For the next five days, the surveillance was as intense as ever. My house was under close supervision. I used that time to assail the KGB with written complaints, specifically about the unlawful confinement they had imposed on me.

Before I knew it, it was the morning of March 10.

Shalaev lived up to his promise. Outside my building, in that early hour of the morning, there was no hustle. The building was waking up one window at a time. It was peaceful. No agents camped out inside their cars. Nobody tailed me on the way to the airport. Better yet, nobody waited for me there. *This is what happiness feels like*, I thought, losing myself in the flow of strangers.

CHAPTER 21

MARCH MADNESS

Riga to Moscow, Moscow to Irkutsk, Irkutsk to Bozoy. I lost track of how many times I traveled there, and although the route took the same amount of time (about twenty-four hours on average), it took less and less effort.

At the headquarters in Bozoy, I showed the letter authorizing the meeting. The guard led me to the meeting room and told me to wait until they brought in Zach. Left alone, trying to calm my nerves of excitement and anticipation, I turned my attention to the room. But there wasn't much to look at. A glass partition divided it into two sections—inner and outer. The chairs for the two of us on each side of the partition faced one another. There was also a chair for a guard inside the inner section, on the left-hand side. Opposite him, on the wall, was a big round clock.

The door opens, and I see Zach accompanied by a guard. Zach is smiling, looking at me, ignoring what the guard is saying—most likely informing him of the rules. I, too, am smiling, looking at him, not quite believing what is happening, trying to keep it together, and yet my eyes are not fully cooperating, as they are tearing up. These were happy tears.

After the initial exchange that I could hardly put into words—nothing but raw emotion—we settled down and started the conversation. Rather, Zach began talking, and I began to absorb word by word, sentence by sentence.

"You should know that nothing has changed since the time we raised hell over the situation with TB," Zach said. "TB inmates are still here with us."

"You are not to talk about this," the guard interrupted, but Zach ignored him.

"Just around me, there are four TB inmates," he continued. "Honestly, it'll be a miracle if I don't catch it."

Having finished with TB, Zach went on to tell me about soap. What about it? It turned out there was a shortage of soap in the camp.

"They give you a quarter pound of soap for the whole month. That's for everything—a wash, shave, shower, laundry—everything! Can you believe it? What am I going to do with that amount? I use it all up in a week, and then what am I to do?"

Another protest from the guard. That one, too, went over Zach's head. He kept talking.

One more interruption and Zach felt he had to address it. He turned to the guard and stated flatly, "We are going to talk about what *we* choose to talk about."

Then it happened. The guard must have pressed an emergency button. The door opened, and another guard barged in. They each grabbed Zach by the wrist and dragged him out of the room. A moment later, he was gone. It happened so fast that I hardly had time to comprehend what had transpired. I remember Zach turning his head to me for a split second and saying something, but I didn't understand what he had said. I was shell-shocked.

The guard came back to inform me that they had canceled the meeting. I looked at the clock. The two-hour meeting got canceled ten minutes into it.

It took me a few minutes to regain my ability to speak. Then I went to the headquarters. *Now it is my turn to barge in*, I thought, and barge in I did—straight into the office of the head of the camp. He must have authorized breaking up the meeting, as the guard would never have done so on his own, not in our case, anyway.

"I am not asking you why this happened. I am just telling you what will happen next," I said indignantly. "I am declaring a hunger strike effective immediately. It will take place here in Bozoy and will last however long till you authorize your people to resume my meeting."

I'd said what I needed to say and left the office.

Still shaking, I parked myself on a chair in the reception area. I needed to calm down. I had hours to do so and even more hours to kill until closing time. I would then move to the hostel and continue with the hunger strike. In the morning—back to the headquarters. *Was I ready to go on indefinitely?* you might ask. I suppose I was. Now that I'd announced it, I had no choice. But did we think it through? Not this time, no. We both acted on a gut instinct. Zach protested the conversation being stifled; I was protesting it being cut short.

As time dragged on, I was wishing for the day to end so I could move to the hostel and curl up in bed. *Spending the rest of the evening in bed*, I thought, *would help preserve my strength. God knows I need it.*

The next morning, I was at the headquarters as soon as it opened, back in my chair for the second day of the hunger strike. I was not yet terribly hungry, but I knew that, as the day progressed, the hunger would set in. I had done it before and had learned this much: the first two days were always the hardest. On day three, the hunger diminished. On day four, it dissipated. But let's not go that far.

The day lived up to its expectations. It was long and tedious. I was getting ready to leave for the hostel when, minutes before 6:00 p.m., an officer came by and told me that the head of the camp wanted to see me.

"Hello. You wanted to see me? What is it?" I asked, entering his office.

"Yes, I did," he said. "Well . . . we are going to allow you and your husband to resume your meeting. First thing tomorrow."

I'll be darned! Does that mean whatever we did worked? Who would have thought? Not us, that's for sure!

"This is great news," I said to him, trying not to show too much glee in front of him, "but I do want to let you know that I will keep my hunger strike going until *after* the meeting. Just to be on the safe side, you know."

That night at the hostel, I told everybody about it. I was giddy. *It worked! It truly did!* I still went to bed early—not because I was hungry, but because I wanted tomorrow to come sooner.

When Zach and I saw each other in the meeting room the next morning, we couldn't help but burst into laughter.

"Can you imagine? It worked!"

"I can't believe it!"

"We did good!"

"We did, didn't we?"

We picked up where we'd left off. Where were we? Ah, soap! The guard didn't interfere. We went on. Having decided to resume the meeting (or somebody had decided for them), the administration must have given up on the idea of stifling our conversation. The guard sat silently, staring at the clock, allowing us to discuss every subject. Soap was just the beginning.

Zach had been feeling decent. His liver had not bothered him for a while. I asked him if he knew how he'd contracted hepatitis, and he gave me a shocking answer: "The people who administered my intravenous blood tests didn't have medical training. They were inmates."

"Inmates?" I gasped. "Administering injections? No wonder they lacked the training to sanitize needles properly!"

He hadn't been thrown into a punishment cell since he'd contracted the disease seven months ago. He was still on a special diet, but the word was that it was coming to an end.

We moved on to anti-Semitic antics. Those were gone! They stopped cold turkey. This was a clear result of our publicity campaign, and I couldn't have been prouder. I threw my hands up in the air. Yesss!

We touched on the subject of Zach's relationship with other inmates. At its core, he said, was respect for his willingness to stand up for himself and his determination to demand his rights. At times, even those who had sold him out in exchange for early release showed a little remorse. Just recently, one of them reached out to Zach and apologized: "Hope you forgive me. I did it because I saw no other way."

We went on talking till the end of our two-hour slot.

The last moments are always crushing. The guards are in. I see him get up and turn around. The guards are on both sides of him. He walks toward the door and quickly looks back, smiling. I am glued to the glass separator with my hands on it. I bang on the glass and keep saying things, hoping he hears me, watching them take him away.

After my meeting with Zach, the Union of Councils distributed a packet of information to their branches. It contained an account of my conversation with Zach. Soon, Operation Soap was launched.

WASHINGTON COMMITTEE FOR SOVIET JEWRY
8402 Freyman Dr., Chevy Chase, MD 20815

. . . SEND A BAR OF SOAP TO ZACHAR ZUNSHINE! . . .

. . . Tatiana Zunshine has requested that thousands of bars of soap be sent to Zachar in the labor camp. The Zunshines are hoping that this flood of soap will motivate the camp authorities to provide this basic hygienic item to Zachar.

You can help Zachar Zunshine by mailing a small bar of soap in an envelope, via air mail, to him. His address is: Zachar Zunshine, Uchr. 272/40, Posiolok Bazoi [Bozoy], Ekhyrit Bulagatsky Rayon, Irkutsk Oblast 666111 USSR.[78]

In my later conversations with Pam, I learned that our supporters had sent thousands of bars of soap. They flooded the camp with it, just like they had with cups and spoons. The message was similar and equally effective: *Due to the reported shortage of soap in your country, we are happy to assist in supplying soap to your camp.*

Later, Zach recalled that even though he never saw a single bar of foreign soap, there was no longer a shortage of domestic soap in the camp.

In early April, I received a letter from Zach. As colorful as ever, it contained much-needed information about his bout with hepatitis. The curious thing about it was that despite the danger of getting infected, the post-recovery regimen became somewhat of a shield, protecting him from exceptionally strenuous labor, malnutrition, and, most importantly, from being thrown into the punishment cells. I was sad to see it go.

April 6, 1986

Dear Tan'ka,

The day has just begun. The sun has risen. The radio is playing softly. Breakfast just ended.

---

78   Archives, Center for Jewish History, New York, NY.

In the canteen, the entire left half of the wall—the right half, for whatever reason, was spared of it—is occupied by a mural. From where I sit (despite the column blocking the view), only its leftmost part is visible, but I know what is depicted in the whole piece. Every time, by partially imagining it, I find in its simplicity and artlessness, in the meekness of the paints—obtained in the camp setting with much difficulty—and in the plot itself, I find something special, something which not only contributes to the secretion of gastric juices but also adds a certain mystical tone to the whole camp existence.

Almost the entire space of the mural is occupied by water. There are no waves. Nothing indicates the slightest attempt to give the piece some kind of dimension. Everything is level and flat, and on the sides are rocks and slopes, brown and green. But either because there is so much water, as flat as it is, and so few rocks and slopes, or for some other unclear reasons, you feel that in all this incompleteness, in this emptiness, there is something quite significant, and, may I suggest, fundamental. The skill here is not as much in the ability to portray but rather in the ability to under-portray, shield, and hide. Something worrisome is felt in this deliberate calmness and tranquility. As it happens, tension subsides, but you can still feel it through subtle signs and empha-sized silence. You wonder if something has happened here. Could it be that somebody drowned, or, perhaps, some action unraveled on the shore?

If this mural, say, for some unknown reason, were painted over—it would be a big loss.

Life is going on as usual. On the morning of March 29, I was summoned to the prosecutor, Vakhrushkin. He was surprisingly quiet, one could even say, preoccupied.

He came over to address my statement dated January 12, 1986, to the minister of internal affairs of the USSR. Prosecutor Vakhrushkin collected, as usual, a bunch of counterstatements. He even read one of them out loud, the one from the head of the medical unit. I asked him, "Do you want to see that what's been written here has nothing to do with reality? Let me show you. The weaving shop is a three-minute walk." And you know,

Prosecutor Vakhrushkin was so quiet and preoccupied that he didn't utter his usual, "What grounds do I have not to trust an official statement?" To my surprise, he did go to the shop and saw things with his own eyes.

On March 28, Prosecutor Vakhrushin addressed the inmates of unit #3: "Yes, there have been instances of insulting of ethnic dignity in your unit. A carelessly thrown word can be hurtful." So now, in a report to the higher-ups, he can state that having visited an on-site location, he has taken all measures needed: questions clarified and shortcomings eliminated.

On March 14, exactly four months after my discharge from the hospital, they summoned me to the medical unit to meet the head of the Infectious Diseases Department. He checked me out and stated that my liver was still in place, which I consider a good thing. And then it turns out that what I had on March 14 was a formal exam and that they no longer consider me a hepatitis patient. Consequently, on April 1, they took me off a special diet and canceled an extensive medical examination slated for mid-May.

I received greetings from one guy from the transitional prison in Irkutsk; somebody who had seen him there brought back a hello for me. Undoubtedly, this was Ari Volvovsky, in the process of etap, on the way to Yakutsk. I was told he was not thin, did not look sick, wore civilian clothes, and had a beard. He was of medium stature and prayed before meals.

Greetings and best wishes to him and to all and everywhere.

Z.[79]

Now that Zach has mentioned Ari Volvovsky incidentally passing through the same transitional prison he went through, let me talk about a circle of friends I acquired through my activities on behalf of Zach.

---

79   Tatiana Zunshine's personal archive.

First, let me spotlight the families of the Jewish prisoners of conscience who selflessly supported each other in their mutual struggles. I was a part of that group, lending a helping hand to other wives while feeding off of theirs. These families included Ari (mentioned in Zach's letter) and Mila Volvovsky, Dina Zisserman and Vladimir Brodsky, Natasha Ratner and Alexei Magarik, Evgeny and Irina Lein, Vladimir and Anya Lifshitz, Roald and Galina Zelichenok, and others.

In Riga, with Sasha Balter gone, my new friends Cooper and Fanya assumed his role and provided me with their invaluable support. In Leningrad, with Yakov Gorodetsky gone, his friend, Grisha Vasserman, took over Yakov's role as my mentor. That, too, was of tremendous help. Other friends extended their helping hand as well. These were Nadezhda Fradkova, Boris Vainerman, and his wife, Tanya, to name a few.

When Yakov Gorodetsky left, my focus inevitably shifted to Moscow. While spending most of my time with Dina Zisserman and Olga Medvedkov, I also hung out with Natasha Ratner, whose husband, Alexei Magarik, would soon be arrested and sentenced to a three-year term for so-called drug possession. In addition, my circle included a group of Jewish refuseniks willing to go above and beyond to help us—the prisoners' wives—pursue our husbands' freedom. These were Natasha Beckman, Alla and Lev Sud, Alla and Leonid Praisman, Sasha Murinson, Misha Shipov, Evgeny Briskin, Lev and Katya Gorodetsky, Ira Soschina, Inna Badanova, and Natasha Khassina.

Had I not had this indispensable support system, life—hard as it was—would have been unbearable. These people were my lifeline, for which I am forever grateful.

Another April 20 was coming up. Another birthday for Zach spent behind bars. This one was going to be his thirty-fifth. In my conversations with Pam, I mentioned my intention to go to Bozoy, just like

I had on April 20 the previous year. Her office immediately issued a press release:

FROM CHICAGO ACTION / APRIL 14, 1986

Zachar Zunshine's (POC[80]) birthday is April 20 and Tatiana plans to go to Irkutsk to pass him some flowers, as Katherine [sic] Porter tried to do on March 6. She asked that she receive support for her actions by having both flowers and telegrams and letters sent to the Soviet Embassy with birthday greetings for Zachar. She also requests that medicine to prevent TB be brought to the Soviet Embassy in the name of Zachar.[81]

On Monday, April 21, the 1986 Call to Conscience Vigil took place on the floor of the US House of Representatives. Briefed by Pam Cohen and Marillyn Tallman, our friend Representative John Porter made the following statement.

On the Floor of the US House of Representatives—John E. Porter (R-IL).

April 21, 1986

Mr. Speaker, it is an honor for me to participate in this year's call to conscience vigil. This annual event reinforces the congressional commitment to working on behalf of the hundreds of thousands of Soviet Jews who desire to emigrate to Israel but cannot. However, despite the optimism that surrounded the atmosphere in Geneva and the symbolic presummit gestures, and even despite the recent release of Anatoly Scharansky, the overall situation for Jews living in the Soviet Union remains dismal. Monthly emigration levels are very bleak and

---

80   Prisoner of conscience.

81   Archives, Center for Jewish History, New York, NY.

harassment of people expressing their religious beliefs is a constant occurrence.

I would like to, once again, call my colleagues' attention to the problems facing Tatiana and Zachar Zunshine. The Zunshines first applied to emigrate to Israel in 1981. Their nightmare began on March 6, 1984, when Zachar began serving his 3 year sentence for alleged crimes committed against the Soviet state. Mr. Speaker, the only crime Zachar committed was that he expressed a desire to leave the Soviet Union and go with his wife to live in Israel . . .

Tatiana is also regularly harassed and threatened by the Soviet authorities. Earlier this year, she was isolated from her Western contact and her travel within the Soviet Union was restricted. Later this week Tatiana will attempt to visit Zachar, on his birthday, but this simple request will no doubt cause the officials of the camp some problems.

The situation facing Tatiana and Zachar Zunshine reminds us that we must continue to join in efforts with the brave individuals of the Soviet Union, who are fighting for their freedom and survival every day . . .[82]

---

82 Tatiana Zunshine's personal archive.

CHAPTER 22

BIRTHDAY ADVENTURE

On Sunday, April 20, I was back in Bozoy.

The weather was warm—between 60°F and 65°F. The sun was timid, lacking the intensity of the summer months. I stood there, turning my face to the sun, feeling its gentle brushstrokes against my skin. For a moment, I almost forgot where I was. Spring had made it here, giving the dreadful place the little color it so badly needed. The tree buds swelled from the inside; the birds chirped vigorously. A new circle of life swept in, and with it came a renewed sense of hope.

The recently installed head of the camp, Mr. Mouzh, passed by, bringing me back to reality. He was in a hurry, walking toward the headquarters with a few pieces of luggage in his hands. *Must have been about to leave town*, I thought. I followed him for a few steps, initiating a conversation.

"Any chance I could see you today?" I asked, just in case.

"No." That's all he said. Whether he was leaving or not, his whole demeanor screamed reluctance to engage.

That soap campaign must have gotten under his skin, I thought, letting him get away from me.

Then I went to the central gate.

At the gate, about ten inmates were painting the fence under the supervision of two escorts. I stood there, watching. From a distance, dressed in asphalt-gray quilted jackets, with their heads shaved, they were hard to tell apart. Although I was out of their earshot, I could still see what they were doing. A few minutes passed, then one of them shouted, "Did you come for Zach?"

"Yes!" I shouted back. "Do you know him?"

"Who *doesn't* know him?"

I expected the escorts to interfere, but they didn't. The guy must have had some standing among the guards. Sensing that he would not get in trouble for talking to me, I continued.

"Please tell him I'm here."

"Will do."

"How is he? Is he healthy?"

"Seems to be."

"Not in the punishment cell, I hope?"

"Nope, not right now." Then he added, "He probably already knows you are here and is standing on the other side of the gate."

I later found out he was right. Zach stood there for two hours, just like I did.

While hanging by the gate, I spent time analyzing the situation. The head of the camp, Mr. Mouzh, seemed set on avoiding any interaction with me. And he was not alone. I spotted two officers walking from the headquarters toward the gate, only to see them suddenly give a wide berth to the area where I was standing.

Why were they trying to avoid me? The explanation is twofold.

The information leak remained an open wound. It just wouldn't heal. According to Zach, the camp administration was "plowing the ground with their noses," looking for a hole to plug. But they hadn't found it. Despite their effort, the leaks persisted, exposing violations steadily. That brought in scrutiny the administration desperately tried to avoid. And that, in turn, caused notable heads to roll. Take the former head of the camp, Mr. Stepanenko. Once the biggest fish in a small pond, he didn't just lose his job; he lost it all. He had been thrown out of his eight-room house, which—although made entirely of wood—was the best in Bozoy. And who, you might ask, lived in that house now? The new head, Mr. Mouzh.

While Zach leaked information via letters, I did my part. Traveling to Bozoy and having countless conversations with the locals was invaluable; there was nothing the administration could do to stop it. What they, perhaps, were trying to limit were my meetings with camp officials. For them, meeting me was like twisting a knife in their wound. But for me? It was an opportunity to *work* them into something they didn't want to do. Those encounters served me just right. How many times did they produce quite unexpected—but welcome—results? How many times have I benefited from human beings' inability to control a slip of the tongue? More than I could count. (A subsequent conversation with a camp official at the headquarters would illustrate that.)

No wonder they were reluctant to see me.

The head of security came by and asked why I was standing there.

"You being here won't help him," he said.

"It won't make things worse either," I responded. "Will it?"

"Well . . . then . . . carry on if you choose to."

We were approaching two hours when an off-putting character came by. Judging by the uniform, he was an unescorted inmate. Judging by the vibe he gave out, he had achieved this position by snitching his way up. He was dressed to a tee—in a Gulag-y way—wearing a new quilted jacket, a new uniform, and shiny boots. His round face revealed the fact that he was well-fed.

"Are you Zach's wife?" he asked me.

I didn't know his game and wouldn't have played it anyway. There was something inexplicably repellent about the man, enough for me to want to get away, and I did.

At the headquarters, I asked for the officer on duty. And who do you think that was? One of the two officers who—just a few hours earlier—had been trying to avoid me like the plague. His name was Plashalin.

Entering his office, I saw a man with a nervous but piercing gaze. At that moment, I wished the appeasement phase was still on. *This guy*, I predicted, *is going to sing a different tune.*

He, in fact, did not want to sing any tune at all.

"Has the administration isolated the TB inmates from the rest?" I asked.

He mumbled something incoherent.

"How much soap does the administration provide for the inmates?" More mumbling.

I asked him about living conditions, explanatory notes, our private meetings (or rather, the lack of them), and scores of other questions. I got nothing.

Finally, I said, "You can refuse to answer my questions all you want, but please know that you will hear the same questions from our supporters on the other side of the pond."

And that's when he broke the pattern and responded quite candidly.

"I don't want to give you any information as I don't want to get on the radar of your dear Pamela."

Ha! My dear Pamela! Not only did he know who she was, he also admitted his unwillingness to get on her radar. I found it amusing and somewhat satisfying. And, by the way, that's what I meant by their inability to control a slip of the tongue. He gave me a sound bite I knew I could use.

He went on. "How long are you gonna worry about your husband? Don't be so worried about him all the time!"

"Say you get arrested, convicted, and sent away to do hard labor," I responded rhetorically. "Would you wish for your wife not to worry?"

"I will not get arrested," he retorted. "Instead, I will get shot." (Another sound bite.)

He must have realized he'd said too much and visibly shut down.

At that point, I knew I wouldn't get more out of him. There was no upside to continuing.

Back in the hostel, a chance conversation with the wife of an inmate opened up an opportunity for a major spill of information. She told me her husband was scheduled for release the next morning. Better yet, he happened to have served his time in the same unit as Zach. What an unbelievable stroke of luck that was, wasn't it? She offered me a chance to talk to her husband, and I seized it. A conversation with him would overshadow any conversation I could have had with the camp administration.

The next morning, we stood in the headquarters, waiting for her husband to emerge from behind the doors. Finally, he did, accompanied by an officer. The officer told them to wait for the release of the paperwork. Once the officer had left, the wife introduced me.

Hoping to beat the time before his papers arrived, I let the guy do all the talking. He talked, and I listened, turning myself into a sponge, absorbing every bit of information he shared.

"They have isolated TB inmates from the rest of us," he said. "Those got transferred to a separate unit."

I wanted to squeal with excitement but was afraid to distract him. I let him continue.

The orderlies, Levashov and Biryukov—the main protagonists of the anti-Semitic games—were released on parole. "They 'earned' it by writing denunciations of Zach," the man said. "Their spot is now taken by the world's biggest jackass—Igor Stepanov. This one exceeds all expectations. A total wretch."

"And don't forget the head of the unit, Officer Baranov," the man added, "another character to watch."

The camp was considered "red." There were 670 inmates in total. Except for ten to fifteen, everyone was a collaborator, a.k.a. "red."

The situation around Zach was tense. Those working toward parole, especially Stepanov, scribbled denunciations against him.

There was a kiosk on the campgrounds where inmates were allowed to buy snacks using the money they had earned. But Stepanov, whose job was to ensure the inmates got paid (a maximum of seven rubles[83] a month), wouldn't sign the work orders. That piece of crap!

"The guys are not able to get any money. Not even three rubles a month," the man said. Then he added, "Could you please take care of it?"

Is this what they think of me? That I can "take care" of things? I was flattered, and I said I would certainly try. I would include the money situation in the next round of complaints.

We got lucky. A few people passed by, but nobody interfered until the head of the Regime Department, Urmaev, walked in on us and ordered the guy into his office. He went in but left the door slightly open, and we could hear Urmaev questioning him: "What were you talking to her about?" The guy made excuses, saying we were chatting, nothing serious. Urmaev handed him his release papers, and, at that point, the couple left.

I was on the way back to the hostel when the same character from the day before reappeared, the one with the round face. This time, he suggested that I write a letter to Zach, and he would pass it on. On his quilted jacket, the name tag read IGOR STEPANOV. Now I knew who he was—"the world's biggest jackass." I said, "No thanks," and hurried up.

---

83 At the time, equivalent to about seven dollars.

On the way home, I decided to stay in Moscow for a few extra days. On April 28, a special Passover Seder was going to take place there, with the wives and relatives of political prisoners participating.

I wanted to be a part of it, but it wasn't in my stars.

What messed up my plans was yet another abduction. How many of those would I have to live through? Too many to count. Their details might vary, but the essence remained the same: having been dispatched to Moscow, Riga's KGB officer, the all-too-familiar First Lieutenant Narnitsky, would apprehend me and bring me back to Riga.

This abduction was no different from the earlier one in February, and, therefore, I will spare you the details. But one detail I want to mention is the hilarious behavior of my friend Dina, who, once again, happened to witness it. What did she do when the KGB agents descended upon us? Appealing to a few bystanders, she yelled, "Comrades! Help! Help!" Narnitsky couldn't help but snarl, "They are not *your* comrades!" I couldn't help but laugh. What did Dina do? She tried to get inside the car I was being shoved in, and it took the agents an effort to peel her away from it.

While escorting me back to Riga, Narnitsky stole my passport. He asked for it to get me through airport security and never returned it. Upon arrival at Riga Airport, he simply disappeared. This was not the first time he pulled that stunt, making me fight hard to get my passport back.

I am not gonna let him get away with it this time, I thought, and went straight to the airport's police station.

"I am here to report a robbery and to press charges against a certain individual," I said to the officer on duty, Captain Maidan.

"What happened? Who robbed you?" he asked.

"The first lieutenant of Riga's KGB, named Narnitsky." As I was saying those words, I noticed a question mark appear on the captain's face, but I ignored it and continued. "This is a repeat offense, and I will not let it slide this time around. I am here to press charges against him. Please give me a pen and paper to make a written statement."

I could tell that the police officer wasn't sure how to react. Had he known anything about me, he would have opened his door and asked me to leave. But he didn't. He gave me pen and paper, and I wrote a statement detailing Narnitsky's actions. I left one copy with him and sent two others to the prosecutors general of Latvia and the entire USSR. Lastly, I asked Pam to pass it on to the attorney David Feuer, who, as a volunteer with the Chicago Action for Soviet Jewry Legal Association, kindly agreed to represent me.

In the last days of April, I received a letter from Zach.

April 27, 1986

Dear Tan'ka,

On April 20, last Sunday, when I woke up in the morning, I said to myself everything you used to say to me on such an occasion.[84] It was a clear day, and I got outside—they were repainting the walls inside the unit—and began to write you a letter. And then they came, and they told me,[85] and it completely knocked me out of my thoughts, and I could no longer write anything, so I decided to postpone this letter until next Sunday.

My unit was taken over by a first lieutenant with the last name of Baranov. He is still young, and who, in his youth, doesn't want to prove himself? A few days ago, right after the evening roll call, he sent me to the office of the head of the camp, showed

---

84 Zach's birthday.

85 They came and told Zach that I was there outside the gate.

up himself, plopped in a chair, and reported: "Inmate Zunshine ignores the marching order, does not raise his leg high enough."

From his facial expression and uncontrollably twitching eyes, it became increasingly clear that he was no longer satisfied with just amusing himself, that more was needed or expected, and that he would be offended if I did not play along, mumble all sorts of excuses, and stand with my head down, putting on the airs of someone overwhelmed with repentance.

It also turned out that my stance was not up to par—my heels were not together, and my toes were not apart. And the head of the camp began lecturing me on how I was supposed to stand in front of them.

I don't remember where I read this—whether it was Confucius or some other smart guy—but the gist is that too many people are being driven by ordinary stupidity and that their grand idea of trying to realign my stance has no chance of succeeding.

The same evening, in my complaint #40 (I have been numbering everything for a while now so that they don't throw it away), I wrote to the head of the camp that the usual and most favorite pastime of the first lieutenant with the last name of Baranov fits into Article #206, Part 2 of the Criminal Code of the Russian Federation: disorderly conduct of a particularly impudent and cynical character. Every time and everywhere, including regular roll calls, the first lieutenant with the last name Baranov gets off by choosing one of the inmates and, with the apparent goal of demonstrating his might, begins to spray insults, flavoring them with swearing and sexual undertones. If ever again—I wrote—I witness such actions, I will not remain silent and will act accordingly.[86]

In mid-April, Literaturka[87] published an essay by O. Tchaikovskaya about professional liars. It would be helpful for you, Tan'ka, to read it so that you best understand the work of their apparatus.

---

86   That is, he would set in action a lawsuit against Baranov under Article #206, part 2 of the criminal code of the Russian Federation.

87   The slang name for newspaper *Literature*.

I always knew that by keeping silent about some essential elements of the situation, by placing the accents in a certain way, one could—and would be able to—create a picture directly opposite to reality. But only when they put me in jail in Riga did I comprehend the full depth of how shameless their lies could be.

One of the answers from the Medical Department stated that the bed linens are changed here every seven days. In fact, the linens are being changed every two weeks, while a shower is allowed once every nine days. I am mentioning this to emphasize that I would not be surprised to see an answer from the Medical Department stating that the change of linens takes place daily.

A washbasin was installed in the weaving shop not so long ago, and in mid-April, the TB inmates were transferred to another unit.

To everyone, everywhere, my personal regards and best wishes for Pesach.

Z.[88]

I had heard about First Lieutenant Baranov from the newly released inmate I spoke with in Bozoy a week earlier. Now I knew I needed to pay special attention to him, as somebody eager to "prove himself" was capable of causing a lot of damage. Another detail that needed my attention was the cruelty of allowing inmates to shower only once every nine days. *More proof of them treating people like animals*, I thought. *One more hurdle to overcome.*

And then there were wins to celebrate. The fact that a washbasin had been installed in the weaving shop might not have sounded like a big deal, but it was. In fact, every deal was a big deal. But the biggest deal of all was the removal of TB inmates. That wouldn't have happened without us banging our heads against the wall, so to speak.

---

88   Tatiana Zunshine's personal archive.

CHAPTER 23

CAN YOU IMAGINE

It had been a few weeks since KGB officer Narnitsky disappeared from Riga's airport, carrying away my passport. I was pushing for formal charges against him when a postcard arrived inviting me to the police station to reclaim my passport. I would have ignored any other pretext to lure me into the police station, but not this one.

To no one's surprise, instead of a police officer, I was greeted at the station by the KGB Lieutenant Colonel Shalaev. I rolled my eyes just at the sight of him. *What is it that he wants from me now?* Little did I know that this would be one of the most significant conversations I'd ever have.

"Here is your passport back," he said, handing it to me. "You can now stop fussing about it."

"Not so fast," I warned him, accepting the passport. "The crime has still been committed, regardless of the fact that—"

He stopped me with an outstretched arm. "Drop it," he said. "And listen to me."

What happened next was nothing short of remarkable.

"It has been a tug of war between us for the last two years or so," he said. "I am offering you a deal. You can maintain your position, and we will maintain ours. But if you stop attacking *us*, we will stop attacking *you*."

I stared at him for a few seconds, wondering if I had gone mad and only imagined what he had said.

"What did you just say?" I asked him. "If I stop attacking you, you'll stop attacking me?"

"That's right."

I couldn't help but burst into laughter.

"You are basically offering me a cease-fire, is that right?" I asked, trying to suppress my laughter.

"Call it whatever you want."

It was time to get serious, and I did.

"Here is my response," I said to him. "You are criminals. And by 'you,' I mean your institution. You committed crimes against my husband when you arrested him for no reason whatsoever and when you convicted him and sentenced him to three years of hard labor. You are committing crime after crime against him while he is serving his term. And he is not alone. The same goes for all the other prisoners of conscience. So, to answer your offer, I do not make deals with criminals. Thank you for thinking of me, but I'll pass."

"This is it!" he shouted, startling me. He banged the table with his palm while rising out of the chair and then leaned forward. "We are through with you! You've gone over the limit! We are DONE!"

Seeing him lose his cool and go red in the face, I wondered: *What did he think I was gonna say?*

The threats continued, but they didn't matter to me. As far as I was concerned, this might have been the most extraordinary encounter with the KGB I'd ever had. I stopped listening to him. Instead, I was talking to myself: *They offered you a cease-fire. How about that?* Years later, I am still wearing it as a badge of honor.

In October 1985, before my friend Sasha left, we came up with an open letter—a plea for help. It was designed for wide circulation and covered the highlights of what had happened to Zach in the course of his incarceration. Titled "Can You Imagine," this became my signature letter.

CAN YOU IMAGINE

Can you imagine being arrested and thrown behind bars simply for your desire to leave the country you were born in?

Can you imagine being tried behind closed doors, with no legal defense, doomed for conviction for a crime you didn't commit?

Can you imagine being ill yet deprived of basic medical care, left to wallow in sweat and fever on a bug-infested mattress in a cramped prison cell?

Can you imagine having to resort to a hunger strike of protest just to obtain a few Aspirin to squash your raging fever?

Can you imagine being forced to rot in an unheated, unlit, and unventilated special security ward, also known as a punishment cell, sack, and coffin?

Can you imagine, after a term in a punishment cell, daylight cutting into your eyes like a sharp-bladed knife?

Can you imagine your willpower and self-control tested with the kicks of the boots, your ribs cracking under their blows?

Can you imagine having to drink water from radiators or take cold showers in a harsh Siberian climate?

Can you imagine having to use one spoon between you and four other cellmates?

Can you imagine being forced to work under such conditions when you are just one step away from wearing a high-voltage electricity cable around your neck like a bow tie?

Can you imagine this happening to you day after day, hour after hour, minute after minute?

You must imagine all this. And once you imagine it, you will not be able to disregard my plea for help for my husband, Zachar Zunshine, imprisoned on trumped-up charges of defamation of the Soviet state, as you would agree with me that at stake is his honor, dignity, and life itself.[89]

I consider this the most successful letter Sasha and I have ever written. Concise but punchy, it had the power of a pamphlet, and I am happy to report that it served its purpose. It landed in many people's hands, turning them into our supporters. One of those people was a true legend, French actor and singer Yves Montand.

Discovered in the mid-1940s, Yves Montand shot to stardom and became the French version of Frank Sinatra, as renowned in French music as he was in cinema. In the United States, his fame was boosted by his well-publicized 1960 affair with Marilyn Monroe. And how did he get involved with us? I learned he had come across the "Can You Imagine" letter and was moved enough to take up our case. The next thing I knew was that, on the eve of the second anniversary of Zach's imprisonment, Montand had appeared on French TV, publicizing our case and appealing to the Russian authorities for Zach's immediate release.

I later came across a letter Pam had sent to Yves Montand, thanking him for his involvement.

To: Mr. Yves Montand
Place Dauphine
74000 Paris
FRANCE

89   Tatiana Zunshine's personal archive.

Dear Mr. Montand:

I am writing to you with regard to Tatiana Zunshine with whom I have been in direct contact since the day after her husband's arrest. As Co-Chairman for Chicago Action for Soviet Jewry and as Vice President of the Union of Councils for Soviet Jews, an international membership organization, I am vitally interested in the support you have provided for Zachar Zunshine in particular, and the human rights issue in general.

I have been given to understand that you have published their case on European television. We are deeply encouraged by your commitment and determination. I am anxious to convey your interest, personally, to Tatiana; as well as to bring to you, consistently, the most recent news from each of them.

I am enclosing for your information, the documentation of Zachar's case which we have reproduced based on his letters.

Please let us know in what way we can best be of help to you in your very remarkable efforts.

Sincerely,

Pamela B. Cohen,
Co-Chairman, Chicago Action for Soviet Jewry
Vice President, Union of Councils for Soviet Jews[90]

Yves Montand's involvement culminated in June 1986 when he went to Israel to participate in a Jerusalem rally on behalf of Soviet Jewry. The rally took place on June 2. In his speech, delivered by the walls of the Old City, Montand talked about his solidarity with Jewish prisoners of conscience and, specifically, with Zachar Zunshine. On June 6, a full-page interview appeared in a Russian-language Israeli newspaper called *Our Country*. Montand, then sixty-four, talked about his aspirations for the presidency of France, his love for his wife of thirty-six years, actress Simone Signoret, his grief at losing her the

---

90   Archives, Center for Jewish History, New York, NY.

previous year, his relationship with Israel, and scores of other topics. Among them, once again, was his support of Zach.

June 6, 1986

... Not only do I want to talk about it, I want to do something about it. Like, to go to Oslo with my friend Elie Wiesel[91] to support Zachar Zunshine. To me, it's very important ... Or, to come to Israel and show my solidarity with him ...

The Soviet rulers pursued the signing of the human rights accords. Once they sign them—they do not fulfill them. But worse: in a conversation with the former Soviet ruler (not with Andropov, but with the one who was after him—the sick one[92]) he reportedly said: "Human rights? I don't give a damn about them!" And when Mitterrand courageously tried to talk to him about Sakharov's[93] plight, he ridiculed our president ...

However, I am only human and have my own life. I only do what I can get my hands on. And when I received a letter from Zachar Zunshine's wife, I publicly read it in Oslo. "Can You Imagine . . ." This is the leitmotif of her letter. "Imagine what my husband has to endure 24:00 a day . . . If you can't put yourself in his shoes, so be it . . . But if you can, please do something about it . . ."[94]

I carry an immeasurable sense of gratitude for Yves Montand's involvement in our campaign. Once the biggest fan of his talent as a singer and actor, I am now in awe of him as a human being. He will forever have a place in my heart.

---

91   Author and future Nobel Peace Prize winner.

92   Yves Montand refers to President Chernenko.

93   Andrei Sakharov, an exiled prominent nuclear physicist, dissident, and Nobel Prize winner.

94   Tatiana Zunshine's personal archive.

CHAPTER 24

DOGS TO THE RESCUE

Back home, I received notification that Zach and I would be allowed another two-hour meeting. Overjoyed, yet reserving a grain of caution based on my previous experience—the meeting in March had been interrupted after ten minutes, followed by a hunger strike, and only then resumed for the full allotted time—I knew I had to prepare for the worst-case scenario. I needed to secure Pam's support before I went to Bozoy.

I happened to possess a direct phone number for the prosecutor general of the Irkutsk region and was ready to use it as my weapon. I had the phone numbers of other functionaries in the prosecutor's office as well. I gave them all to Pam and told her, "If and when you receive a go-ahead from me, please have our supporters call these numbers in solidarity with me. The more phone calls we generate, the better. Let their phones ring off the hook!" For fear of our conversation being bugged, I did not give her the details of how I would deliver the "go-ahead" to her.

A friend of mine, a refusenik from Leningrad, Boris Vainerman, volunteered to accompany me on the trip. He would be the one to deliver the go-ahead. If there were any problems with our meeting, whether it was interrupted or not allowed at all, Boris would send a telegram to a refusenik friend of his in Leningrad. Regardless of the text (for example, "Arrived safely, all is well"), just the fact of receiving the telegram would mean: "Let Pamela know to initiate a storm of phone calls."

Boris and I flew to Irkutsk and headed to Bozoy, arriving on June 4. At the headquarters, I presented the letter authorizing the meeting.

"You are gonna have to wait," the officer on duty said, feeding my suspicion that something was cooking.

The administration dragged their feet for a couple of hours until they declared that the meeting could not possibly occur because Zach was serving an eleven-day term in a punishment cell, which began on May 31 and would end on June 11.

I knew it. I just knew it! Over the past few years, I had developed an intuition that hardly ever failed me. This time, in particular, I knew something was fishy about it. I could smell it!

They must have expected me to storm into some office, as usual, and start demanding things, but that wasn't my plan. My plan was to leave. (This must have surprised everyone, and that, too, was part of the plan. It's good to throw them off once in a while; the less they can read you, the better.)

By the time Boris and I were back in Irkutsk, the workday was ending. I stayed in the hotel while Boris went out to send the telegram. Tomorrow would be the start of a new battle.

The next day, June 5, I went to the prosecutor's office in Irkutsk and took a seat in the reception area. I asked the prosecutor general's secretary to let him know I was there to stage a sit-in strike to protest the denial of the supervised meeting. I offered her a copy of the letter authorizing the meeting and detailed the administration's actions resulting in this denial.

"I will be here day after day until my husband and I get our meeting," I added. "Please let the prosecutor know. Also, while you are at it, please let him know that our supporters from the United States are about to start calling and demanding our right to the meeting. I gave them the numbers of various people here in this office. Be prepared for a storm of phone calls."

I knew this was going to be an uphill battle. Zach was serving time in the punishment cell. What could they possibly do to satisfy my demands? Release him ahead of time? Cut his term short so that they could give us a meeting? *C'mon*, I said to myself, *be realistic*. They would much rather remove me from the premises by giving me a fifteen-day jail term for disorderly conduct. That option put me at the mercy of our supporters—the more phone calls they made, the less chance I had of being thrown in jail. As for a third option, I didn't see it. What else could they do? I was willing to find out.

I was there for hours. Time crawled, just as it had on every other similar occasion. The only entertainment I had was observing employees coming into the reception area. The way they looked at me, I swear, they must have made up an excuse to go there. For them, this was entertainment as well.

More hours passed, and the workday was coming to an end. On my side, it felt anticlimactic. Not much was happening. The critical part was what—if anything—was happening inside those offices. Did their phones ring off the hook the whole day long? Did they have to answer to our supporters? Did that make any difference? I was in the dark about it.

Meanwhile, as I was sitting in the prosecutor's office, there was a flurry of activity in the Union of Councils for Soviet Jews. In a memorandum to UCSJ member councils, the Chicago branch included the following news release:

FROM CHICAGO ACTION / JUNE 5, 1986

Zachar Zunshine's (POC)[95] wife, Tatiana, is in Irkutsk attempting to have a meeting with Zachar. The camp administration has denied the meeting and informed her that Zachar was placed in a punishment cell. In response, Tatiana went on a sit-down strike in front of the Irkutsk prosecutor's office until she can meet Zachar. Telegrams should be sent questioning why Zachar is in a punishment cell and protesting the denial of the promised meeting between Tatiana and Zachar. The address of the Irkutsk prosecutor:

Prosecutor of the Irkutsk Region
Mr. Rechkoff
Proletarskaya Street 10
Irkutsk, RSFSR, USSR[96]

Following the UCSJ's recommendations, US representative John R. Miller, a Republican from the state of Washington and an advocate for human rights in the Soviet Union, sent the following letter to Prosecutor Rechkoff.

Congress of the United States
House of Representatives
Washington, D.C. 20515

June 5, 1986

Prosecutor Irkutsk Region Mr. Rechkoff
Proletarskaya Street 10
Irkutsk RSFSR USSR

Dear Mr. Prosecutor:

---

95   Prisoner of conscience.

96   Archives, Center for Jewish History, New York, NY.

I am writing to inquire why prisoner Zachar Zunshine has been put into isolation. I am concerned about his well-being and would like an immediate response from you.

I understand that Mrs. Zunshine was granted a visit with Zachar and that when she arrived at the camp, she was denied the visit. I protest such treatment of Mrs. Zunshine.

I look forward to your immediate reply.

Yours truly,

John Miller
Member of Congress[97]

The next morning, I was back in my seat at the prosecutor's office. By then, Boris had already left, making me promise to call him in Leningrad every night. He would pass my information on to Pam.

Halfway through the day, the secretary came out of the office with a piece of paper in her hands; she handed it to me.

"What is it?" I asked, glancing at the paper. Before I realized what it was, she answered: "Newly signed authorization for your meeting with your husband tomorrow, June 7, at 7:00 p.m."

Stunned, I looked at the paper to make sure it did say that, and yes, there it was: "June 7, at 7:00 p.m." This was the best possible outcome. I simply couldn't believe it!

"But wait a minute!" It dawned on me. "He is in the punishment cell!"

"It's all in there," she said, pointing at the paper. "A decision has been made to limit his term to what he's already served and to allow the meeting."

Hallelujah! They were cutting Zach's punishment short just to give us the meeting. Now *that* was a cause for celebration! *That* could have only happened in my wildest dreams!

---

97 Archives, Center for Jewish History, New York, NY.

I thanked the secretary and hurried out of the office. I needed to let Boris know what had just transpired so he could report it to Pam. My heart was full of gratitude for her, the Union of Councils, and all our friends and supporters, without whom we would not have achieved this remarkable result.

Around 7:00 p.m. the next day, I arrived at the Bozoy headquarters. A guard took me to the meeting room. It was the same room as before, of which I had already studied every inch. I had been there for a few minutes when a man came in and took the chair by the wall on the inner side of the room. He introduced himself as an officer from the Operative Department.[98] He would be present at the meeting, he said. Back in March, that chair was occupied by an anonymous guard. *I hope he's not here in an attempt to stifle our conversation; not again*, crossed my mind.

Then the door opened, and Zach stepped in, accompanied by two guards. He was smiling, but I couldn't help but notice he was visibly shaking.

"What happened? Why are you shaking?" I yelled, banging my hands on the glass partition.

"Freaking punishment cell, that's what happened," Zach said, settling in his chair. "It was pure torture. No other way to describe it. Torture by cold."

"Animals!" I exclaimed angrily. "What animals!"

"They got me out of there this morning. Gave me a hot shower —all because they didn't want you to see me like this. But that didn't do squat. Sometimes the shaking lasts for days, but it'll go away eventually," Zach added. "But how in the world did you get me out of there?"

---

98   An arm of the KGB.

I described the events of the last two days to him, and it cheered him up immensely.

"This is remarkable, simply remarkable!" he said, laughing. "You, my dear Tan'ka, have officially kicked ass. And hats off to Pam and everybody else involved. Tell them I send my very best."

We went back to torture by cold, as I needed to know all about it. To beat the cold, Zach told me, he had to get creative. He asked the guards to bring in newspapers, and the "nicer ones" did. He used the newsprint pages to wrap his feet. That helped a bit, but not much. After the first two days in that cell, with the cold overpowering his body, he had to resort to a hunger strike of protest. As a "solution," the administration put several inmates in the cell with him. Why? So that they could cling to one another and warm each other up.

"You cannot make these things up even if you try," Zach added. "That was their solution? I actually felt guilty for those guys suffering because of me."

While Zach was saying this, I looked at the officer in attendance. Could it possibly cost us the meeting? The guy showed no emotion, looking straight ahead at the opposite wall.

The next revelation was nothing short of a bombshell.

The hunger in the camp was rampant. The daily food ration, so minuscule it amounted to a whooping fifty kopeks worth of food,[99] served only as an appetizer for the herd of grown men, leaving them perpetually hungry. Zach said his body had adjusted—his stomach must have shrunk—and he no longer felt the hunger. But that was not the case for the rest of them. How did those inmates overcome the lack of food? By resorting to eating . . . dogs!

"Eating . . . WHAT?" I almost jumped out of my chair.

"Those savages would eat anything that moves or makes sound," Zach said. "But it's not all their fault. The hunger here is out of control."

---

99   At the time, equivalent to about fifty cents.

"How? How do they get hold of the dogs? Who brings them in?"

"The guards do. They catch stray dogs and sell them to the inmates."

I again looked over at the officer. He was still staring at the wall. *If that disclosure doesn't bring our meeting to an end*, I thought, *nothing will.*

But there was more. In desperation, the inmates would fight each other over a dog. One would claim it was his, while others challenged him. To prevent the fights, the guards had started attaching the inmate's name to the dog's hind leg.

We moved on from dogs to the matter of beatings by the camp administration. These were rampant. They hadn't laid their hands on Zach since his first day in the camp in September 1984, but almost everyone else had been a victim. There was even a term for it—to get beaten up was to get "rejuvenated."

Zach asked me about things at home, and I told him all about the campaign, the support we were getting, the presence of the KGB, and the constant bumping heads with KGB Lieutenant Colonel Shalaev. I mentioned our latest encounter and his offer of a cease-fire. Zach couldn't get over it. He just couldn't stop laughing, and I joined in.

"He asked you to stop attacking them, and then they won't attack you?" he marveled. "And you shut him down. How did he think you were gonna respond?"

"I have no idea!"

The tears of laughter were still in my eyes when we began to say goodbyes. Good tears turned into sad ones, and that was inevitable. I asked him to be careful, and he promised he would. He asked me the same, and I said I would, too. I would also raise hell about dogs, torture by cold, and other matters.

The cruelty of being separated by a glass wall with no ability to touch, hug, and kiss goodbye is never as evident as in those last minutes. It breaks your heart and leaves it bleeding for days on end.

Upon my return to Riga, I got in touch with Pam. In my conversation with her, I relived every detail of my trip—my sit-in strike and the administration's decision to cut short Zach's confinement to give us the meeting. I thanked her from the bottom of my heart and emphasized that, without their incredible support, I might not have been talking to her right now. I, most likely, would have ended up in the county jail, charged with disorderly conduct. I also told her about torture by cold, hunger, dogs, and everything else I had learned from Zach. Soon, a press release was disseminated among the branches.

TORTURE BY COLD IN THE GULAG

A rare report of Soviet labor camp conditions, including the practice of the eating of dogs was revealed at Bazoi [Bozoy]. Bazoi is located about 90 kilometers from Irkutsk according to Chicago Action for Soviet Jewry, the Highland Park based human rights organization.

After a two day sit-in strike in Siberia Tatiana Zunshine, wife of the Soviet Jewish Prisoner-of-Conscience, Zachar Zunshine, forced her husband's Soviet captors to release him from his punishment cell and provide them with a two hour meeting. Zachar was placed in a Special Security Ward on May 31, where prisoners are tortured by such extreme cold. To protest the frigid temperature of the cell, Zunshine began a hunger strike after the second day despite the already reduced food rations which are limited to every other day . . .

To supplement the meager food rations which cost 15 rubles a month or 50 kopeks a day, prisoners are eating dogs which are sold by prison guards. The dogs are brought by guards to special work detachments and are bought for cash by Reds and other activists [collaborators] in the camp who are given, among other privileges, money for their willingness to carry out the orders of the prison administration. Terrible fights among the prisoners occur over the dogs who now are brought to the work assignment details with the name of a prisoner attached to its hind leg. Beatings of prisoners are commonplace and these beatings are called "to make younger."[100]

To protest the treatment of the prisoners (as well as the endangerment of dogs) in the USSR, our supporters held rallies in front of the Soviet embassies in Washington, DC, and Bonn, Germany. In London, a rally took place in front of the headquarters of Aeroflot—the official Soviet airline. A letter from Rita Eker, a cofounder of the London-based 35's—Women's Campaign for Soviet Jewry—appealed to the public to participate in the rally.

35's
WOMEN'S CAMPAIGN FOR SOVIET JEWRY
Co-chairmen: Rita Eker, Margaret Rigal
755A Finchley Road, London, NW11 8DL

June 5, 1986

Date: Wednesday, 25th June 1986
Venue: Aeroflot, Piccadilly, London W1
Time: 10:30am

Dear Member of the Public,

This is a Demonstration with Dogs, but it is a very serious occasion!

We have just learned that innocent Jewish Prisoners of Conscience, together with Christians and other political prisoners are being systematically starved in the Soviet labor camps. So appalling are the conditions that the prison guards are now selling to the prisoners live dogs for food.

We are here to mark the second anniversary of Zachar Zunshine's trial in Riga . . . Zachar and other Soviet Jews are

---

100   Archives, Center for Jewish History, New York, NY.

being persecuted because they insist on their right to live according to their religious beliefs and because they demand exit visas.

We're asking that the Soviet authorities should honour their obligations under existing treaties before they negotiate new international agreements and, most of all, we demand Human Rights for Soviet Jews and Christians imprisoned by the KGB.

If you agree with us that human beings should not be starved and ill-treated, please fill in the slip below and hand it to us or send it direct to the Soviet Ambassador.

To:

> H.E. Mr. Leonid Zamyatin
> The Soviet Ambassador
> The Soviet Embassy
> 18 Kensington Palace Gardens
> London W8

Please urge your Government to observe the Human Rights Charter and stop starving innocent prisoners. Let Soviet Jews who wish to emigrate to Israel have exit visas.[101]

Indignation over the practice of eating dogs would not wind down. My friend Sasha Balter, now a resident of Tel Aviv, organized an event dedicated to the second anniversary of Zach's trial. Everyone was invited, especially dog owners and their respective dogs (I learned that bringing dogs to protests was his idea in the first place). Chicago Action for Soviet Jewry issued a statement supporting Sasha's actions.

---

101   Tatiana Zunshine's personal archive.

From: Chicago Action for Soviet Jewry

To: All Councils
RE: Zunshine Action on June 25
Date: June 18, 1986

June 25 marks the 2nd anniversary of Zachar Zunshine's trial. Alexander Balter in Israel has organized petition drives and demonstrations. In Tel Aviv he is setting up a table on the street from which he will gather signatures. Nearby there will be a demo held in conjunction with the 35's which will include dogs (a reference to the new information that the Bazoi [Bozoy] guards are selling dogs to prisoners to supplement their diet).

Balter has requested international support on the 25th. Enclosed are petitions for circulation. Please distribute as widely as possible. Because of the close time schedule, feel free to extend the deadline.

Further suggested activities:

1. Telephone campaign to the Soviet Embassy enquiring into the reason for the cancellation of the private meeting between Tatiana and Zachar.[102]

2. Telephone to the Minister of the Interior Alexander V. Vlasov protesting the practice of eating dogs in the labor camp of Bazoi as well as expressing extreme concern as to the seriously unsanitary conditions inside Bazoi labor camp.

3. Other relevant phone numbers and contacts for enquiries and protests:

Head of Bazoi Camp, Moush [sic]
E.K. 272/40: Posiolok Bazoi
666111 Irkutskaya Oblast', USSR

---

102 While Zach and I had just had a two-hour supervised meeting, we had not had a private meeting for almost two years. The last one—and the only one—had taken place in September 1984.

Chief of Men's Division – same address

Chief Management of Labor Camps
Mr. Bolangen
Irkutsk Region
Litvinova 15, Irkutsk, RSFSR

World Health Organization
20 Avenue Oppia
1211 Geneva, Switzerland
Soviet Mission: 212/861-4900[103]

I also learned that, on more than one occasion, people brought their dogs dressed in little jackets with DON'T EAT ME written on them. Soon after, when the KGB Lieutenant Colonel Shalaev had another opportunity to confront me, he uttered the words: "We will *never* forgive you for those dogs!"

---

103 Archives, Center for Jewish History, New York, NY.

CHAPTER 25

NIGHTMARE TO REMEMBER

July 4, 1986, was approaching. The joy of celebrating the Fourth the year before in the American consulate in Leningrad stayed firmly engraved in my memory. But this year's celebration was not for me. I had a different event to attend—a protest.

On July 5, 1986, an international multisport event, the Goodwill Games, was opening in Moscow. An alternative to the 1980 Olympic Games in Moscow and 1984 Olympics in Los Angeles (both boycotted by the opposing side), this event—created by Ted Turner—was intended to demonstrate the willingness of the Soviets and the Americans to build a bridge of understanding by participating in a major international sporting competition. This Goodwill Games opened its doors to 3,000 athletes from 79 countries.

Knowing how inundated Moscow would be with tourists and members of the foreign press, we felt this would be a great time to bring attention to our cases and stage a protest. By "we," I mean Olga, Dina, and me. The timing coincided with Olga's husband, Yuri, serving another fifteen-day "tour" in a county jail. Dina's husband, Vladimir, was still serving his three-year sentence, and so was mine.

We cooked up a plan: we would each sew a husband's photograph onto the front of a T-shirt; underneath the photo, we'd sew on a message: FREE [HUSBAND'S NAME]; we would choose a busy part of Moscow, like New Arbat; we would invite the media to attend our event; before leaving home, we would put on those T-shirts and then regular ones over them; we would arrive at New Arbat, take off our top layer to reveal the signs and photographs, and start making statements to the journalists on behalf of our husbands.

It sounded like a plan, but for me, there were a lot of challenges to overcome and questions to answer. *Would I be able to leave Riga? Say I escaped Riga ahead of time; would I be able to stay in Moscow without being tracked down?* Knowing all too well that I would use the Games to get the media's attention, the KGB was sure to start looking for me all over the place.

I left Riga two weeks before the event. I went to Leningrad and camped out there, staying with a refusenik family of a slightly lower profile. Closer to the event, I started making arrangements to go to Moscow. *I will go there by train, that's a given. Except*, I was thinking, *I would rather not depart from the central train station. Is there another way?* The friend I was staying with said, "Yes. There is a way." He would help me get on a train that bypassed the central station in Leningrad.

I was interested. "Tell me more!"

"I know of a place on the outskirts of Leningrad where an obscure train stops nightly en route from Helsinki to Moscow. That train," he added, "stops there at around 1:30 a.m., picks up a few passengers, and heads to Moscow."

"Wow!" I exclaimed. "That'll work."

"I'll take you there in the daytime to show you the surroundings so that you are familiar with it. This way, you'll get no surprises when you are there by yourself past midnight. Sounds good?"

Sounded good.

I did have one event to attend before I left Leningrad. Having rejected the idea of going to the American consulate for the July Fourth celebration, I accepted an invitation to a small get-together on July 5—the night of my departure—at the apartment of an American diplomat, Vice Consul Daniel Grossman.

Twenty-seven-year-old Daniel Grossman had been appointed to the consulate in 1985. In just one year, this handsome and personable Yale graduate—who spoke fluent Russian—had acquired many friends in the Leningrad refusenik community. There was an undeniable poise to him to which we were all drawn. An invitation to celebrate a belated Fourth of July with him and a few of my refusenik friends was hard to resist. Should I have resisted it? I should have, but I didn't.

On the afternoon of July 5, my host took me to the train stop. To get there, we took public transportation, schlepped on foot for a little longer, and found ourselves at the city's edge. The train tracks were in front of us, surrounded by wooded areas. Next to the tracks was a ticket booth and a platform. And not a soul around.

I started feeling uneasy about the whole idea, but my friend assured me I had nothing to worry about.

"Everything will look the same as it does now, only it will be late at night. But the lights on the platform will be on," he told me. "There will be quite a few people hanging out on the platform waiting to board."

That convinced me. With the lights on and people around, I was game.

"Okay," I said to him. "I'll do it."

The evening at Daniel's was fabulous. The place was spacious, modern, and furnished in a minimalist style. There were eight of us there that night. With cocktails in our hands, we parked ourselves on a couch and chairs surrounding the coffee table. The conversation was effortless, flowing from topic to topic, and it was a perfect prelude to what would turn out to be a perfect storm.

I told the group about my plan and shared my reservations regarding the train. I admitted I would probably be nervous about it until the minute I got on board. They all assured me it was going to be fine. One guest said he'd done it in the past. There were enough people to feel safe, he said, and the place was well-lit.

We stayed late. In fact, I was the first one to say goodbye.

"Time to go," I said, getting up. "Need to catch a cab and be on my way."

I thanked Daniel, hugged everyone goodbye, and went outside.

It didn't take me long to catch a cab. I gave the driver the name of the station and got cozy in the back seat.

Driving through the city took a while. Tucked in the back, I wished I was still in the comfort of Daniel's apartment, surrounded by friends. *Oh, well,* I thought, *let's get it over with. Best not to work myself up.*

The cab was now on the outskirts of the city. We wobbled along the road, away from the residential sector, entered the wooded area, drove a short distance, and stopped, with the car facing the train tracks.

"Here," the cab driver said, "as you requested."

I looked around. Nothing looked the same as it had during the day. Nothing.

"Wait a minute!" I exclaimed anxiously. "I was here during the day today. This doesn't look the same, not one bit!"

"Of course," the guy said. "You were here in the daylight. How do you expect it to look the same?"

"There was a ticket booth there."

"There is your booth," he said, pointing at some structure about fifty yards away. "You must have come from the opposite direction. I can't get you any closer because of the tracks, but if you cross the tracks on foot, you'll see the same station you visited before."

I should have stayed in the car and asked him to take me back to the city, but I didn't; I got out. The driver took off.

To get to the tracks, I had to climb a slightly raised embankment. I did that, crossed the tracks, and found myself on the other side. I looked around. No, nothing—nothing whatsoever—looked the way it had before. I wanted to scream. *What is going on? Where am I?* My heart was picking up speed at a scary rate. *The ticket booth!* I remembered. *There might be somebody in the booth! A sales clerk, maybe?* The booth was about thirty yards away. *Move!* my mind shouted, but my legs, as if stuffed with cotton wool, were not obeying.

I did make it to the booth, except a booth it was not. It was a shack, abandoned, boarded up, completely void of life. It was at that moment—the moment I saw the shack the way it was—when reality kicked in: no booth, no platform, not a soul, darkness, and woods all around me. At that very moment, I felt the fear overpowering me, penetrating every particle of my body.

Somehow—even though I don't remember moving—I ended up at the back of the shack. I must have walked around it in a zombie-like state. There, I slid down the wall of the shack, my back propped against it. Sitting on the ground, I felt my body racked with uncontrollable tremors. I don't know how long that lasted—minutes? Hours? It felt like an eternity.

I am delirious, stuck somewhere in a parallel universe, where—in true Orwellian spirit—only one emotion is assigned per person, and mine happens to be FEAR. I am consumed by it.

Suddenly, I heard voices. Voices! That jolted me up. *Could these be the passengers?* I thought to myself, ignoring the fact that without a platform, at a minimum, this could not be a train station.

I peeked my head around the back wall, just enough to see where the voices were coming from, and pulled it back in horror. It was a group of young men—boys, teenagers. Each carried a flashlight. With them was a large dog.

I froze behind the back wall. As they spoke, I could hear them slurring their words. *They are drunk!* They were laughing, swearing. The dog was barking hard.

I knew I only had a few seconds to think. *What do I do? Try to hide? Or step out? If I hide, and they find me—the dog might smell the presence of a stranger and lead them to the back—then I am prey. The rest is up to them. So what do I—*

I stepped out.

"Aah, look who's here!" one of them cheered, elbowing another. "Look!" He pointed at me. "Where did she come from?"

I didn't stay from where I had emerged. Trying to project that I was in control, I walked a few yards toward them, stopped in front of them, and started talking. I told them about the train, the station, about me being here in the daylight, how the platform was there, the booth was too, and so were the lights, and how they all have disappeared. *I don't understand*, I said, *please help me understand what has happened*. I was trying not to stop talking so that I didn't give them a break.

They did not need a break. While I was talking, some of them were laughing, ridiculing what I had said. ("The train? What are you talking about, sweetheart? Who needs to take a train when we can have a good time?") I felt hands on my body, touching me.

Guided purely by a survival instinct, I scanned the group man by man, face by face, from one set of eyes to another. Then I chose *him*. I chose one guy, and I chose him for his eyes. There was something in them that the others lacked. Maturity, perhaps. He may have had some alcohol, but he wasn't drunk, not like the rest of them, anyway. He was older than the others—maybe twenty or twenty-one. It was his dog that had been barking hard before I started speaking. By now, the dog had calmed down.

"You," I said, looking straight into his eyes. "Can I talk to you alone? Can you please tell them to stop? And please explain to me where I am!"

My gut didn't fail me. He happened to have some sway over the group, and he told them to quit. We stepped a few yards away from them.

"I hear what you are saying about the train," the guy said, "but there is no such thing as a train around here. These tracks have been abandoned for as long as I can remember."

I felt I was losing my mind.

"If you don't believe me," he added, "I can take you to the cabin where I live, about a mile away. My wife is there, sleeping. We'll wake her up, and you can ask her yourself. Wanna do that?"

A chance of getting away from the pack of drunk teenagers was all I could hope for. *If something happens to me on the way to the cabin or inside the cabin, let it be just him, one guy—not the whole gang,* I thought.

"Yes," I said to him. "I do."

He told the group he was taking me away. He said it quite sternly, so they got it. And we left—he and I, and the dog.

We were walking through the woods, talking. I tried to stay in the present and not let my mind wander. Did I know there was a cabin in the woods with his wife in it? Even if there were, was he taking me there, or were we going deeper into the woods? There was no point in asking myself these questions. I had chosen him for his eyes because I saw decency in them. I was hanging tightly on to that, realizing it was my only choice. Having come from the party—which seemed to be a lifetime ago—I was wearing high heels. That didn't help, but I didn't care; I kept walking. Occasionally, I would follow in his footsteps and climb over fallen trees. He'd offer me a hand to get over the hump, and I would take it, trusting him. We kept walking. And then we reached the cabin, as he had promised.

Once inside, I stayed in the tiny hallway while he went in. In a few minutes, he returned, accompanied by a girl about his age. Wrapped up in a robe, she looked like she wasn't quite sure why she was being woken up in the wee hours of the night, but despite that, she didn't look mad. Seeing her, I started to tear. *Aah, what a relief!* I wanted to hug her just for being there.

"This is my wife," he said. "You can tell her what happened and ask her yourself. And you will see that I was telling you the truth. So tell her!" He addressed me, pointing at her.

I started telling her about my ordeal, and midway through, the girl said, "He was telling you the truth. The tracks over there have long been abandoned."

In the end, they offered me a choice. I could stay with them till morning or walk with the guy for another five minutes to a nearby road, where he would help me hitch a ride back to the city.

I chose the latter. I just wanted the nightmare to end. I needed to be out of the woods like I needed air to breathe.

I thanked his wife for being so gracious, and we left. Standing by the side of the road, we signaled for cars to stop. Having passed on a few of them, we settled for one with a sleepy woman in the front passenger seat.

I told the guy I would be forever grateful. I hugged him, said goodbye, and got inside.

Once in the car, I realized I had never asked for his name.

I gave the driver the address of my refusenik friends who had hosted me before this nightmare unraveled. Sitting in the back seat, I thought of one thing, and one thing only: *I won't tell them what*

CHAPTER 25: NIGHTMARE TO REMEMBER

happened. Not now. I can't! I will crawl into bed and close my eyes. That's
all I want. Or else my heart will break into a million pieces.

The car stopped by the building where my friends lived. I paid
the driver and got out. Going up the stairs, I kept saying to myself,
Crawl into bed and close your eyes. I got to the door and rang the bell.
Nobody answered. I waited a minute and rang again. And again. I
rang it for a continuous stretch. Nothing. I began to knock. I knocked
till I realized that no one was going to open that door.

That's when the floodgates opened. I didn't just cry—I sobbed
inconsolably. I banged my head on the door, talking through a flood
of tears. If what had happened in the woods was terrifying, what
happened at that door was devastating. I thought my heart would
not survive—that it would break.

By the time I re-emerged on the street, I was a shell of my former
self. I hitched another car ride and asked the driver to take me to the
airport. I no longer cared what would happen. If the KGB caught me
at the airport on the way to Moscow, so be it.

At the ticket counter, the agent said, "No seats available for the
next thirty-six hours. You still want it?"

"Sure."

And so for the next thirty-six hours, I stayed at the airport, but I
don't remember much about it. I sat on a bench, staring ahead. I felt
hollow inside. Hollow and numb.

After landing in Moscow, I took a cab to Dina's apartment.

"Tan'ka, what happened?" she asked, alarmed by the way I looked.

By then, I had been away from that horrific scene for a while.
Sitting alone at the airport had given me time to process. My senses
slowly started coming back to me, and I felt that I was able to talk. I

sat Dina down and recounted the whole story. I had no tears left in me. But her? She was crying. She was crying *for me*, and for that, I would be eternally grateful.

I have been revisiting the events of that night for years. And for all of those years, I have not been able to say with certainty whether those events were random or staged. As much as I would like to say, "The KGB did it," the truth is, I don't know. I wish I did. Had I known it was *them*, I wouldn't have beaten myself up for getting out of the car—the "cab driver" would have kicked me out anyway.

There is a chance it may have been accidental. How? Back at Daniel's apartment, I had told the party about the station. I mentioned its name (which my memory has conveniently erased). The conversation moved on to other train stations previously serving similar goals. A few names were thrown in. This may sound like a stretch, but could I have picked up the wrong name? I don't know.

A few things I do know. The encounter with the drunk teenagers was entirely random, and because it was random, it added the most terrifying element to the whole ordeal. And lastly, a split-second decision to step out from behind the shack and, subsequently, to go for the right pair of eyes may have been one of the most consequential decisions I've ever made.

Ah, and the reason my friends' door didn't open? They had spent the night at their dacha.[104]

By the next day, I felt life flowing through my veins again. When Olga and Dina asked me about our planned demonstration—guessing I might not have been up to it—my answer was, "Oh, yes, I am going." Considering what it had taken to get there, would I bail out now? No!

---

104 A summer house in the country.

"Let's do it!" I said.

We did everything we'd planned: got the T-shirts ready, put them on, put other ones on top. Unfortunately, coming to Moscow via plane increased my chances of getting caught. So as not to risk the demonstration's success for all three of us, we decided that Olga and Dina would go together while I would go alone. They left long before the 4:00 p.m. meeting time. Perhaps they went shopping first, I don't know; I would have if I were them.

I wasn't entirely on my own. Dina and Olga's friend, a young member of the Trust Group, Kolya Khramov, had come to the house to accompany me out of the door. Somebody to witness my abduction if that was in the cards.

Kolya and I waited till 3:00 p.m. and then went out. I was almost certain a human tornado would descend on us downstairs, but it didn't. Nor did it happen by the entrance to the building. So far, so good! We made it to the subway station, but while walking down the stairs, we encountered a human barrier of men—about five of them—taking up the entire width of the stairway. One of them was, you guessed it, KGB Lieutenant Colonel Shalaev.

Now, let me explain something. Who was previously dispatched to Moscow to retrieve me and take me home to Riga? First Lieutenant Narnitsky of the KGB. And who had dispatched him? None other than his boss, Lieutenant Colonel Shalaev. Seeing Shalaev on the steps of the subway made me realize that he had been dispatched there by his own superiors—that he had been humiliated, reduced to the role of an escort, which constituted some kind of punishment, and that he was hardly happy about it.

Surrounded by KGB agents, Kolya and I found ourselves in the center of a circle (or a circus?). Surprising myself, I turned to him and said, "Kolya, please meet Lieutenant Colonel Shalaev. He is head of the Jewish Department of Riga's KGB."

I must have struck a nerve. The agents grabbed me by my wrists and began to wring my hands behind my back while dragging me a short distance to the car. Following Dina's example, I yelled, "Comrades, help!" That caused a barrage of insults to fly out of Shalaev's mouth. He must have lost it. Hearing him swear at me, I have to admit, I lost it, too. I answered him in kind.

In the car, sandwiched between him on my left-hand side and another agent on my right, I was holding on to my shoulder bag, but not for long. Two more agents got in the front, and the car took off. Once we started moving, Shalaev tore the bag off me and began throwing stuff out, frantically looking for my passport, repeating, "Where is your passport? Where is it?"

The passport was at the bottom of the bag, but he hadn't seen it. *Some sleuth he is*, I thought. He then decided that I must have been hiding the passport in my clothes, and that's when it got physical. Both of them, on either side of me, started touching me, hands landing on my chest and my thighs. *What did I do?* With all my strength, with everything I've got, I buried my nails into one of the men's arms. He screamed in pain and, while swearing at me, pulled his hands back. It turned out it wasn't Shalaev's arm. It was the other guy's. Shalaev pulled his hands back, too. We were all sitting there in the back seat, breathing heavily.

After a minute or so, the other guy said, "I felt something firm in the front." He must have touched the photograph.

"No worries. We'll get it off of her once we arrive," Shalaev responded.

They did find my passport, eventually. We drove for quite a while. Shalaev spoke on and off.

"You've crossed the line; in fact, you've crossed all lines," he said. "We've tolerated you for as long as we could, but no more; we are done with you. And you are done coming here, too. Forget about getting your passport back for a long, long time."

"Why don't you take it away for good?" I asked him. "That's what we've been asking for all along. Take away our citizenship, give us exit visas, and we'll be out of your sight."

He ignored that and continued talking at me.

"You've gotten completely out of hand. And, by the way, the scheme you pulled off regarding dogs? You will regret that. We will *never* forgive you for those dogs.

"For as long as you were fighting for your own husband, we were sort of tolerating it. But now that you've started coordinating the efforts of other wives? That is pushing our patience like nothing else. Mila[105] should be on her own, Anya[106] should be on her own, and so should Olga and Dina.

"Nobody acts with such audacity like you do. You've got it into your head that you can free your husband. Dream on! He'll be there until the last roll call, and that is if he is lucky. Just hope his term doesn't get extended.

"You think if you are serving your time, you will be somewhere close to him? Think again. You can end up in Kamchatka or, worse, in Kolyma.[107]

"Even though you have some understanding of what the Gulag is about, you still don't know what true prison or torture feels like.

"What good will it do if Zach gets out and you go in? You guys will have to do it all over again, only in *your* defense."

Judging by the surroundings, we weren't going to the airport. I didn't have to guess for too long before the car stopped at the

---

105 Mila Volvovsky, the wife of the prisoner of conscience Ari Volvovsky.

106 Anya Lifshitz, the wife of the prisoner of conscience Vladimir Lifshitz.

107 Areas in the far northeast of Russia.

entrance of the Hotel Izmailovo. Shalaev was staying there and needed to check out.

All four men got out of the car, leaving me to myself. Shalaev went inside the hotel.

Left alone, I looked at the clock and saw that it was just minutes away from 4:00 p.m., the planned starting time of our demonstration. Shalaev's words, "We'll get it off of her once we arrive," alluded to the possibility of a body search. *Well*, I thought, *if they do search me, they'll find the photo and rip it off. Why not use it while I still can? Even if it is strictly symbolic, in solidarity with my girls?*

At 4:00 p.m. sharp, I took the top layer off.

I had been in the car for about five minutes when Shalaev opened the door to throw in his bag. Seeing me sitting in the T-shirt with Zach's photo and a sign attached, he stared at me in shocked silence, shaking his head in disbelief.

"Either you put your top layer on," he said irately, barely controlling himself, "or I will personally take the bottom layer off of you." He slammed the door, and I saw him say something to the other men, who took a peek into the window one after another. He went back into the hotel.

I sat there for another ten minutes until, by my calculation, the girls' demonstration would be over, and I put my top layer back on.

More time passed before Shalaev came back to the car. Everyone took their seats, and we drove off. This time, I could recognize the route leading to the airport. There was quite a way to go, and Shalaev resumed his spiel. Except, he changed his tune.

"You are one of a kind; you are one in ten million; you are the only one in Riga; you are ours." He leaned closer and whispered, "In fact, you are not ours; you are *mine*."

My face said it all. I was appalled. He then said he was joking and kept quiet for a while.

Once we reached the airport, Shalaev took me to the police station and into a built-in detention center. There, he ordered a body search. Two female guards proceeded with a search, confiscating my inner T-shirt.

I spent five long hours at the police station before Shalaev came back to retrieve me. We walked to the gate and boarded the plane.

He kept talking for most of the flight. To summarize, this is what he said:

He understood us—Zach and me—in fact, he respected us and perhaps was ready to acknowledge the strength of our position. ("Don't wanna give up? Good for you! Don't give up.")

Why was I looking at them like they were some kind of animals? They were people, just like everybody else.

They knew Zach was a force to reckon with, but me? They'd misread me, that's for sure. If only they had known what a nightmare I would turn out to be.

I had to interrupt to ask, "Then what? Would you have not chosen him as a target?"

He didn't answer, but to me, this was an answer in itself. They might not have. Wow.

He resumed but changed his tune again.

"Okay, maybe things will end up the way you want. Maybe Zach gets released, and you get permission to leave the country. Maybe, hypothetically. But mark my words: you and Zach will not stay together."

"WHAT?" I almost hit the ceiling. "Who do you think you are telling me things like that?" I was furious. Oh, how I wished I had scratched *his* arm!

"You are not the only ones who have gone through this," he said. "There have been other couples, and they ended up in shambles. You'll see."

"Please stop talking to me."

The last thing he did before landing was give me a warning: I could not leave the vicinity of Riga till July 20—the end of the Goodwill Games. If they saw me attempting to contact foreign tourists, his "boys would handle it." And lastly, he had no intentions of returning my passport any time soon, "until further notice."

I wondered what had happened to Olga and Dina. I later found out they had reached New Arbat without any problems. The hurdle occurred when they realized that the reporters were nowhere around. It turned out there had been a miscommunication, and the reporters were waiting on a different corner of the street. Unfazed, at exactly 4:00 p.m., the girls took off their outer layers and stood there, anticipating the police emerging. After about five minutes, the police arrived, shoved them into a car, and drove them to police headquarters. Several hours later, they let them go.

Back at Olga's apartment, a group of reporters covered a press conference conducted by the Trust Group. Needless to say, once the girls arrived, the spotlight was on them. And in the end, our demonstration received the publicity it deserved.

CHAPTER 26

RED BOOTS

Meanwhile, the Soviet Jewry Advocacy Center in Waltham, Massachusetts, approached the office of Senator John Kerry (D-MA) to propose becoming our "sponsor and attorney of record." I was happy to learn that Senator Kerry had kindly agreed to take up the case.

United States Senate
Washington D.C. 20510

July 16, 1986

Ambassador Yuri V. Dubinin
Embassy of the U.S.S.R.
1825 Phelps Pl., N.W.
Washington, D.C., 20008

Dear Ambassador Dubinin:

I am writing on behalf of Tatiana Zunshine, a citizen of the Soviet Union whom I am representing as an attorney. I am enclosing a legal petition on behalf of Mrs. Zunshine, which is directed to the Procurator [Prosecutor] General of the U.S.S.R. I respectfully request that you forward this petition to the Procurator General in Moscow.

Briefly, Tatiana Zunshine is the wife of Zachar Zunshine, a Jewish citizen of Riga in the Soviet Union. Mr. Zunshine is presently imprisoned in the Soviet Union under a court judgment entered June 28, 1986 [1984], sentencing him to three years imprisonment in a labor camp. Mr. Zunshine's sentence was appealed, and the appeal denied, on July 26, 1984.

It is my firm belief that Mr. Zunshine has been unjustly punished for nothing more than attempting to exercise his legal right to give up his Soviet citizenship and emigrate to Israel. Since his arrest, Mr. Zunshine has been subjected to inhuman conditions in prison, and his wife has been harassed and intimidated by Soviet authorities. This treatment of the Zunshines is in direct violation of the obligations of the Soviet Union under the Helsinki accords and the United Nations Charter, as well as a violation of Soviet law itself.

I join with the Soviet Jewry Legal Advocacy Center of Boston, Massachusetts, and with the Jewish community and all concerned Americans in requesting an immediate end to these violations of basic human rights for Zachar Zunshine and Tatiana Zunshine. At a time when the Soviet Union is endeavoring to meet the concerns of the international community on human rights and other issues, I believe that a review of the Zunshine case would be a step in the right direction.

I would appreciate your assistance in conveying this petition on behalf of Zachar and Tatiana Zunshine to the proper authorities in the Soviet Union, and in facilitating the prompt release of Zachar Zunshine. I look forward to hearing from you.

Sincerely,

John F. Kerry
United States Senate[108]

The twenty-seven-page petition was drafted by the Soviet Jewry Advocacy Center, signed by Senator Kerry, and delivered to Soviet Ambassador Yuri Dubinin in Washington, DC.

108   Archives, Center for Jewish History, New York, NY.

PETITION

To: Prosecutor General of the U.S.S.R.
FROM: Tatiana Zunshine, on behalf of her husband, Zachar Zunshine, by Her Attorney, John F. Kerry

The Petitioner, Tatiana Zunshine, is a citizen of the Soviet Union. She is the wife of Zachar Zunshine, a citizen of Riga, Soviet Union, presently confined under a court judgment entered June 28, 1984, sentencing him to three years imprisonment in a labor camp. Zunshine's sentence was appealed and the appeal denied on July 26, 1984. Petitioner, Tatiana Zunshine, deprived of the companionship of her husband as a result of his present confinement under the judgment and denial of appeal, hereby submits this Petition by her attorney John F. Kerry for relief as hereinafter set forth.

The undersigned, John F. Kerry, is a citizen of the United States and duly accredited attorney under the laws of the Commonwealth of Massachusetts. He is a duly elected member of the United States Senate from the Commonwealth of Massachusetts.[109]

Back in 1985, Zach told me about his desire to become a lawyer. For his law degree, he wanted to study at no other than Yale University. The Union of Councils for Soviet Jewry contacted Yale on my behalf, asking them to accept Zach as their student. In the end, enrolling him as a student turned out to be too ambitious—he needed to get out of prison first—but the school remained involved in Zach's case for the rest of his term.

---

109 Tatiana Zunshine's personal archive.

Yale Law School
401A Yale Station
New Haven, Connecticut 06320

August 4, 1986

His Excellency Mikhail Gorbachev
General Secretary
Central Committee of the Communist Party of the U.S.S.R.
The Kremlin, Moscow

Dear Mr. Gorbachev:

In view of your splendid decision, published in today's New York Times, to allow the family of Anatoly Scharansky to emigrate to Israel, I am hopeful in writing to you on behalf of Zachar Zunshine of Riga and his wife, Tatiana. Zachar Zunshine is a prisoner in the Irkutsk camp, having unsuccessfully sought for more than six years to exercise the right to emigrate to Israel. I would like to bring some of the facts of the Zunshine case to your personal attention, so that you can understand why I appeal to you on humanitarian grounds to permit the Zunshines to emigrate.

More than two years ago, Zachar Zunshine was arrested and accused of anti-Soviet slander and sentenced to three years in prison. Since his imprisonment, the conditions of the prison, combined with the harsh treatment that Zachar has received, have contributed to the deterioration of Zachar's health. In December [August] 1985, he contracted infectious hepatitis "B" and has had to receive a special diet and rest in order to overcome this dangerous disease.

Tatiana's struggle on behalf of her husband has not been easy. Earlier this year, she began a hunger strike in Riga to protest Zachar's situation. She is fighting not only for her husband's life but also for her own survival. Soviet officials are determined to break her spirit, whether it be by obstructing her travel, monitoring her actions or isolating her from communicating with people from the West. But her spirit will not be broken. She will continue her struggle until her husband is released and they realize their dream of living together in Israel.

In anticipation of the summit conference now being planned and in recognition of the compelling humanitarian claims in this case, I call upon you to use your influence to intervene to ensure that the Zunshines are accorded their basic rights under Soviet and international law. As our two countries seek improved relations, it is vital that the Soviet Union take steps to demonstrate its commitment to peace through humanitarian gestures. In that spirit, I appeal to you to release Zachar Zunshine from his imprisonment, to end the harassment and repression of Tatiana Zunshine, and to allow them to emigrate to Israel.

Sincerely,

Peter H. Schuck, Simeon E. Baldwin Professor[110]

Meanwhile, at the camp, things were worse than I'd expected. While I was riding my high horse about the fact that, back in June, the administration had succumbed to my demands and given us the meeting, they had regrouped and gone on the offensive. A short note smuggled from the camp arrived in late August. It listed punitive measures taken against Zach from mid-June till mid-August:

June 20–28: eight days in a punishment cell for refusing to participate in a nonobligatory meeting

July 4–13: nine days in a punishment cell for refusing to participate in a nonobligatory meeting

July 18–August 18: one month in an internal labor camp prison for refusing to perform a job that is considered shameful

---

110 Tatiana Zunshine's personal archive.

Not again! I saw a reference to an internal labor camp prison, and it brought back the scare we had gone through at the beginning of the previous year, when, having locked Zach up for six months, the administration laid the groundwork for an additional three-year term. Since then, things have seemingly quieted down in regard to the second term. We had not heard them mention it for a long time. Until now. Had they finally decided to pursue a new term? This once again emphasized the never-ending volatility of the situation—one moment, having gained some ground, you were elated; the next, you were digging yourself out of the hole of despair.

I knew I needed to fire up my guns and start attacking them for these alleged intentions. I did not have the luxury of sitting there, guessing: were they pursuing the second term or not? *Assume the worst,* I said to myself. If I were wrong, I'd welcome it with all my heart. But if I was right, the time to act was *now.* With six months left to serve, we had to address that threat head-on.

I started another letter-writing campaign dedicated to the issue of a potential second term. In my letters, I raised suspicion about Zach getting a one-month term in the internal camp prison. *Who gets one month?* I asked. It felt nominal; it felt like it was serving a purpose other than punishment. What was their purpose? What were they cooking up?

I was in the middle of my campaign when I learned that a prominent American diplomat, a former ambassador to the United Nations, Jeane Kirkpatrick, was planning to visit Riga. I couldn't believe my luck. In my experience, when people of her stature came to Moscow or Leningrad, there were serious hurdles for someone like me to overcome to gain access to them. Most often, if not captured ahead of time, I would be expelled from whatever city the guests visited. But Riga? I didn't have to go anywhere. I lived in Riga! Try to expel me from here!

I found out who was bringing her. The Chautauqua Institution–Eisenhower Institute Conference on US–Soviet Relations was supposed to take place in Jurmala (a seaside Baltic community outside of Riga) on September 15–19. It was set up as an international town hall with 2,000 Latvians and 200 Americans participating. Among notable invitees on the American side were former Ambassador Jeane Kirkpatrick, Assistant Secretary of Defense Richard Perle, and former National Security Advisor Robert McFarlane.

I started making arrangements to see Ms. Kirkpatrick. I called Pam. "She is a rare guest here in Riga," I said, "and I need to use that to our advantage."

I was pushing all buttons to secure my meeting with Ambassador Kirkpatrick when, out of nowhere, I received a letter authorizing a two-day private meeting with Zach on September 15–17.

I could not believe my eyes.

I was grateful to have seen Zach twice since March, but nothing could compare to *this*! This was the private meeting we were talking about! We have not had a meeting like that for two long years. I had exhausted all my means to get it and had practically given up. And now they were offering it to me on their own? And not for one day, but for two?

I was over the moon, waltzing around my apartment with the letter in my hand. My head was spinning, but I didn't care. I would stop from time to time, laughing at my inability to keep straight, prop myself against the wall, and read the note again. Yep, it still said, "September 15, 1986." I wasn't imagining it.

I quickly realized whom I should thank for it: Ambassador Kirkpatrick. Remember what I said: *I live in Riga! Try to expel me from here!* There was no need for the KGB to expel me. *Entice her with a private meeting,* must have been the thinking, *and she will leave Riga voluntarily.* It worked! So all I could say was: *Thank you, Ambassador*

*Kirkpatrick, for your visit and everything you have already done for us! I
am forever grateful to you.*

I flew to Moscow a week early, on September 8, so I could take time
to collect everything I needed for the meeting.

While staying at Dina's, I was drawn into conversations regarding a rumor circulating among Moscow refuseniks. The rumor was
that Dina and Olga, with their respective families, would soon be
allowed to leave. That rumor had flown around several times before, but nothing ever happened. And how could it? Dina's husband,
Vladimir Brodsky, was still in prison with about two-thirds of his
term left to serve. Whoever had started the rumor was being ridiculous, to say the least.

I went on preparing for my meeting. Olga and Dina shook it off
and went on with their lives.

The three of us had a lot in common. Besides being fighters and
sharing a slew of other traits, there was something else that we each
had—a pair of red boots.

About a year earlier, Olga, Dina, and I had bought the same pair
of boots. Red, Austrian-made, midcalf lambskin boots, to be exact.
That purchase did not come without an effort. To explain, let me
present a scenario inherent to the Soviet lifestyle: Say you spot a
long line of people stretching over a few city blocks. What do you do?
Go to the front of it to see what's for sale? No. First, you secure your
spot. Then you ask people around what they are in line for. If the answer fits your fancy, you stay in line for hours, praying that the item
you are after doesn't run out of stock. And if the stars align, you get
your "trophy," coupled with the satisfaction of a day well spent.

I stood in line for those boots like everybody else. On a separate occasion, the girls spotted a line while driving around Moscow
in search of prison clothes for Dina's newly imprisoned husband,

Vladimir. Having learned it was for Austrian boots, they looked at each other: *Austrian boots or prison clothes?* They went for the boots. We laughed about it, but hey, the boots were a one-time deal, whereas prison clothes were widely available.

I had worn my boots down to the ground. In fact, I no longer owned them, as I had had to throw them away. Dina and Olga wore theirs on occasion. We called ourselves "red boot buddies."

I left my red boot buddies on the evening of September 12 and took a red-eye flight to Irkutsk. Arriving the next morning, I had given myself plenty of time to get to Bozoy by September 15.

When I finally showed up at the headquarters in Bozoy, I presented my letter to the officer on duty. He studied the paper and then told me to stop by the head of the camp's office.

"What for?" I asked. "All you need is this letter."

"Yes," the man said, "but the head of the camp wanted to talk to you first. He is expecting you."

Slightly alarmed, I went next door to the office of the head of the camp, Mr. Mouzh.

He was sitting at his desk, and when he saw me, he put a smile on his face. That alarmed me even more.

"Hello. You wanted to see me. What for?" I asked suspiciously.

"Don't you worry. Everything is on track with your meeting," he assured me.

"Okay. Then why did you want to see me?" I asked.

"It's not me who wanted to see you," he said. "It's the head of the Gulag office in Irkutsk."

Hmm. "Okay," I repeated. "I will see him on the way back. Anything else?"

"No, you don't understand," the guy said. "He wants to see you *before* your meeting. As a precondition to the meeting."

"What!?" I erupted. "If he wanted to see me, he could have informed me beforehand, and I would have seen him before coming here."

"Something has come up just now. It's just a formality . . . You are going to have your meeting, I promise. It's really no more than a formality . . ." he mumbled.

Oh, I was furious! This time, with the visit of an American ambassador triggering the meeting, I didn't think they would be playing games. Not again!

"I can't say no to them when they ask for it," he confessed. *Am I supposed to sympathize with him?* crossed my mind. "I will lend you my car and a driver," he added pleadingly. "He will take you to Irkutsk, stay until you see the head of the department, and will take you back."

From his conciliatory tone, I knew he was in a tough spot. He wouldn't be able to approve my meeting, I concluded, even if he wanted to. I decided to take a chance.

"If I go, I go in your car with your driver," I said.

"You got it."

On the way to Irkutsk, I wondered if I had made the right decision. If I'd stayed, would I have been able to force them into giving me a meeting, like I had before? Somehow, it felt like this time was different. It felt like the head of the camp had no say in it. Or did he?

We shall see . . . We shall see . . . I repeated to myself nervously.

We arrived at the Gulag office, and I told the driver, "Wait for me, please; it won't be long."

I got inside the building and went straight to the Gulag office. I grabbed the handle to open the door—it wouldn't open. I shook it a few times. No movement. The door was locked.

LOCKED!

I flew out of the building and into the car still hanging by the entrance—the driver hadn't parked it yet. I yelled, "Please go!" and he agreeably started moving. My heart was jumping up and down. I could not believe the trap I had allowed myself into. *How did that happen? Why, all of a sudden, would you start trusting them? What made you think this time was different?*

"Please, please, please, could you go faster," I begged the driver. My goal was to return to the camp before the end of the day at 6:00 p.m.

We arrived at the headquarters with the clock showing 5:57 p.m. I thanked the driver, flew out of the car, and into the building. I ran down the hallway to Mouzh's office and paused in front of his door for a split second. The door was open, but Mouzh was not there. Two female inmates assigned to cleaning the headquarters stood in the doorway, laying out their tools: a bucket, mops, and cleaning supplies. I went through the doorway, leaping over the bucket, pushing the women aside, and plopped myself down in the chair by the wall across from the desk.

Phew! That was close.

"What the hell are you doing? Get out!" the women yelled in one voice.

"I am here to stay indefinitely," I proclaimed, trying to catch my breath.

What started then can hardly be described in words. Not in literary words, anyway. Using a full arsenal of curses, the two women screamed at me, their eyes popping with rage. One woman or the other would stick her face inches away from mine, yelling profanities and threatening me with a fight. I didn't quite understand why they were so immensely mad at me, and I had no chance to dwell on it. I froze. I didn't try to calm them down; I just waited for their anger to subside.

It then occurred to me: the women needed to report the fact that there was an intruder in Mr. Mouzh's office and that it, unfortunately, had happened on their watch.

That's what it was! I got it. Having a job as a cleaning person must have been the cushiest way to serve out the remainder of one's term. These two must have had to snitch, lie, betray, and bend over backward to get there. And out of nowhere, there I came, rushing through the doorway, pushing them aside, jeopardizing everything they had achieved up to this point in their merciless lives.

Eventually, the women realized that yelling at me would not solve their problem. They argued about the phone call for a few minutes and opted to start with an officer on duty. One of the women placed a call and offered a lengthy explanation of what had happened. The way she described the events confirmed my conclusion. The fear of being punished for letting me jump over the bucket and into the room—that was what had driven their anger.

The voice on the other end of the line told her to stay put. They would get back to her.

The women were no longer yelling. But they were still spewing insults while vigorously moving their mops around, salvaging their attempt to clean the room. I'd made an impromptu decision not to respond. I just needed to ride out the storm.

A phone call came in. Judging by the tone of the conversation on our side of the line, it must have been Mr. Mouzh. The woman who took the call detailed all that had happened, emphasizing how much the two of them had been caught by surprise.

"She ran over us!" she exclaimed. "There was nothing we could do!"

The conversation seemed to have put her at ease. She said okay a few times and hung up.

"He wants us to remain here with her, for now," she said to her partner, "while they are trying to decide."

By now, the cleaning was over. The women sat down, prepared for a long wait. They still looked at me like I was an eyesore, but at that point, they were no longer as generous with the insults. They talked on and off between themselves, leaving me to my thoughts.

This is the most surreal, out-of-this-world experience, something I myself have a hard time believing. Had I arrived ten minutes later, this might not have happened. But the driver was a good sport, bringing me back on time. And I've been able to hijack the head of the camp's office for my sit-in strike. At home, on his off-hours, he is wracking his brain, trying to decide how to get out of it. He can't hush it up, that's for sure. He has to report to his superiors, which puts him in a ridiculous position. Ha! That'll teach him! He was the one to lie to my face. He deserves every bit of it.

We had been there for a few hours when another phone call interrupted our sojourn. One of the women rushed to get it. Listening to someone on the line, she nodded and said yes a few times. Once the call ended, she announced, "We will be guarding her here for the rest of the night."

"Yesss!" I exclaimed.

She looked at me for the first time with a grain of interest. "Who are you, anyway?" she asked.

As I had broken the silence between us, I told them about myself, about Zach, our fight with the KGB, and what had brought me there to the head of the camp's office. We went on talking for hours. They told me about themselves: what crimes they had committed and what terms they were serving.

Sometime in the middle of the night, one of the women suggested we get some hot tea.

"There is a room in the basement," she said. "We have a kettle there; we can make some tea. You want some?"

Oh, I wanted it. I wanted it so much! But how could I? Going with them meant leaving the office. It meant trusting them to let me come back there.

They must have sensed my hesitation.

"C'mon," one of the women said. "Let's go. You can trust us."

I looked at them, assessing the situation. Then I realized that I owed them my trust.

We went. We had tea. And we all came back to the office.

The three of us dozed off on the chairs until the phone rang again in the early morning hours. "This one's for you," one of the women said, handing me the phone.

For me?

The head of the camp, Mr. Mouzh, was on the line, informing me of my three-day meeting with my husband, effective immediately.

"Three days!?" I exclaimed in disbelief. "This is not a mistake?"

Not a mistake, he confirmed. Three days it was. I thanked him for the wonderful news and assured him that my taking over his office was by no means the fault of my two companions.

A guard took me to a room in the barracks designated for private meetings. Zach was already in, he said. I waited for the guard to leave, then knocked on the door. The door opened, and we lost ourselves in one long embrace.

Ask me to describe our meeting, and I will be at a loss for words. That whole encounter was nothing short of emotional fireworks. It was saturated with happiness but blemished by an awareness that the end time was near. It was a feast for the body, the mind, and the soul. It was full of laughter, and yet, sometimes, the tears of laughter would turn into tears of sorrow. But laughter prevailed.

Zach told me he knew about what had happened the previous night.

"When did you find out?" I asked.

"From the minute you guys made the first phone call, the whole camp was in stitches." He wanted more details, and I told him all about it. He was laughing hard, and I was, too.

"That's the best weapon, isn't it?" We both agreed it was.

We came to the same conclusion: Mouzh had tricked me into going to Irkutsk on the orders of the KGB. He had been told to push back the start of the meeting by about two days. *Why?* you might ask. Because of Riga's town hall, scheduled for September 15 to 19. They wanted me out of Riga for its entire duration. Having sent me to Irkutsk, they succeeded in postponing the meeting by one day only. That wasn't enough. They now had no choice but to give us an extra day. That's how we ended up with a three-day meeting. Mystery solved.

We went on talking about other stuff. Things that were no laughing matter.

According to Zach, the head of the Men's Division, Major Korenev, had made it his life's mission to extend Zach's term for an additional three years, and he didn't care to hide it. Thus, on August 5, he solemnly declared, "I will do everything in my power to give you, Zunshine, a second term."

What had preceded this was yet another provocation. The head of the unit, Officer Valeev, had ordered Zach to clean the campgrounds using a short-handled broom made of grass (to use it, one had to bend in half to get close enough to the ground). Zach said, "No, not happening," giving Valeev two reasons. First, it hit too close to home. It reminded him of the Jews in Nazi Vienna being forced to scrub the streets, kneeling on the ground at their captors' feet. Second, this job was considered shameful, and the administration knew it. Ordering him to do it was nothing less than a provocation.

For refusing to obey their orders, the administration had sentenced him to one month in the internal labor camp prison. "Why is the term so short?" Zach wondered out loud, to which Korenev responded, "It's enough for what I intend it to be."

"I knew it!" I jumped in. "I knew it the minute I received your note. The one-month prison term is just a building block for him. He seems to have made up his mind." Zach agreed.

"He is insane," he added. "You should have seen him. He's morphed into a convict, and it shows."

Speaking of insane, Zach had spent that month in the internal prison in the company of two mentally ill inmates who had just been brought back from an asylum. One of them was quiet, but the other was quite aggressive. Was Korenev trying to get to Zach with the help of mentally unstable patients?

This was beyond scary.

"Everything we've got," I said to Zach, "should be directed at this psychopath." I told him I had already started the campaign, and boy, would I come out with guns blazing the minute I got back. "And I will do everything in *my* power to expose him and his rotten ideas," I promised.

We moved on to talk about the letters, the leaks, and the lengths to which the administration went trying to find them.

"They're worried so much about the leaks," Zach said, "that they assign people to be by my side on a rotating basis. They hope to catch me eventually. All I can say is: Best of luck!"

Clueless about the existence of our secret code, they allowed letters with hidden messages to escape censorship. In addition, numerous letters went through a back door. The administration knew he was relying on helpers to smuggle them, but they couldn't figure out who those helpers were. It turns out the helpers were "double agents"— their own collaborators, colluding with Zach. These guys were beyond suspicion, and the administration ended up spinning their wheels.

We touched on the subject of shameful jobs. "They keep throwing shameful jobs at me," Zach said. "It gives them an excuse to punish me for rejecting them. They know I can't accept them. That would undermine my standing among other inmates, which is quite high; high enough to get help smuggling letters to you."

The conversation moved on to the living conditions, and I was delighted to hear that things had improved. Our battle over the cups, spoons, soap, TB inmates, showers, drinking water—all of those issues—had borne fruit. The conditions had improved so much that there was hardly anything to complain about. Wow. That was a big win!

We talked for hours and hours, and it wasn't all Zach telling me what was happening. I told him about my life, our campaign, and the friends we had acquired whom he had yet to meet. We talked about Pam, Marillyn Tallman, John and Kathryn Porter, Martin Gilbert, Konnilyn Feig, Yves Montand, and an army of other supporters to whom—we both agreed—we owed more than we could ever repay.

The three days evaporated before we knew it. Near the end, the inevitable sadness set in. We were saying our goodbyes, promising to stay strong, knowing there were only six months left until the nightmare ended—praying that it did—swearing not to let the worst happen.

We were holding each other close when the guards showed up, signaling our time was up.

Straight from the barracks, I went to the headquarters and requested a meeting with Major Korenev. I hadn't dealt with him before, and I needed to see with my own eyes who this guy was, the one who, according to Zach, had "morphed into a convict" and professed his hatred of him.

I entered his office and announced my name. The guy sitting at the desk looked at me with curiosity. Standing in front of his desk—standing up helped channel a warrior in me—I confronted him right off the bat.

"I know what you said to my husband: that you would do everything in your power to give him a second term. But I have a question for you."

"What's that?" he asked without contradicting me.

"Aren't you afraid to overestimate your power?" I asked. "After all, you are just the head of the Men's Division. There were stronger pieces on this chess board that got knocked over."

To my astonishment, he replied, "Yes, I am afraid. I am afraid to overestimate my power, but I am willing to take a risk." He paused. "I am only human," he added, "with all my faults. Whether right or wrong, I can do a lot at my level, and if I fail, let them punish me for that."

While he was talking, I paid attention to his eyes. His pupils were moving quite rapidly, and his eyes were somewhat bloodshot. I remembered Zach saying, "He is insane. You should have seen him." Well, now I'd seen him. He struck me as someone weak and unstable yet with a Napoleon complex. *And that's a dangerous combination*, I thought.

"We'll see who wins this battle," he concluded.

"We will," I said, and I left.

After arriving at Moscow Airport, I grabbed a cab to Dina's. I had been absent for less than five days, but it felt like an eternity.

I was in the elevator going up to Dina's apartment when suddenly it hit me: *The rumor! What if it wasn't a rumor, and they had let Dina and Olga out of the country?* I calmed myself down, thinking, *Don't be ridiculous. It hasn't been five days since you left. Nothing could have happened in five days. Plus, Brodsky is still serving his time.*

I came to the door and heard voices. *Phew! They're there.* I rang the bell, and the door opened; our friend Natasha Beckman was standing at the door. The apartment was empty, with the floors full of clutter, which Natasha and other friends were disposing of.

"Tan'ka . . ." Natasha said, opening her arms to me. We stood there, holding each other, our eyes tearing.

"When?" I asked her.

"Right after you left for Siberia. Both Olga and Dina and their families. They were given forty-eight hours to leave."

I had never heard of anybody being given forty-eight hours to leave the country. How was it possible?

"But what about Brodsky?" I asked. "He was still in prison when I left."

"They let him out. It was surreal. He just knocked on the door."

"That does sound surreal!" I exclaimed. "Dina must have lost her mind!"

Then Natasha said, "Hold on. The girls left you something." She found a big plastic bag and handed it to me. I looked inside and saw some clothes—a few pieces from each of my girls. Silk dresses, blouses, and such—all hardly worn—and underneath them all . . . was a pair of red Austrian boots.

And that's when I lost it.

I spent that night at my friend Natasha Ratner's apartment. She, too, was the wife of a political prisoner. Her husband, twenty-seven-year-old Alexei Magarik, had recently received a three-year sentence in the Gulag on trumped-up charges of "drug possession."

Natasha was highly intelligent and fascinating to talk to, yet she was humble and unpretentious. But above all, she was a loyal friend;

she'd drop everything to rush to your rescue. Her generosity of heart made people flock to her, and she was always there for them.

The den in Natasha's apartment reminded me of the one at Yakov and Lina's in Leningrad. It, too, was long and narrow, with bookshelves wall-to-wall. Opposite them was a couch.

I'd received an open invitation from Natasha to stay with her whenever needed. And so had her other friends, Mila Volvovsky—the wife of the prisoner Ari Volvovsky—and their daughter Kira, and Nadezhda Fradkova, a former prisoner herself, who had just recently finished serving a two-year sentence for "social parasitism." We shared that den on more than one occasion, but more importantly, we shared some truly fascinating stories, stories you couldn't find in any of those many books lining the wall.

CHAPTER 27

DESPERATE MEASURES

By the time I landed back in Riga, I knew exactly what my next move would be.

I remembered Zach calling Korenev "insane." In my conversation with Korenev, I, too, thought he was deranged. My thought was, *If the KGB is "qualified" to question the mental health of refuseniks and political prisoners, why couldn't we re-pay them in kind?* What was stopping me from questioning the mental health of Major Korenev?

Nothing.

Based on this conclusion, I launched a massive letter-writing campaign with an all-out attack on Korenev. I wrote letters to the Human Rights Commission of the United Nations, Amnesty International, the International Commission for Protection of Prisoners, the Supreme Soviet of the USSR, the head of the KGB, the head of the national Gulag, the prosecutor general of the USSR, Secretary-General Mikhail Gorbachev, and anyone else I could think of.

I wrote, "I have irrefutable testimony that the head of the Men's Division of the labor camp #40 of the Irkutsk region, Major Korenev, is manufacturing a reprisal against my husband, prisoner of conscience Zachar Zunshine." I quoted every word Korenev had said regarding this matter, first to Zach and then to me: "I will do everything in my power to give you, Zunshine, a second term," "Yes, I am afraid to over-estimate my power, but I am willing to take a risk," "I can do a lot at my level, and if I fail, let them punish me for that."

I went on:

According to my husband, Major Korenev hates him so much that he's ready to risk it all. His constantly wandering, red-tinged eyes tell the tale and give away his determination and fear in the face of punishment. His dangerous actions and reactions—his whole demeanor—compel me to doubt his sanity.

Recently, it seems, it got into Major Korenev's head to rid himself of my husband with the help of others. In August of this year, he confined Zachar in a cell with two mentally disabled inmates, recently released from an asylum. One of them showed violent behavior.

Thus, Major Korenev deliberately created a situation he could not control, which could have resulted in unforeseeable consequences.

Therefore, based on the facts mentioned above, I strongly appeal to you to set up a medical commission to examine the mental health and professional fitness of the head of the Men's Division of the labor camp #40, Major Korenev.[111]

For the next four weeks, I did nothing but expand my campaign. I added the deputies of the Supreme Soviet to my list. Despite the KGB's stark warnings ("Stop it, or else"), I never stopped sending postcards to them. This time, I listed juicy quotes from Major Korenev and let the leaflets fly.

On October 14, I received some truly inspiring news: the Nobel Prize committee awarded the author Elie Wiesel the 1986 Nobel Peace Prize. The committee's press release stated:

---

111 Tatiana Zunshine's personal archive.

"It is the Committee's opinion that Elie Wiesel has emerged as one of the most important spiritual leaders and guides in an age when violence, repression and racism continue to characterise the world. Wiesel is a messenger to mankind; his message is one of peace, atonement and human dignity. His belief that the forces fighting evil in the world can be victorious is a hard-won belief. His message is based on his own personal experience of total humiliation and of the utter contempt for humanity shown in Hitler's death camps. The message is in the form of a testimony, repeated and deepened through the works of a great author."[112]

Once his award was announced, Elie Wiesel, in turn, announced his plan to visit Moscow. As chair of the US Holocaust Memorial Council, he hoped to meet with Secretary-General Mikhail Gorbachev.

Among us refuseniks, there was pure jubilation. This gentle man—a Holocaust survivor and the author of *Night* (among other novels)—deserved nothing less than the Nobel Peace Prize. He was worshiped in Jewish communities around the world. And to hear that he was coming to Moscow? What an honor! But for the families of political prisoners, it meant something more: a chance—however slight—to meet with Elie Wiesel in hopes of having him put their loved ones' names on his list and present the list to Mr. Gorbachev, asking for their release.

It sounded like a long shot, but it was worth a try.

I called my friend Dr. Konnilyn Feig, whom I have mentioned several times. In the summer of 1985, she and her partner, Lisa Wilhelm, visited me in Moscow, and then later, in March 1986, she was among those who'd organized a vigil in front of the Soviet consulate in San Francisco. Knowing her as a writer and historian, I thought she could perhaps find a way to approach Mr. Wiesel.

112 https://www.nobelprize.org/prizes/peace/1986/summary/.

She did:

Wednesday, October 15, 1986

To: Mr. Arnold Thaler and
    Mr. Professor Elie Wiesel
From: Dr. Konnilyn Feig
About: A Direct Message from Tatiana Zunshine, Riga, Latvia

I have always been grateful that you both have given me your phone numbers to use if I felt an urgent situation existed. I believe such a situation exists, and that you may be able to help.

At 6 a.m. today, Tatiana Zunshine called me at home from Riga, Latvia. She had just that moment, returned from Siberia from her visit to her husband, Zachar Zunshine, a well-known Prisoner of Conscience who is serving a 3 year term to end supposedly in March 1987.

The purpose of Tatiana's call was to urge me to get 2 messages to Elie Wiesel at once. Those messages which I recorded are:

1. "Zachar and I wish to offer our warmest and deepest congratulations to you, Elie Wiesel, on receiving the Nobel Prize. For Zachar, you are a constant inspiration as he tries to live out the brutality of his existence in your image—with dignity and strength, giving not one inch to his captors, remaining true to his humaness [sic] and his Jewishness at every moment . . . No Nobel selection could mean as much to us."

2. "Konnilyn, please urgently request of Professor Wiesel the following:

    "'When you come to the Soviet Union, I urgently wish to meet with you in Moscow. It is so very important... I will risk everything to meet with you. I have much information. And it will give Zachar such a renewed spirit.'"

Why did Tatiana call me? . . . In the past 1½ years on my salary, I have paid for myself and the team to go into the Soviet Union 4 times. No one knows (not the Embassy or the Consulate) why the KGB keeps warning me and then allowing me to return. The KGB detains me when I walk off the plane in Moscow, strip searches me on exit, pulls me in for questioning, follows and harasses me unrelentingly, threatens and calls in for interrogation my Russian friends, etc. But still they allowed me to return.

I meet with Refusenik leaders, give "underground" lectures on the Holocaust, sponsor, support, fund special vital research on the Holocaust in Russia (working with Martin Gilbert— and with your help, Elie. You may recall that you have written encouragement notes to them in their work which I have smuggled into the Soviet Union along with 40 copies of your books). Most important is my organizing of and continuing caring for the activist women . . .

The KGB, in its last "meeting" with me, told me that Tatiana Zunshine was the leading woman activist in the SU, or in their words, "the most serious violator of Soviet principles." She is in great danger.

Please. I know how many thousands of demands are on your shoulders. I feel deeply your burden . . . Yet, perhaps, just perhaps, your effort will make a difference—"if only" for a Sakharoff and a Zunshine. Thank you so very much for caring.[113]

Calling Konnilyn, I had no idea whether or not she knew Elie. Not only did she know him, but he had given her his phone number to use if she felt "an urgent situation existed." My wanting to meet Elie, in her mind, constituted such an urgent situation. For that, I was grateful beyond words. From this letter, I learned details about the consequences of Konnilyn's own activities in Russia—the strip searches, interrogations, and harassment she had endured by

---

113 Tatiana Zunshine's personal archive.

coming to see the refuseniks in her attempts to rescue them from the oppressive Soviet regime. I learned about the lectures she had given on the Holocaust, and I found it remarkable. I felt honored to be Konnilyn's friend. I also felt honored to hear that the Soviets considered me "the most serious violator of Soviet principles."

Elie Wiesel came to Moscow on October 22, 1986, accompanied by an entourage: the director of international concerns of the National Jewish Community Relations Advisory Council, Abraham J. Bayer; a survivor who chaired the US Days of Remembrance, Sigmund Stratcher; and a Roman Catholic nun, Sister Carol Rittner.

I received a phone call from one of Elie's companions. The circumstances around the call have escaped my memory—I don't recall whether I was still in Riga or already in Moscow. I do remember, however, that the man on the other end of the line gave me details on my upcoming meeting with Elie Wiesel. We were to meet on October 24 in a group setting—with other wives of the prisoners of conscience—at an apartment belonging to one of the American diplomats in Moscow.

"Bravo to Konnilyn!" I exclaimed, hanging up the phone. "She did it! That is incredible. I am so grateful!"

Whether the meeting would happen with me or without me was another matter. Would I be able to join the other wives, or would I get apprehended on the way over? Nobody knew.

On the 24th, in Moscow, I kept a low profile in anticipation of the meeting. I wanted it so badly, but I also knew that had the KGB decided to prevent me from going, it would happen no matter what. For that reason, I was keeping my expectations low.

To my delight, nothing happened on the way to the diplomat's house. Nobody pounced on me at the entrance to his building. Better yet, there wasn't anybody waiting for me inside the entrance, in the elevator, or by the door. I hurriedly rang the bell, and the door opened. I saw people in the living room—quite a crowd—with drinks in their hands, mingling with one another. Stepping through the doorway, I knew I was safe.

We waited about forty-five minutes in that room, anticipating Elie's arrival. The place was buzzing with conversation about recent events. Just two days before, on October 22, the Soviets had ordered five American diplomats to leave the country in retaliation for so-called "anti-Soviet actions by the United States." (In reality, the diplomats were expelled as a part of the game of petty reciprocity for the Americans' expulsion of Soviet spies.) Among those expelled were the Moscow embassy's Michael Matera—the human rights officer—and Daniel Grossman, a vice consul from the Leningrad consulate. This was the same Daniel Grossman who had hosted me, among others, for a small gathering in Leningrad on July 5 that year and whose apartment I had left to catch an early-morning train to Moscow—the event I called a "nightmare to remember."

We were sad to hear about the expulsions, especially considering that those diplomats had established a record of defending human rights in the Soviet Union and, by doing so, had made friends with people from the refusenik community. I was particularly sad to hear about Daniel's departure.

Word got around that Elie was on his way. Everyone moved closer to the door. Soon, the door opened, and a small-framed man came in, surrounded by a few of his friends. This was Elie. He was handsome, dark-featured, distinguished, and carried an abundance of grace. He was only fifty-eight years old at the time, but on his face was the wisdom of centuries. *What a face!* I said to myself, getting to the end of the line of those wishing to greet him. These were mostly the wives of the prisoners of conscience, but also some long-term refuseniks. Being last in line, I watched him shake hands and have short conversations, making the person on the other side of a hand-shake feel that they were the only one that mattered, assuring them that things would improve.

When he finally got to me, somebody from the embassy intro-duced me: "Mr. Wiesel, this is Tatiana Zunshine."

"Nice meeting you," Elie said, shaking my hand. "A few days ago, we had a chance to talk to your mother."

My mother? How in the world did he get hold of my mother? She is in Tallinn helping my sister, Lora, with the babies. What?

"My mother?" I asked out loud, with a bewildered look on my face.

"Yes, your mother. We talked on the phone with her," he repeated.

After a moment of silence, everybody burst into laughter. We all got it at the same time. Though I was about to turn thirty-one, I looked at least ten years younger. While Elie knew they had talk-ed on the phone with Zachar Zunshine's wife, looking at me, he couldn't place me as anybody's wife; in his mind, I must have been the daughter.

"Oh, no, no, no, the person you talked to was *me*," I told him, try-ing to quash my laughter. "I am the wife of Zachar Zunshine."

That moment was special. It created an additional layer of con-nection, I thought. I talked to Elie on and off during the rest of his stay, telling him about Zach's situation and the need for help pre-venting the administration's intention to give him a second term. He listened attentively and promised to do his best.

Once Elie and his companions left, the party wound down. People started leaving one after another. I can't speak for the others, but I left with the understanding that I had met a true icon—one of the most fascinating humans I may have ever crossed paths with. And I knew I would not have traded my place with anybody else at that party and would cherish that "mother" story for the rest of my life.

The next day, many refuseniks gathered at the American ambassador's residence, Spaso House, for a special event—a monthly screening of an American movie. Not being a Moscow resident, I rarely had a chance to attend those events, but on this visit, I did. My trip coincided with the screening of the newly released *Children of a Lesser God*.

After the movie, there was, as always, a little reception, and without prior warning, who do you think showed up? Elie Wiesel again, with his entourage. That created quite a stir. Everybody wanted to meet him. Before I had a chance to say hello to Elie, one of his companions approached me.

"After this, we are heading to the synagogue for the celebration of Simhath Torah. Do you want to join us?" he asked.

"Of course!" I exclaimed. "It would be an honor."

He warned me that, for religious reasons, they were not able to take transportation. "We'll have to walk," he said, and my response was, "Not a problem."

I immediately went looking for my friend Sasha Murinson. I found him in the crowd and pulled him aside.

"Elie's friend just asked me to accompany them to the synagogue," I said to Sasha excitedly. "You are going with me whether you want to or not."

Sasha Murinson was my close friend and a designated translator. He knew English better than any of us. His English was idiomatic, grammatically correct, and enriched by the use of slang. He was my go-to man for translating letters from Russian into English. Sometimes, when I was out of reach for Pam, Sasha would take my calls and dictate my letters to her. In addition to being a great friend, he was a genuinely nice guy.

I didn't have to ask Sasha twice; he was happy to join. But I didn't recruit him for his English. I needed directions. Having not lived in

Moscow, how would I know the walking route from Spaso House to the synagogue?

It was about a fifty-minute walk, and along the way, we all talked to each other—Elie, two or three of his friends, Sasha, and I—exchanging conversational partners, following Sasha's lead. Suddenly, I saw one of the men sidle himself up to Elie and whisper something in his ear. The two of them stopped for a second and looked back. I saw the expressions on their faces turn serious.

"What is it?" I asked. "Is there a problem?"

"We think we are being followed," either Elie or the other man said.

I looked back and saw some familiar faces.

"Aah, no worries at all!" I exclaimed in relief. "Those are *mine!*"

They looked at me, perplexed.

"They are *yours*? What do you mean, they are *yours*?"

"Yeah, yeah, they are totally after me," I assured them, laughing. "You have nothing to worry about."

Maybe because I was laughing about it, I was able to put them at ease, and we continued walking. By then, we were close to the synagogue. We soon reached it and found an enormous crowd encircling it. There must have been thousands of people there. We stood at the outer edge of the crowd, realizing that once we stepped in, there would be no way to stay together. We needed to say our goodbyes before that happened.

And so we did. It was incredibly sweet. Elie promised to do everything he could to bring Zach's case to the attention of whichever Russian leader he got the opportunity to see.

"Everything will be okay, you'll see," he said warmly.

We hugged each of our walking companions and parted ways.

I later learned that Gorbachev declined Elie Wiesel's proposal to meet. But that visit was by no means in vain, for the simple reason that the press was all over it, and the Soviets got an earful. Here is how the *New York Times* reported Elie Wiesel's experiences:

WIESEL ENDS HIS SOVIET VISIT WITH PLEA FOR RELEASE OF JEWS

October 27, 1986

Elie Wiesel, winner of the 1986 Nobel Peace Prize, concluded a five-day visit to the Soviet Union today with an appeal to the Soviet authorities to release Jews seeking to emigrate.

"I say without any anger, without any animosity, with deep compassion, that it would be to the honor of the new style of leadership to allow these men, women, and children to be happy again," Mr. Wiesel said at the news conference shortly before his departure.

The Nobel laureate, a survivor of the Auschwitz and Buchenwald death camps who has dedicated most of his life to perpetuating the memory of the Holocaust, spent much of his time in Moscow meeting with Jews, both at private homes and at an emotional celebration of the feast of Simhath Torah on Saturday night at the main Moscow synagogue.

"I had a feeling of walking in a sea of tears," he said of the experience at the synagogue, "tears of joy, as well as tears of nostalgia and sorrow . . ."

He said he had hoped to meet with Mikhail S. Gorbachev, but had received a message from the Soviet leader Saturday saying he could not see him at this time, though a meeting in the near future remained possible.

For the Simhath Torah, or Rejoicing in the Law of the Torah, that concludes the three-week-long Jewish High Holy Days, Mr. Wiesel and the small delegation accompanying him received a rapturous reception from several thousand Jews who had gathered at the synagogue and on the street outside to celebrate what has evolved into one of the main holidays of Soviet Jewry.

"I'm not embarrassed to say I broke up in tears," Mr. Wiesel said at the news conference today. "I attended something that will stay with me for years, just as the first time I attended the Simhath Torah in 1965 stayed with me for years." The visit was Mr. Wiesel's fourth to the Soviet Union . . .[114]

Meanwhile, in Chicago, my tireless hero Pam led the campaign to prevent the Bozoy administration from giving Zach a second term. I dictated a letter to her, detailing my doubts about Major Korenev's sanity and demanding an examination of his mental health and professional fitness. Based on that letter, Chicago Action for Soviet Jewry issued an emergency alert:

EMERGENCY ALERT TO FRIENDS OF ZACHAR AND
TATIANA ZUNSHINE

November 3, 1986: The attempts by Major Korenev to fabricate a second trial against Zachar continues.

Only your immediate cables can have impact. Since these actions have been taken against Zachar, other actions against Jewish prisoners demonstrate that new trials for prisoners will become routine in the official repression of Jewish prisoners.

If Zunshine is to be retried, we can expect new trials for all Jewish men who have been arrested.

Please cable the head of the camp, Mr. Mouzh, U.K. 272/40, Posiolok Bazoi [Bozoy], Ekhirit Bulagatsky Rayon, 666111 Irkutskaya Oblast, USSR, expressing your outrage and call upon him to fire Major Korenev, who has said he will go to the wall if he has to, to convict Zachar in a second trial.

We also urge you to send cables to Politburo member Geidar Aliev, the Kremlin, 103132 Moscow, USSR, calling upon him to personally inquire into the excessive violations of Soviet Law in Bazoi Camp No. 40.[115]

---

114 From *The New York Times*. ©1986 *The New York Times* Company. All rights reserved. Used under license.

115 Archives, Center for Jewish History, New York, NY.

People started flooding the camp with cables. Our friend and supporter, a professor of chemistry at Pennsylvania State University, Dr. Julian Heicklen (who in October 1985 had written a letter to Secretary-General Gorbachev on our behalf), sent two cables. One of them went to the head of the camp #40, Mr. Mouzh:

"THE BEHAVIOR OF MAJOR KORENEV TOWARD PRISONER OF CONSCIENCE ZACHAR ZUNSHINE IS DEPLORABLE. I URGE YOU TO FIRE MAJOR KORENEV."[116]

A second one went to a prominent member of the Politburo of the USSR, Mr. Geidar Aliev:

"I URGE YOU TO LOOK INTO THE EXCESSIVE VIOLATION OF SOVIET LAW PERPETRATED BY MAJOR KORENEV AGAINST PRISONER OF CONSCIENCE ZACHAR ZUNSHINE IN BAZOI CAMP NO. 40."[117]

Unfortunately, the Gulag administration was not backing down. I received two responses from Gulag officials, both hinting at the possibility of a second term.

From: The Head of the Gulag Office of the Irkutsk region, Vitaly Balandin

Your statement that there is deliberate preparation for the institution of criminal proceedings against Zachar Zunshine for malicious disobedience to the legal demands of the administration of Institution UK272/40 is not based in reality. At the

---

116 Tatiana Zunshine's personal archive.
117 Tatiana Zunshine's personal archive.

same time, we inform you that the convict, Zachar Zunshine, continues to transgress maliciously the requirements of the regime of his confinement. He deliberately refuses to fulfill the legal demands of the administration (which does not exclude the possibility of an additional term of confinement according to Article 188.3 of the Russian Criminal Code).[118]

From: The Head of the Gulag Office of the USSR, Skriprikov

During his term in the places of confinement, your husband systematically and maliciously broke the requirements of the regime. For that, he was repeatedly and justly punished in a disciplinary way by the institution's administration. The head of the institution has warned Zunshine that in case of his unwillingness to fulfill the legal demands of the administration, he will be made answerable for criminal punishment according to Article 188.3 of the Russian Criminal Code.[119]

That sounded dreadful. I realized I needed to go back to Moscow and see the Gulag officials in person. I had one last trick up my sleeve and needed to give it a shot.

I arrived in Moscow and went straight to the Gulag office of the USSR. I asked to see Mr. Skriprikov—the author of one of those threatening letters—but they let me see his deputy instead.

Entering his office, I went up to his desk and put my letter in front of him. It contained quotes from Korenev: "I will do everything in my power to give you, Zunshine, a second term," "Yes, I am afraid to overestimate my power, but I am willing to take a risk," "I can do a lot at

---

118 Archives, Center for Jewish History, New York, NY.

119 Archives, Center for Jewish History, New York, NY.

my level, and if I fail, let them punish me for that." It also contained my demand for an examination of Korenev's mental health.

I asked the guy to read it, and he didn't object. He finished reading and raised his head to look at me.

Desperate times require desperate measures, I thought to myself, and said:

"This conversation with Major Korenev has been recorded. I have it on tape, which is safely secured. If you give my husband a second term, I will immediately release the tape in the West, and everyone will see what stands behind that infamous second term. Nothing more than a personal vendetta, the attempt of a deranged psychopath to square accounts with his subject—a political prisoner."

It was a total bluff. There was no tape. But there was no other way out, either. Looking back, of all the things I had resorted to, bluffing about the tape might have been the most outrageous. What could I say? *You gotta do what you gotta do.*

In late December, I received a small note from Zach, smuggled out of the camp. In it, he let me know that the threats about giving him a second term had ceased and that the administration couldn't wait to get him out. I no longer have that note, but I do have Zach's contemporaneous notes echoing its contents.

> *The bluff worked. The head of the Men's Division, Korenev, was now a changed man. Since then, no one has ever talked to me about the second term. Furthermore, a representative of the Gulag office of the USSR was dispatched to the camp with the evident goal of convincing me that no one had any desire to give me an additional term and that they were all waiting for my term to end so that they could finally get rid of us. By the end of my term,*

I knew so much about everything and everyone that the admin-
istration was clearly getting a little scared of me.[120]

Reading Zach's note, I knew *this* was the turning point. It all
came down to that moment. Not only had they ceased pursuing the
second term, but they had practically admitted their inability to
muscle us down. At that thought, I sat in a chair with my hands over
my eyes as if trying to stop the tears from coming. They wouldn't
obey. These were happy tears, tears of relief, tears of vindication. I
felt a bit sorry for myself, but not in a bad way. What we had gone
through to get here—that's what the sorrow was about. But it didn't
matter; it didn't last. An overwhelming feeling of joy and relief came
over me. I sat there, my hands still covering my eyes, endlessly repeating, *Oh, my god.*

Was it the bluff that tipped the scale in preventing the second term?
Who knows? Even if it was, a bluff alone would not have done it. The
campaign led by Pam, the publicity, the cables—all of those combined must have contributed to it. And there was another factor: In
the fall of 1986, the liberalization campaign in the USSR was gaining
momentum. Gorbachev's socio-economic reform, called Glasnost
and Perestroika,[121] first announced at the beginning of 1986, was
slowly picking up steam. With it came signs—or rather, hints—of
the easing of the iron grip. With all that in mind, I could confidently
say that the tide had finally started to turn.

---

120 Tatiana Zunshine's personal archive.
121 Openness and Reconstruction.

PART 4

1987

CHAPTER 28

TO PAINT OR NOT TO PAINT

In early January 1987, I started preparing for Zach's upcoming release, scheduled for March 6. I wanted to get our apartment ready—it needed a fresh coat of paint—and asked around for a painter. A friend recommended hiring a Latvian man named Jānis Jurkāns.

When Jānis appeared at my door, I had to tilt my head to say hello. He was over six foot six. A handsome, broad-shouldered guy in his early forties, he didn't look like a typical house painter. I couldn't quite put my finger on what set him apart, but I sensed some mystery associated with him.

Jānis turned out to be a highly intelligent man. We spent hours talking, discussing wide-ranging subjects. One subject we tried to avoid was politics; not knowing each other through social circles, we were both playing it safe.

On day five, Jānis ran out of paint. He asked me to get him another bucket. I said, "Of course, but I need to stop by this one office first before I get it." Which office? The emigration office, to be exact, but I wasn't getting my hopes up. They had been playing jokes on me for a while, and I needed to put an end to it. Let me explain. This was not the first time. They would summon me to the office only to ask some silly invented questions and make it look like that was the sole purpose of it. After receiving yet another summons, I was annoyed.

At the office, I asked to talk to the person in charge of this charade. They showed me to a room. I entered and saw a woman sitting at the desk. Before I could open my mouth to start giving her a piece of my mind, she said, "Sit down, please." She sounded somewhat convincing, and I sat down in front of her.

"The decision has been made," she said, "to grant you and your husband exit visas. You are free to leave the country upon his release. In fact, you *have* to leave within three days of it."

"Huh?"

I am looking at her without blinking, and I don't understand what she is saying. What does she mean we are free to leave? It's been six years. Is this really the end of it? Or is it another joke? That would be cruel. And what about remodeling? The paint! Jānis asked me to get him some paint. What do I do about that?

This was not the reaction she thought she would get. She said something about it while I remained silent. At least, by then, I started blinking again. This was not the reaction I'd thought I would have, either. Astounded, I simply stared at her. I couldn't feel my body. I felt nailed to the chair, unable to get up.

I did get up, eventually. I left the office and stood outside, unsure of where to go. The house was in one direction, the paint store—in another.

We no longer needed the paint. But I had promised. *What should I do?*

I went to get the paint.

I came home with a bucket of paint and handed it to Jānis. For the next hour or so, I sat quietly, watching him diligently paint the walls.

"Something happened?" Jānis asked. "You've been awfully quiet."

I then opened up my cards, telling him about my husband, a political prisoner finishing his three-year term in the Siberian Gulag, due to be released in a few weeks. "But that's not the whole story," I added. "I just received permission for us to leave the country. In fact, we have to leave within three days of his release. Which means you don't have to toil on those walls. We no longer need them."

It turned out he had a story of his own. (I knew it!) A former professor of English at Latvian State University, he had been fired from his position for, in their words, being too sympathetic to Jews. He was now painting apartments, trying to make ends meet. Unsurprisingly, he held anti-Soviet sentiments, supporting people like us in any way he could.

Needless to say, my reaction was delayed.

It was not until Jānis left that I started to comprehend the enormity of what had just happened. And then it hit me. It's hard to describe the way I felt, but let me try: It felt like some imaginary guests had paid me a visit all at once. These were Joy, Gratitude, Pride, Hope, and Vindication, among others. With them crept in Bitterness, Anger, and Sorrow.

Bitterness, Anger, and Sorrow? Why did they have to show up? Here's why. The events of the last six years were flashing through my mind like the frames of a moving picture. The brutal battle we'd had to engage in, the three rotten years in the Gulag for Zach, the chases, the woods, the beatings, the punishment cells, the threats, the abductions, the hunger strikes, the sit-in strikes—all of it. Had they uttered the same words—"You are free to leave"—six years earlier, as they should have, none of that would have happened. Yes, we had won many battles and achieved what we wanted, but did we win the war? The answer is no. We didn't. If you ask me why, I'll tell you: it is because of the casualty of that war we'd had to endure—the death of Zach's mother, Dora.

And yet.

Joy, oh Joy! I wish, dear reader, you had been there to share it with me. You would have heard me sing; you would have seen me dance. You would have heard my voice coming through my window:

"THEY ARE LETTING US GO! WE ARE FREEEEEE!"

I called my family.

"Mom, are you sitting down? I have great news! We are free! They are letting us leave the country!"

"Lora, did Mom tell you? We got our permission to go! We are leaving as soon as Zach gets out! Hurrayyyy!"

"Gena, I have great news! You won't believe it! I just received permission for us to leave the country. This is incredible!"

I sent a note to Zach telling him that we had received permission to leave. I put it in our secret code to ensure he gets the message:

"THEY ARE LETTING US GO! WE ARE FREEEEEE!"

I called Pam to tell her the news and to congratulate her on our mutual victory:

"Pam, I have great news! They are letting us leave the country! We did it, Pam! We did it!"

I was proud of the campaign we had built together. And who were "we"? Zach on one side of the wall, me on the other; Pam Cohen, Marilyn Tallman, the Union of Councils for Soviet Jews, other Jewish and human rights organizations, members of the US government, celebrities, and activists across the pond. That campaign provided us with invaluable support, without which—I can say with confidence—the two of us would not have made it. And that's why Gratitude settled in my heart, an immeasurable Gratitude toward all who participated in our rescue.

It's March 6, 1987. I am in Bozoy, standing in front of the gate, antici-pating it opening at any moment. In a state of pure exhilaration, I can't stand still. I pace around: back and forth, back and forth. I don't know how long it has been since I came to the gate. In my mind, time stands still. It doesn't move. The gate doesn't move, either. I find myself talking to it: "C'mon, open up! Open up!" More time passes.

Then I hear the cracking sound of the gate opening. I turn toward it, and I freeze.

I see Zach coming out of the gate.

EPILOGUE

The road to freedom was winding—Bozoy to Irkutsk, then Sverdlovsk, Moscow, Riga; back to Moscow; then to Vienna, Jerusalem, and finally, the United States.

In 1988, once Gorbachev's reforms took hold, the door to emigration was flung wide open. Did the refusenik movement have anything to do with it? I'd like to think we helped pick the lock. My family applied for emigration and soon left Russia once and for all. Seeing each other on American soil for the first time was truly a dream come true.

I asked Mom, "When did you decide to leave?"

"The minute your plane was up in the air," she said.

Meanwhile, the Soviet landscape was changing. Latvia, Lithuania, and Estonia—formerly independent countries annexed by Stalin in 1940 and subsequently forced to become a part of the Soviet Union—were spreading their wings of independence. Peaceful protests were sprawling across the Baltic lands. The Singing Revolution in Estonia—a model for bloodless, orderly uprising—set the stage, with Latvia and Lithuania following suit. On August 23, 1989, a demonstration called The Baltic Way took place. Walking hand in hand, about two million people formed a 370-mile-long human chain across three Baltic states, protesting the forceful annexation and nearly half-century-long occupation by the Soviet Union.

On a curious note: When thousands of people were gathering at the central squares of Riga, who do you think stood in front of them with a loudspeaker in his hands? My painter, Jānis Jurkāns. And when, in August 1991, Latvia had attained full independence from the Soviet Union, who do you think became the first minister of foreign affairs of the newly sovereign country of Latvia? You guessed it—my painter, Jānis Jurkāns.

By November 1989, the entire Eastern bloc was in the flames of change. Following the fall of the Berlin Wall, one state after another declared its independence from the Soviet Union. One by one, the statues of Vladimir Lenin were hitting the ground, head down. For us, the newly minted Americans, barely one foot out of the Iron Curtain, it felt like nothing short of a miracle.

When we first arrived in the United States, Zach and I embarked on a three-month speaking tour, traveling nationwide to promote human rights, participating in dozens of speaking engagements, and giving numerous interviews to the media. Once the dust settled, we began putting down roots in our new adoptive country. In 1990, our son, Phillip, was born. (My sun and my moon, he is the best gift the universe has ever given me.)

A few more years passed, and our path took an unexpected turn—it split. *We* split.

I remembered the words of KGB Lieutenant Colonel Shalaev, predicting that outcome for the two of us. Oh, how I hated him for being right! But the truth is, it happens more often than you think—people are able to survive the war, but not the peace. And so it happened. Who was to blame? Life itself.

We both went on with our lives. Zach became a lawyer and remarried. He and his wife, Jill, were together for twenty years, most of which they spent in New York City, in their apartment near Central Park. His favorite pastime was taking long walks in the park. Sadly, he passed away in 2021 after a long battle with cancer.

As for me, I once again found love. My husband, Miles, is my heart and my soul. A true one-of-a-kind, he is hard to define. But if I had to, I would describe him as a man of brilliant mind, generous heart, and a big appetite for life. With him by my side, I can finally say: "All right."

My mother, Frieda Pertsovskaya.

My father,
Alexander Kremnev.

My family: Mom, Dad, my twin sister Lora (left), my brother Gena, and I (right).

Zach at the age of twenty-four, about the time he and I met.

Zach and I (center)
in Israel, a few weeks
after his release,
with Yakov and Lina
Gorodetsky.

In Israel, a few months
after Zach's release, with
the supporter

Pamela Cohen in Congressman John Porter's office, on the phone with me while I was still in Riga.

Martin Gilbert.

Sasha Balter.

Dina Zisserman (left), Olga Medvedkov (right).

ACKNOWLEDGEMENTS

This book would not have seen the light of day if not for my son, Phillip, who, persistently, over the years, kept reminding me that I had a story to tell. This book would have been different had he not assumed the role of an editor later in its development. His help was invaluable, and I am at a loss for words. I am beyond proud of him and am so very grateful to him.

This book would not have been possible without the unwavering love and support of my husband, Miles. As a newbie writer, I often found myself overwhelmed with self-doubt, but Miles was always there to build me up with his constant words of encouragement. I am forever grateful to him.

This book (and my very existence) would not have been possible without the tireless efforts of my hero, my savior, Pamela Cohen. Her role in ensuring Zach and I survived the grueling three years of our battle with the KGB is beyond words. I am eternally indebted to her.

Pam's co-chair, the late Marillyn Tallman, and other members and volunteers of the Union of Councils for Soviet Jewry, along with members of their sister organizations, were indispensable in their noble fight to free the Soviet refuseniks from the claws of the oppressive regime; so were members of the US Congress. I am forever grateful to all of them.

In addition to those mentioned above, my heartfelt gratitude goes to: Lenny Cohen, Hon. John Edward Porter (R-IL), Kathryn Cameron Porter, Hon. Mario Biaggi (D-NY), Alison Smale, Michael J. Freed, Esq.,

Hon. Robert J. Lagomarsino (R-CA), Hon. Ted Weiss (D-NY), Senator Alfonso D'Amato (R-NY), Hon. Edward F. Feighan (D-OH), Sir Martin Gilbert, Dr. Murray Peshkin, Dr. Thomas H. Stix, Hon. Steve Bartlett (R-TX), Hon. Barbara Mikulski (D-MD), Hon. Ben Erdreich (D-AL), Hon. Michael Bilirakis (R-FL), Hon. Louis Stokes (D-OH), Hon. Jim Moody (D-WI), Senator Paul Simon (D-IL), Dr. Julian Heicklen, Dr. A. P. French, Dr. Konnilyn Feig, Lisa Wilhelm, Herbert L. Adams, M.D., Rabbi Mordecai Simon, Rabbi Samuel Fraint, Rabbi Stuart Weiss, Devra Noily, Stephanie Hunt, Bill Peters, David Feuer, Esq., Yves Montand, Hon. John R. Miller (R-WA), Rita Eker, Senator John Kerry (D-MA), Dr. Elie Wiesel, Abraham J. Bayer, Sigmund Stratcher, Sister Carol Rittner, Harvey Barnett, Esq., Hinda Cantor, Howard Cantor, June Daniels, Ron Daniels, Judy Balint, Morey Schapira, Lynn Singer, Sandy Spinner, Rabbi Abie Ingber, David Waksberg, Glenn Richter, Frank and Bunny Brodsky, Daniel Grossman, Sasha Balter, Yakov Gorodetsky, Polina Gorodetsly, Nadezhda Fradkova, Michael Vinover, Evgenia Vinover, Mikhail Tsivin, Ari Volvovsky, Mila Volvovsky, Olga Medvedkov, Yuri Medvedkov, Dina Zisserman-Brodsky, Vladimir Brodsky, Natasha Ratner, Alexei Magarik, Evgeny Lein, Irina Lein, Vladimir Lifshitz, Anya Lifshitz, Roald Zelichenok, Galina Zelichenok, Alik ("Cooper") Kupershmidt, Fanny Kupershmidt, Grigory Vasserman, Boris Vainerman, Natasha Beckman, Alla Sud, Lev Sud, Alla Praisman, Leonid Praisman, Alexander Murinson, Misha Shipov, Evgeny Briskin, Lev Gorodetsky, Katya Gorodetsky, Natasha Khassina, Irene Badanova, Caroline Leavitt, Peri Gabriel, and Tenyia Lee.

Two more heartfelt thanks: to Olga Medvedkov for initiating a flurry of activities to bring us to the United States and to our three adoptive American families—Bernie and Miriam Yenkin, Howard and Sondra Fink, and Jacques and Laura Zakin—who, through their collective efforts, went above and beyond to make it happen.

Lastly, thank you to all my family for their unwavering love and support.

ABOUT THE AUTHOR

TATIANA ZUNSHINE was born and raised in the Soviet Union. When her husband became a political prisoner serving time in the Siberian Gulag, Tatiana built an effective international campaign on his behalf. This campaign, a testament to the power of collective action, mobilized an army of supporters from diverse backgrounds, including US members of Congress and a host of prominent personalities.

Throughout the years, Tatiana's son asked her if she intended to write a book about her fight with the Soviet KGB. Her answer always was, "Not really." But one day, Tatiana surprised herself, uttering, "I don't think I have a choice. The story needs to be told." That came as a shock to her. She had no idea where the words came from. But as they flew out of her mouth, Tatiana knew she would be writing a book. Soon, Russian President Vladimir Putin ordered a full-scale invasion of Ukraine, starting an unprovoked and unjustified war with a sovereign neighbor. That solidified Tatiana's desire to show the true colors of Russia's authoritarian regime. Her goal is to remind her audience of the dangers of authoritarianism and the need to preserve democracy at all costs.

www.ingramcontent.com/pod-product-compliance
Lightning Source LLC
Chambersburg PA
CBHW020148090426
42734CB00008B/738